MW01010702

Bach: The Orgelbüchlein

BACH :

The Orgelbüchlein

— ❧ —

Russell Stinson
Lyon College

Monuments of Western Music
George B. Stauffer, Series Editor

SCHIRMER BOOKS
An Imprint of Simon & Schuster Macmillan
NEW YORK

Prentice Hall International
LONDON   MEXICO CITY   NEW DELHI   SINGAPORE   SYDNEY   TORONTO

Copyright © 1996 by Schirmer Books

All rights reserved. No part of this book may be reproduced or transmitted in any form or by any means, electronic or mechanical, including photocopying, recording, or by any information storage and retrieval system, without permission in writing from the Publisher.

Schirmer Books
An Imprint of Simon & Schuster Macmillan
1633 Broadway
New York, NY 10019

Library of Congress Catalog Card Number: 96–94581

Printed in the United States of America

printing number
1 2 3 4 5 6 7 8 9 10

Library of Congress Cataloging-in-Publication Data

Stinson, Russell.
     Bach, the Orgelbüchlein / Russell Stinson.
         p.   cm. — (Monuments of western music)
     Includes bibliographical references and index.
     ISBN 0-02-872505-0 (alk. paper)
     1. Bach, Johann Sebastian, 1685–1750. Orgelbüchlein.   2. Chorale prelude.
     I. Title.   II. Series
ML410.B13S87   1996
786.5'18992'092—dc20   96-24581
                                                                                   CIP
                                                                                    MN

This paper meets the requirements of ANSI/NISO Z39.48-1992 (Permanence of Paper).

To Laura, Matthew, Rachel, and Patrick

Contents

Abbreviations

BWV   *Bach-Werke-Verzeichnis.* Wolfgang Schmieder, *Thematisch-systematisches Verzeichnis der musikalischen Werke Johann Sebastian Bachs* (Leipzig: Breitkopf & Härtel, 1950; revised edition, Wiesbaden: Breitkopf & Härtel, 1990)

BWV Anh.   BWV Anhang (appendix to the *Bach-Werke-Verzeichnis*)

KB   *Kritischer Bericht* (critical report of the *Neue Bach-Ausgabe*)

NBA   *Neue Bach-Ausgabe. Johann Sebastian Bach: Neue Ausgabe sämtlicher Werke* (Kassel: Bärenreiter; Leipzig: VEB Deutscher Verlag für Musik, 1954–present)

P   *Partitur* (music score—abbreviation used by the Staatsbibliothek zu Berlin—Preussischer Kulturbesitz, Musikabteilung)

SBB   Staatsbibliothek zu Berlin—Preussischer Kulturbesitz, Musikabteilung

Foreword

———————— ✌ ————————

The *Monuments of Western Music* series is devoted to the examination of single works, or groups of works, that have changed the course of Western music by virtue of their greatness. Some were recognized as masterpieces almost as soon as they were written. Others lay in obscurity for decades, to be uncovered and revered only by later generations. With the passage of time, however, all have emerged as cultural landmarks.

The *Monuments* volumes are written by historians and performers, specialists who bring to their accounts the latest discoveries of modern scholarship. The authors examine the political, economic, and cultural background of the works. They consider such matters as genesis, reception, influences, and performance practice. But most importantly, they explore the music itself and attempt to pinpoint the qualities that make it transcendent. The result is a series of comprehensive, engaging books that are of interest to students, performers, scholars, and devotees alike.

No other volume of music is so well known to organists as the *Orgelbüchlein* of Johann Sebastian Bach. For generations of players it has stood as the first resource for honing manual and pedal skills. As Bach's Two-Part Inventions, Three-Part Sinfonias, and *Well-Tempered Clavier* are to pianists and harpsichordists, so the *Orgelbüchlein* is to organists: it is central to the educational process, a pedagogical *vade mecum* that no student or instructor can be without. Indeed, for this editor and organist, the *Orgelbüchlein* was a constant companion during high school and college days. Settings such as "Ich ruf zu dir, Herr Jesu Christ," "Der Tag, der ist so freudenreich," and "Christ lag in Todesbanden" served as my introduction to the rigors of strict part-playing, the demands of obbligato pedalling, and the art of the chorale prelude itself. Later, settings such as "In dulci jubilo" and "In dir ist Freude" served as "display pieces" in my first college recitals. Since then, the *Orgelbüchlein* has remained at the top of my stack of Bach organ music, a collection constantly consulted, played, and assigned to budding students.

But the *Orgelbüchlein* is much more than music for teaching and performance, of course. As Russell Stinson shows in the present volume, the collection also played a central role in Bach's own development, serving as a critical testing ground for the forging of his highly personal idiom. In this group of forty-six pieces we see the composer formulating a new type of organ chorale, one in which the pedal is treated in a fully obbligato manner. In seventeenth-century organ music, the pedal was handled in an *ad libitum* way, even in the works of Buxtehude, Bruhns, and other North Germans. In the *Orgelbüchlein*, Bach assigns the pedal its own independent line, notating it unambiguously and thus placing it on an equal footing (one might say) with the manual parts. In this sense, the *Orgelbüchlein* represents the first "modern" organ music. But of equal importance is Bach's approach to the manual parts. Here, too, one finds fully independent lines: the soprano, the alto, and tenor each have a melodic say. This disciplined part-writing, still missing in Bach's Mühlhausen cantatas, marked the beginning of the composer's mature writing style. It paved the way not only for the large organ works of the Weimar years, but also for the keyboard collections and chamber music of Cöthen and the vocal masterpieces of Leipzig. The four-part chorales of the Leipzig cantatas have their roots in the controlled part-writing of the *Orgelbüchlein* settings. The pieces are also the first sign of Bach's fascination with the melodic canon, an interest that resurfaces toward the end of his life in the *Art of Fugue*, the *Goldberg Variations*, the *Musical Offering*, and the Canonic Variations on "Von Himmel hoch."

Stinson places the *Orgelbüchlein* in this larger context by outlining the compositional strata in the original manuscript and showing for the first time the order in which the pieces were entered into the collection. In the process, he takes us into Bach's Weimar workshop at a critical turning point in the composer's career and lets us observe the conception and growth of the *Orgelbüchlein* chorale itself. Stinson begins, in Chapters 1 and 2, by looking at Bach's method of composition. He continues, in Chapter 3, by examining the chorale types found in the collection and their distinctive stylistic characteristics. This is followed, in Chapters 4 to 6, by an in-depth survey of the individual settings. Finally, in the closing chapter, Stinson traces the reception of the *Orgelbüchlein* in the eighteenth, nineteenth, and twentieth centuries and demonstrates the music's influence on later composers such as Mendelssohn, Busoni, and Schoenberg. Carl Philipp Emanuel Bach's previously unpublished arrangement of "Ich ruf zu dir" and a list of transcriptions of the chorales appear as appendices at the end of the text.

In this volume Stinson broadens our view of the *Orgelbüchlein*. He reminds us why the collection is of such great importance for organists and other musicians. But by examining Bach's original manuscript and revealing its compositional layers, he also shows us why the music was of such great significance for the composer himself. In Stinson's monograph the *Orgelbüchlein* emerges as a masterpiece that set the stage for other masterpieces. For this reason, it must rank as a monument of Western music.

George B. Stauffer
Series Editor

Introduction

At first glance, J. S. Bach's "Little Organ Book" is not the most obvious choice for a series dedicated to musical "monuments." Appearances, however, can be deceiving: the *Orgelbüchlein* contains no fewer than forty-six compositions and an imposing amount of music. Why Bach chose such a title for this much-beloved collection of organ chorales is not altogether clear. As we shall see in Chapter 1 ("The *Orgelbüchlein* Project"), he may well have borrowed the appellation from a sixteenth-century source. But it may also represent characteristic modesty on Bach's part or constitute nothing more than a description of the autograph manuscript, a volume measuring roughly 6 × 7 inches. Whatever the case, there is nothing at all "little" about the *Orgelbüchlein's* quantity or quality. Both insure the *Orgelbüchlein* a place among Western music's "monumental" works.

The *Orgelbüchlein* is also one of the cornerstones of the organ repertory. It comprises the most frequently performed organ collection ever written, one that virtually every modern organist in the world regularly plays. Given this popularity, it comes as no surprise that the *Orgelbüchlein* has long intrigued musicologists. The literature on the collection is as extensive as it is diverse, to the degree that no other organ music by Bach or anyone else has been pondered more often or from a wider spectrum of historical and analytical perspectives. What is more, much of this literature, particularly that of the past two decades, represents exemplary scholarship.

Although this book has greatly benefited from previous research, its main objective is to show the *Orgelbüchlein* in a new light. This is by no means an impossible goal, for there are vital aspects of the collection that have received only scant attention. For example, even though most of the entries in the autograph contain compositional revisions, the issue of compositional process, which is the subject of Chapter 2 and a recurring theme in Chapters 4–6, has remained relatively untouched by past commentators. The work's reception, the subject of the final chapter, is another unexplored line of inquiry, despite the fact that ever since its inception the *Orgelbüchlein* has played a significant role in the culture of Western church music.

Even more important in this connection, arguably, is the matter of musical style. Although scholars have known for almost four decades that the *Orgelbüchlein* chorales were not composed in their order of appearance in the autograph, the general compositional sequence has been clarified only recently. Armed with this new information, we can now identify ways in which the *Orgelbüchlein* evolved stylistically, an issue that is addressed in Chapter 1 and throughout Chapters 4–6, where for the first time the individual works are discussed in chronological order.

As the first substantial monograph devoted to the *Orgelbüchlein*, the present volume also considers such familiar topics as the collection's purpose and historical context in far greater detail than has hitherto been possible. This level of detail is perhaps most evident in the individual commentaries found in Chapters 4–6. It is to be hoped that these commentaries will, in addition to presenting views of past writers, provide the reader with fresh insights into each of these incomparable pieces, particularly with respect to contrapuntal structure, textual-musical relationships, and performance practice.

I would like to express my sincere appreciation to institutions and individuals for helping me in my work. Thanks are due, first of all, to the Staatsbibliothek zu Berlin, Musikbibliothek der Stadt Leipzig, Öffentliche Bibliothek der Universität Basel, Kunstsammlungen zu Weimar, and Johann-Sebastian-Bach-Institut (Göttingen) for supplying photocopies of sources in their possession. A special word of gratitude goes to the Staatsbibliothek zu Berlin for allowing me to examine firsthand several manuscripts, including the autograph of the *Orgelbüchlein*. I am grateful to John Butt, Delbert Disselhorst, the Rev. T. Carleton Lee, Michael Marissen, Kerala Snyder, Teri Noel Towe, and Harald Vogel for helpful comments; to Joyce Clinkscales, Stephen Crist, Sidney Grolnic, Diane Ota, William Parsons, Donna Sammis, David Schulenberg, Judy Tsou, Kathy Whittenton, Peter Williams, and Barbara Ulman for assistance in locating items in the secondary literature; to Ruben Weltsch for help in translating German; and to Larry Todd and Tilman Seebass for information on Mendelssohn's encounter with the *Orgelbüchlein*. I would also like to thank Lyon College for supporting this project in the form of a Christian A. Johnson Fellowship. My greatest debt is to George Stauffer, for the skill and care with which he steered this book to press.

Russell Stinson
Batesville, Arkansas
Spring 1996

Chapter 1

THE *ORGELBÜCHLEIN* PROJECT

HISTORICAL POSITION

To study the *Orgelbüchlein* is to witness a familiar scene in the history of the Western church: an organist compiling organ music for use during worship. In other words, the *Orgelbüchlein* belongs to the tradition of liturgical organ music. The tradition itself is an ancient one, and its repertory is venerable. The repertoire begins in the fourteenth century with the Faenza Codex, the second oldest collection of keyboard music in existence, and has continued unabatedly until the present day.

A pivotal event in this history occurred in 1517, when Martin Luther founded a denomination, commonly known as the Lutheran Church, distinguished by novel ideas about the function of music in worship services. For instance, whereas singing in church had been the sole domain of clerics and choirs, in Luther's church it became the privilege and duty of the entire assembly. Because the new congregational songs, or chorales, often contained ten or more stanzas, they consumed a sizable portion of the liturgy.

The birth of the chorale as a musical genre changed the role of the organist forever, for in the Lutheran church it became his responsibility not only to accompany congregational singing but also to arrange chorales as organ solos. Thus the inception of the chorale spawned a new keyboard genre, the organ chorale, in which a chorale melody is set for organ. In most instances organists improvised on these tunes, but organ adaptations of chorale melodies were often committed to paper as well, to be preserved for future use.

1

The literature of organ chorales is almost as old as the Reformation itself. From the sixteenth century onward, organ chorales were preserved in both manuscript and print, often in the form of collections designed for year-round use. The compiler of such a collection either composed all the settings himself or mixed his own settings with works by other composers. The order sometimes followed the church year; other times it was entirely random.

By the time of Bach's birth in 1685, the corpus of chorale melodies had grown to gigantic proportions, and one assumes that to maintain some command over this ever-expanding repertory, organists routinely compiled large collections of organ chorales. Of the extant collections from this period, two of the most significant are by organists who worked in Thuringia, the region of Germany where Bach spent approximately his first thirty years: *Choral-Fugen durchs gantze Jahr*, by Johann Pachelbel and *Choraele zum Praeambuliren*, a collection of forty-four fughettas by Johann Christoph Bach (1642–1703). Both composers were a great influence on the young J. S. Bach, and it is possible that the concept of the *Orgelbüchlein* was inspired by these two collections in particular. Johann Christoph Bach was organist in Eisenach, where J. S. Bach was born and spent his first ten years; it was probably Johann Christoph who introduced Johann Sebastian to the organ. The link between Pachelbel and J. S. Bach involves Bach's older brother, a second Johann Christoph Bach (1671–1721), who was a pupil of Pachelbel and, from 1695 to 1700, Johann Sebastian's keyboard instructor.

The Layout of the Autograph

Bach's autograph manuscript of the *Orgelbüchlein*, housed in the Staatsbibliothek zu Berlin under the shelf number *P 283*, yields secrets about the collection that can be garnered from no other source. Only the autograph, for instance, shows that the surviving music is just a fragment of Bach's original plan. Most of the manuscript's pages contain no music, only chorale titles and blank staves (these "titles" are invariably the first line of the first stanza). Bach entered a total of 164 chorale titles, which constitute a comprehensive Lutheran hymnal.[1] The first sixty are designated for a specific time in the church year—either a season or particular festival—and therefore fall into the category of *de tempore*. They follow the order of the church year. The remaining 104 are *omne tempore* chorales, appropriate for any season. They begin with the articles of the Catechism and then move on to such topics as Christian living, the Bible and the Church, and death. Table 1–1 lists all the chorale titles inscribed by Bach, along with their pagination and liturgical association (the headings provided in the table under "Liturgical Association" are not found in the autograph). BWV numbers are given for the forty-six chorales that Bach actually set (or began to set, in the case of the fragmentary "O Traurigkeit"). Bach does not appear to have modelled the design of his collection after any particular hymnal of the day. Rather, he seems to have devised his own scheme, based on his acquaintance with various hymnals and his general knowledge of hymnody. Even though Bach left the *Orgelbüchlein* incomplete, it is the closest thing we have to a hymnal of his own fashioning.

TABLE 1–1.

The Projected Contents of the Orgelbüchlein, *as Displayed in the Autograph Manuscript*

ORDER IN MANUSCRIPT	TITLE	LITURGICAL ASSOCIATION	PAGINATION	BWV NO.
		DE TEMPORE		
1	"Nun komm, der Heiden Heiland"	Advent	p. 1	599
2	"Gott, durch deine Güte" or "Gottes Sohn ist kommen"	Advent	pp. 2–3	600
3	"Herr Christ, der ein'ge Gottessohn" or "Herr Gott, nun sei gepreiset"	Advent	p. 4	601
4	"Lob sei dem allmächtigen Gott"	Advent	p. 5	602
5	"Puer natus in Bethlehem"	Christmas	pp. 6–7	603
6	"Lob sei Gott in des Himmels Thron"	Christmas	p. 7	not set
7	"Gelobet seist du, Jesu Christ"	Christmas	p. 8	604
8	"Der Tag, der ist so freudenreich"	Christmas	p. 9	605
9	"Vom Himmel hoch, da komm ich her"	Christmas	p. 10	606
10	"Vom Himmel kam der Engel Schar"	Christmas	pp. 11–10	607
11	"In dulci jubilo"	Christmas	pp. 12–13	608
12	"Lobt Gott, ihr Christen, allzugleich"	Christmas	p. 14	609
13	"Jesu, meine Freude"	Christmas	p. 15	610
14	"Christum wir sollen loben schon"	Christmas	p. 16	611
15	"Wir Christenleut"	Christmas	p. 17	612
16	"Helft mir Gotts Güte preisen"	New Year	p. 18	613
17	"Das alte Jahr vergangen ist"	New Year	p. 19	614
18	"In dir ist Freude"	New Year	pp. 20–21	615

19	"Mit Fried und Freud ich fahr dahin" [*Nunc dimittis*]	Purification (February 2)	p. 22	616
20	"Herr Gott, nun schleuss den Himmel auf"	Purification (February 2)	pp. 23–23a	617
21	"O Lamm Gottes, unschuldig"	Passiontide	pp. 24–24a	618
22	"Christe, du Lamm Gottes"	Passiontide	p. 25	619
23	"Christus, der uns selig macht"	Passiontide	p. 26	620a/ 620
24	"Da Jesus an dem Kreuze stund"	Passiontide	p. 27	621
25	"O Mensch, bewein dein Sünde gross"	Passiontide	pp. 28–29	622
26	"Wir danken dir, Herr Jesu Christ, dass du für uns gestorben bist"	Passiontide	p. 30	623
27	"Hilf Gott, dass mir's gelinge"	Passiontide	pp. 31–30a	624
28	"O Jesu, wie ist dein Gestalt"	Passiontide	p. 32	not set
29	"O Traurigkeit, o Herzeleid" [fragment]	Passiontide	p. 33	Anh. 200
30	"Allein nach dir, Herr, allein nach dir, Herr Jesu Christ, verlanget mich"	Passiontide	pp. 34–35	not set
31	"O wir armen Sünder"	Passiontide	p. 36	not set
32	"Herzliebster Jesu, was hast du verbrochen"	Passiontide	p. 37	not set
33	"Nun gibt mein Jesus gute Nacht"	Passiontide	p. 38	not set
34	"Christ lag in Todesbanden"	Easter	p. 39	625
35	"Jesus Christus, unser Heiland, der den Tod überwand"	Easter	p. 40	626
36	"Christ ist erstanden"	Easter	pp. 41–43	627
37	"Erstanden ist der heil'ge Christ"	Easter	p. 44	628
38	"Erschienen ist der herrliche Tag"	Easter	p. 45	629
39	"Heut triumphieret Gottes Sohn"	Easter	pp. 46–47	630
40	"Gen Himmel aufgefahren ist"	Ascension	p. 48	not set
41	"Nun freut euch, Gottes Kinder, all"	Ascension	p. 49	not set
42	"Komm, Heiliger Geist, erfüll die Herzen deiner Gläubigen"	Pentecost	pp. 50–51	not set
43	"Komm, Heiliger Geist, Herre Gott"	Pentecost	pp. 52–53	not set
44	"Komm, Gott Schöpfer, Heiliger Geist"	Pentecost	p. 54	631a/ 631
45	"Nun bitten wir den Heil'gen Geist"	Pentecost	p. 55	not set
46	"Spiritus Sancti gratia" or "Des Heil'gen Geistes reiche Gnad"	Pentecost	p. 56	not set

47	"O Heil'ger Geist, du göttlich's Feuer"	Pentecost	p. 57	not set
48	"O Heiliger Geist, o heiliger Gott"	Pentecost	p. 58	not set
49	"Herr Jesu Christ, dich zu uns wend"	Pentecost	p. 59	632
50	"Liebster Jesu, wir sind hier"	Pentecost	p. 60	634
51	"Liebster Jesu, wir sind hier" (*distinctius*)	Pentecost	p. 61	633
52	"Gott der Vater wohn uns bei"	Trinity	pp. 62–63	not set
53	"Allein Gott in der Höh sei Ehr"	Trinity	p. 64	not set
54	"Der du bist drei in Einigkeit"	Trinity	p. 65	not set
55	"Gelobet sei der Herr, der Gott Israel" [*Benedictus*]	St. John the Baptist (June 24)	p. 66	not set
56	"Meine Seele erhebt den Herren" [*Magnificat*]	Visitation (July 2)	p. 67	not set
57	"Herr Gott, dich loben alle wir"	St. Michael and All Angels (Sept. 29)	p. 68	not set
58	"Es stehn vor Gottes Throne"	St. Michael and All Angels (Sept. 29)	p. 69	not set
59	"Herr Gott, dich loben wir" [*Te Deum*]	St. Simon and St. Jude, Apostles (October 28)	pp. 70–71	not set
60	"O Herre Gott, dein göttlich Wort"	Reformation Festival (October 31)	p. 72	not set

OMNE TEMPORE
(*CATECHISM*)

61	"Dies sind die heil'gen zehn Gebot"	Ten Commandments	p. 73	635
62	"Mensch, willst du leben seliglich"	Ten Commandments	p. 74	not set
63	"Herr Gott, erhalt uns für und für"	Ten Commandments	p. 75	not set
64	"Wir glauben all an einen Gott"	Creed	pp. 76–77	not set
65	"Vater unser im Himmelreich"	Lord's Prayer	p. 78	636
66	"Christ, unser Herr, zum Jordan kam"	Holy Baptism	p. 79	not set
67	"Aus tiefer Not schrei ich zu dir" [Psalm 130]	Confession, Penitence, and Justification	p. 80	not set
68	"Erbarm dich mein, o Herre Gott"	Confession, Penitence, and Justification	p. 81	not set
69	"Jesu, der du meine Seele"	Confession, Penitence, and Justification	p. 82	not set

70	"Allein zu dir, Herr Jesu Christ"	Confession, Penitence, and Justification	p. 83	not set
71	"Ach Gott und Herr"	Confession, Penitence, and Justification	p. 84	not set
72	"Herr Jesu Christ, du höchstes Gut"	Confession, Penitence, and Justification	p. 85	not set
73	"Ach Herr, mich armen Sünder"	Confession, Penitence, and Justification	p. 86	not set
74	"Wo soll ich fliehen hin"	Confession, Penitence, and Justification	p. 87	not set
75	"Wir haben schwerlich"	Confession, Penitence, and Justification	p. 88	not set
76	"Durch Adams Fall ist ganz verderbt"	Confession, Penitence, and Justification	p. 89	637
77	"Es ist das Heil uns kommen her"	Confession, Penitence, and Justification	p. 90	638
78	"Jesus Christus, unser Heiland, der von uns den Gotteszorn wandt"	Lord's Supper	p. 91	not set
79	"Gott sei gelobet und gebenedeiet"	Lord's Supper	pp. 92–93	not set
80	"Der Herr ist mein getreuer Hirt" [Psalm 23]	Lord's Supper	p. 94	not set
81	"Jetzt komm ich als ein armer Gast"	Lord's Supper	p. 95	not set
82	"O Jesu, du edle Gabe"	Lord's Supper	p. 96	not set
83	"Wir danken dir, Herr Jesu Christ, dass du das Lämmlein worden bist"	Lord's Supper	p. 97	not set
84	"Ich weiss ein Blümlein hübsch und fein"	Lord's Supper	p. 98	not set
85	"Nun freut euch, lieben Christen g'mein"	Lord's Supper	p. 99	not set
86	"Nun lob, mein Seel, den Herren" [Psalm 103]	Lord's Supper	p. 100–1	not set

(*END OF CATECHISM*)

| 87 | "Wohl dem, der in Gottes Furcht steht" [Psalm 124] | Christian Life and Conduct | p. 102 | not set |

88	"Wo Gott zum Haus nicht gibt sein Gunst" [Psalm 127]	Christian Life and Conduct	p. 103	not set
89	"Was mein Gott will, das gescheh allzeit"	Christian Life and Conduct	p. 104	not set
90	"Kommt her zu mir, spricht Gottes Sohn"	Christian Life and Conduct	p. 105	not set
91	"Ich ruf zu dir, Herr Jesu Christ"	Christian Life and Conduct	pp. 106–7	639
92	"Weltlich Ehr und zeitlich Gut"	Christian Life and Conduct	p. 107	not set
93	"Von Gott will ich nicht lassen"	Christian Life and Conduct	p. 108	not set
94	"Wer Gott vertraut"	Christian Life and Conduct	p. 109	not set
95	"Wie's Gott gefällt, so gefällt mir's auch"	Christian Life and Conduct	p. 110	not set
96	"O Gott, du frommer Gott"	Christian Life and Conduct	p. 111	not set
97	"In dich hab ich gehoffet, Herr" [Psalm 31]	Christian Life and Conduct	p. 112	not set
98	"In dich hab ich gehoffet, Herr" (*alio modo*)	Christian Life and Conduct	p. 113	640
99	"Mag ich Unglück nicht widerstahn"	Christian Life and Conduct	p. 114	not set
100	"Wenn wir in höchsten Nöten sein"	Christian Life and Conduct	p. 115	641
101	"An Wasserflüssen Babylon" [Psalm 137]	Christian Life and Conduct	p. 116–17	not set
102	"Warum betrübst du dich, mein Herz"	Christian Life and Conduct	p. 118	not set
103	"Frisch auf, mein Seel, verzage nicht"	Christian Life and Conduct	p. 119	not set
104	"Ach Gott, wie manches Herzeleid"	Christian Life and Conduct	p. 120	not set
105	"Ach Gott, erhör mein Seufzen und Wehklagen"	Christian Life and Conduct	p. 121	not set
106	"So wünsch ich nun eine gute Nacht" [Psalm 42]	Christian Life and Conduct	p. 122	not set
107	"Ach lieben Christen, seid getrost"	Christian Life and Conduct	p. 123	not set
108	"Wenn dich Unglück tut greifen an"	Christian Life and Conduct	p. 124	not set

109	"Keinen hat Gott verlassen"	Christian Life and Conduct	p. 125	not set
110	"Gott ist mein Heil, mein Hülf und Trost"	Christian Life and Conduct	p. 126	not set
111	"Was Gott tut, das ist wohlgetan, kein einig Mensch ihn tadeln kann"	Christian Life and Conduct	p. 127	not set
112	"Was Gott tut, das ist wohlgetan, es bleibt gerecht sein Wille"	Christian Life and Conduct	p. 128	not set
113	"Wer nur den lieben Gott lässt walten"	Christian Life and Conduct	p. 129	642
114	"Ach Gott, vom Himmel sieh darein" [Psalm 12]	Psalm Hymns	p. 130	not set
115	"Es spricht der Unweisen Mund wohl" [Psalm 14]	Psalm Hymns	p. 131	not set
116	"Ein feste Burg ist unser Gott" [Psalm 46]	Psalm Hymns	p. 132	not set
117	"Es woll uns Gott genädig sein" [Psalm 67]	Psalm Hymns	p. 133	not set
118	"Wär Gott nicht mit uns diese Zeit" [Psalm 124]	Psalm Hymns	p. 134	not set
119	"Wo Gott der Herr nicht bei uns hält" [Psalm 124]	Psalm Hymns	p. 135	not set
120	"Wie schön leuchtet der Morgenstern"	The Word of God and the Christian Church	pp. 136–37	not set
121	"Wie nach einer Wasserquelle" [Psalm 42]	The Word of God and the Christian Church	p. 138	not set
122	"Erhalt uns, Herr, bei deinem Wort"	The Word of God and the Christian Church	p. 139	not set
123	"Lass mich dein sein und bleiben"	The Word of God and the Christian Church	p. 140	not set
124	"Gib Fried, o frommer, treuer Gott"	The Word of God and the Christian Church	p. 141	not set
125	"Du Friedefürst, Herr Jesu Christ"	The Word of God and the Christian Church	p. 142	not set
126	"O grosser Gott von Macht"	The Word of God and the Christian Church	p. 143	not set

127	"Wenn mein Stündlein vorhanden ist"	Death and Dying	p. 144	not set
128	"Herr Jesu Christ, wahr Mensch und Gott"	Death and Dying	p. 145	not set
129	"Mitten wir im Leben sind"	Death and Dying	pp. 146–47	not set
130	"Alle Menschen müssen sterben"	Death and Dying	p. 148	not set
131	"Alle Menschen müssen sterben" (*alio modo*)	Death and Dying	p. 149	643
132	"Valet will ich dir geben"	Death and Dying	p. 150	not set
133	"Nun lasst uns den Leib begraben"	Death and Dying	p. 151	not set
134	"Christus, der ist mein Leben"	Death and Dying	p. 152	not set
135	"Herzlich lieb hab ich dich, o Herr"	Death and Dying	p. 152–53	not set
136	"Auf meinen lieben Gott"	Death and Dying	p. 154	not set
137	"Herr Jesu Christ, ich weiss gar wohl"	Death and Dying	p. 155	not set
138	"Mach's mit mir, Gott, nach deiner Güt"	Death and Dying	p. 156	not set
139	"Herr Jesu Christ, meins Lebens Licht"	Death and Dying	p. 157	not set
140	"Mein Wallfahrt ich vollendet hab"	Death and Dying	p. 158	not set
141	"Gott hat das Evangelium"	Death and Dying	p. 159	not set
142	"Ach Gott, tu dich erbarmen"	Death and Dying	p. 160	not set
143	"Gott des Himmels und der Erden"	Morning	p. 161	not set
144	"Ich dank dir, lieber Herre"	Morning	p. 162	not set
145	"Aus meines Herzens Grunde"	Morning	p. 163	not set
146	"Ich dank dir schon"	Morning	p. 164	not set
147	"Das walt mein Gott"	Morning	p. 165	not set
148	"Christ, der du bist der helle Tag"	Evening	p. 166	not set
149	"Christe, der du bist Tag und Licht"	Evening	p. 167	not set
150	"Werde munter, mein Gemüte"	Evening	p. 168	not set
151	"Nun ruhen alle Wälder"	Evening	p. 169	not set
152	"Dankt dem Herrn, denn er ist sehr freundlich" [Psalm 136]	After Meals	p. 170	not set
153	"Nun lasst uns Gott dem Herren"	After Meals	p. 171	not set
154	"Lobet dem Herren, denn er ist sehr freundlich" [Psalm 147]	After Meals	p. 172	not set
155	"Singen wir aus Herzensgrund"	After Meals	p. 173	not set
156	"Gott Vater, der du deine Sonn"	For Good Weather	p. 174	not set

157	"Jesu, meines Herzens Freud"	APPENDIX	p. 175	not set
158	"Ach, was soll ich Sünder machen"	APPENDIX	p. 176	not set
159	"Ach wie nichtig, ach wie flüchtig"	APPENDIX	p. 177	644
160	"Ach, was ist doch unser Leben"	APPENDIX	p. 178	not set
161	"Allenthalben, wo ich gehe"	APPENDIX	p. 179	not set
162	"Hast du denn, Jesu, dein Angesicht gänzlich verborgen" or "Soll ich denn, Jesu, mein Leben in Trauern beschliessen"	APPENDIX	p. 180	not set
163	"Sei gegrüsset, Jesu gütig" or "O Jesu, du edle Gabe"	APPENDIX	p. 181	not set
164	"Schmücke dich, o liebe Seele"	APPENDIX	p. 182	not set

Remarkable is the emphasis on early Lutheran hymnody: seventy percent of the proposed chorales date from the sixteenth century, and most of the remainder are from no later than 1650. In fact, Bach includes no fewer than thirty of the thirty-six chorales ascribed to Martin Luther himself.[2] Of the chorales that were actually set, over half are from the Reformation era. This emphasis on the early Reformation is likewise a feature of the recently unearthed organ chorales attributed to Bach from the so-called Neumeister Collection.[3] Bach was probably influenced in this regard by Johann Christoph Olearius, an eminent hymnologist and deacon of the Neue Kirche in Arnstadt at the time Bach served there as organist (1703–7). Olearius published scholarly tracts on many early chorales as well as practical editions of them; it is unlikely that Bach was unaware of Olearius's publications. A further bow to the past is the opening placement of Luther's "Nun komm, der Heiden Heiland," traditionally the first chorale in sixteenth-century hymnals. With this chorale at the head of the collection, both the *de tempore* and *omne tempore* sections commence with hymns by Luther, since the *omne tempore* section begins with Luther's "Dies sind die heil'gen zehn Gebot" (no. 61).

The design of the *Orgelbüchlein* is interesting in other respects as well. First, for whatever reasons, there is no section for Epiphany. Noteworthy, too, is the section for psalm hymns (nos. 114–19) and the entry of these hymns in Biblical order. There are exactly three Trinity chorales, exemplifying the composer's well known penchant for numerological—and especially Trinitarian—symbolism. Chorales for miscellaneous needs and occasions are contained in an appendix.

Bach did not inscribe all the chorale titles before entering a single work. For instance, the placement of the title "Lob sei Gott in des Himmels Thron" (no. 6) reveals that the title was penned after the music of "Puer natus in Bethlehem" (no. 5). Still, large sections of the manuscript obviously were ruled with staves and supplied with titles before any music was notated. For most of the projected entries, only one page was allotted; for relatively long chorales, two pages. In deciding between one or two pages, Bach was by no means systematic. To cite just one example, he reserved a single page for "Der Tag, der ist so freudenreich" (no. 8), even though it contains about ten more syllables per stanza than "Gott, durch deine Güte" or "In dulci jubilo" (nos. 2 and 11), both of which were given two pages. He was relying on intuition, and a lot of guesswork must have gone into the operation. Bach's tiny script notwithstanding, his notation of a work sometimes exceeded the one-page limit, forcing him to conclude the entry on the facing page ("Puer natus in Bethlehem," "Vom Himmel kam der Engel Schar," and "Ich ruf zu dir, Herr Jesu Christ") or on a supplementary paper slip ("Herr Gott, nun schleuss den Himmel auf," "O Lamm Gottes, unschuldig," and "Hilf Gott, dass mir's gelinge").

The realization that a chorale's length generally determined the number of pages reserved for it leads to an important conclusion about the organ-chorale types Bach had in mind as he laid out the autograph: on the whole, he must have been considering only those types that call for the complete chorale melody. This excludes the chorale fugue and chorale fughetta, based on only a phrase of the melody. Moreover, the one-page limit imposed for most entries, coupled with the extremely small size of the manuscript (6 × 7.5 inches), allowed only those chorale types in which the chorale tune is set just once and in continuous fashion. This excludes the chorale partita, the chorale fantasy, and the chorale motet. Left are only three types in use at the time: the melody chorale, in which the whole chorale tune appears more or less continuously in the soprano voice, with either very brief interludes between phrases or none at all; the ornamental chorale, identical to the melody chorale except that the chorale tune is greatly embellished; and the chorale canon, in which the entire tune is presented continuously by two canonic voices (because the space between the canonic entries is normally no greater than a measure, the chorale canon is essentially the same length as the first two types).

Among the chorales that were set, the only real exceptions to this list are "Christum wir sollen loben schon," in which the chorale tune is stated by the alto, and "In dir ist Freude," a setting that approaches the chorale fantasy, a chorale type characterized by expansive interludes between chorale phrases as well as multiple statements of the phrases themselves. Such a lengthy work was possible only because Bach had reserved two pages for this relatively long chorale. Had he set the melody "Herr Gott, dich loben wir" (no. 59), and restricted himself to the two pages allocated in the *Orgelbüchlein* manuscript, there would have been a further exception, since at least four pages would have been needed to set this gigantic tune (the longest chorale melody of all?).[4] Perhaps Bach planned on setting only a portion of the tune here, as he did in his cantatas. The hymn tunes "Allein nach dir" (no. 30) and "Wir glauben" (no. 64) would have been similarly problematic.

In three instances Bach planned on setting the same chorale twice. In the case of "Liebster Jesu, wir sind hier" (nos. 50–51), the title was entered on facing pages; in the case of "In dich hab ich gehoffet, Herr" and "Alle Menschen müssen sterben" (nos. 97–98 and 130–31), the title was entered on a first page and the tag *alio modo* ("a different way") on a second. There is one setting each of "In dich" and "Alle Menschen," both notated, inexplicably, on pages with the *alio modo* heading. "Liebster Jesu" was set twice, but the settings are essentially different versions of the same composition.

GENESIS

It was once believed that the *Orgelbüchlein* originated late in Bach's Weimar period (1708–17) or during his years in Cöthen (1717–23). On the title page of the autograph (see Figure 1–3 on p. 32), Bach cites his professional position as Capellmeister at Cöthen. That was evidence enough for Wilhelm Rust, editor of the *Orgelbüchlein* for the Bachgesellschaft, to suppose that the pieces were composed in Cöthen, even though producing organ music was not part of Bach's duties there.[5] (The explicitly didactic title page gave rise as well to the the once popular but now clearly erroneous notion that the *Orgelbüchlein* was conceived as an instructional volume for Bach's eldest son, Wilhelm Friedemann.) On the other hand, the famous nineteenth-century Bach biographer, Philipp Spitta, maintained that the actual composition occurred late during Bach's tenure as court organist in Weimar and that only the title page was penned in Cöthen.[6]

About forty years ago, Georg von Dadelsen demonstrated that the vast majority of the works do indeed date from the Weimar period.[7] For one thing, as Dadelsen observed, there are numerous manuscript copies of *Orgelbüchlein* chorales by Bach's Weimar colleague Johann Gottfried Walther and Weimar pupil Johann Tobias Krebs that were presumably prepared during

Bach's Weimar years—and copied directly from the surviving autograph. Far more telling, though, were two facts uncovered by Dadelsen about the autograph itself. First, the only other Bach autographs bearing the same watermark as the *Orgelbüchlein* date from 1714. Second, of the Bach autographs that can be precisely dated, those whose handwriting most closely resembles that of the *Orgelbüchlein* autograph date from 1713–16. In comparing the *Orgelbüchlein* autograph with these sources, Dadelsen concluded that Bach worked on the manuscript intermittently for a number of years, with some entries originating no later than 1714, others as late as 1715–16. Dadelsen's work effectively disproved Charles Sanford Terry's fanciful, if attractive, theory that the *Orgelbüchlein* was authored late in 1717, while Bach was incarcerated in Weimar after too forcefully demanding his release from Duke Wilhelm Ernst's service.[8] Handwriting evidence also led Dadelsen somewhat unexpectedly to date the entries of "Helft mir Gotts Güte preisen" and the fragmentary "O Traurigkeit, o Herzeleid" to Bach's Leipzig period (1723–50). Furthermore, Dadelsen was the first to show that the works were not entered in the order of their appearance in the autograph and that the autograph contains composing scores as well as fair copies.

Using Dadelsen's findings as a point of departure, Heinz-Harald Löhlein, the editor of the *Orgelbüchlein* for the *Neue Bach-Ausgabe*, has proposed that virtually all the works originated in Weimar during one of three annual cycles—1713–14, 1714–15, and 1715–16—each corresponding to the church year.[9] According to this chronology, Bach began work on the collection in December 1713 shortly after returning from his audition for the organist post at the Liebfrauenkirche in Halle (Peter Williams's idea that the *Orgelbüchlein* somehow originated in conjunction with this audition is supported only by circumstantial evidence).[10] Löhlein's dating has aroused skepticism simply because a chronology this exact is not possible, given the nature of the evidence. Moreover, the organ at the Weimar court church seems to have been under renovation—and therefore out of commission—from soon after Pentecost 1713 until at least Easter 1714, something Löhlein expressly chooses to ignore. It is hard to believe that the ever-pragmatic Bach, in his capacity as Weimar court organist, would have embarked on a large organ collection without even having a serviceable instrument at hand.

But Löhlein's conclusions about the *order* in which the settings were entered into the autograph are generally quite tenable. These findings have allowed him to observe patterns in how the *Orgelbüchlein* developed stylistically. For example, only in the latest entries does Bach tend to write in more than four parts and place the chorale tune in voices other than the soprano.

Löhlein was able to show as well that the revised versions of two settings, "Christus, der uns selig macht" and "Komm, Gott Schöpfer, Heiliger Geist," which Bach notated in the autograph directly on top of the original versions, date from Leipzig.

More recently, Christoph Wolff has argued that the origins of the collection may be earlier still.[11] Citing newly discovered sources unknown to Dadelsen, Wolff maintains that during Bach's first seven years in Weimar his script was extremely stable, and that handwriting evidence is therefore insufficient to assign works to specific years. A biographical factor that Wolff finds chronologically suggestive is Bach's appointment on March 2, 1714, as *Konzertmeister* in Weimar, a position that he added to his continuing duties as court organist. The new post entailed composing church cantatas at the rate of one per month, thus reducing the amount of time at Bach's disposal for writing organ music. To Wolff, this means that Bach did not continue work on the *Orgelbüchlein* beyond March 1714 (except in the case of the Leipzig entries). Wolff also argues that the initial entries in the autograph may have been made as early as 1708–10, when the new court organist would have had an immediate need for a large chorale repertoire. (In this connection, Robert Marshall has recently suggested that the *Orgelbüchlein* was Bach's first systematic attempt toward a "well-regulated church music," the goal that he set for himself in 1708 upon resigning his position as organist in Mühlhausen.)[12] There are no dated autographs from 1708–10 that might support this idea, however (the earliest dated autograph from the Weimar years is from 1713, which poses a fundamental obstacle in assigning any autograph to the early Weimar period). Wolff also voices doubt that the chronological layers detected by Dadelsen and Löhlein can be dated with any degree of precision.

Wolff's point about the uniformity of Bach's script from 1708 to 1715 is well taken. Nonetheless, the present writer has formulated a chronology of the *Orgelbüchlein* by closely comparing the handwriting of the autograph with Bach's script in all manuscripts written before 1718, paying special attention to: the method of sharp cancellation (whether by naturals or flats); the symbols used for half notes and whole notes, soprano clefs, and common-time signatures; the size of the script in general; and, to a lesser extent, the type of pedal cues used (*ped.* versus *p.*) as well as their presence or absence.[13] This chronology is given in Table 1–2. There is no clear evidence of annual cycles (although they may have existed), but there were apparent-ly general phases of compilation: an early phase from approximately 1708–12; a middle phase that can be broken down into early (1712–13) and late (1715–16) stages, designated in Table 1–2 as "Middle I" and "Middle

II"; and a late phase from approximately 1716–17. The late stage of the middle phase appears to have begun in 1715 rather than 1714 because of the renovation of the Weimar court organ, which seems to have extended well into the spring of 1714; with the organ under repair for the first three or four months of 1714, it seems unlikely that Bach would have composed the Purification and Passiontide chorales BWV 616–19 during that year. The Leipzig entries may not be dated any more specifically than after 1726.

TABLE 1–2.

A Proposed Compositional History of the Orgelbüchlein

BWV NO.	TITLE	LITURGICAL SEASON OR FESTIVAL	COMPILATION PHASE	PROPOSED DATE	PROPOSED ENTRY TYPE
601	Herr Christ, der ein'ge Gottessohn	Advent	Early	1708–12	fair copy
603	Puer natus in Bethlehem	Christmas	Early	1708–12	composing score
604	Gelobet seist du, Jesu Christ	Christmas	Early	1708–12	composing score
605	Der Tag, der ist so freudenreich	Christmas	Early	1708–12	composing score
606	Vom Himmel hoch, da komm ich her	Christmas	Early	1708–12	revision copy
608	In dulci jubilo	Christmas	Early	1708–12	composing score
609	Lobt Gott, ihr Christen, allzugleich	Christmas	Early	1708–12	composing score
621	Da Jesus an dem Kreuze stund	Passiontide	Early	1708–12	revision copy
622	O Mensch, bewein dein Sünde gross	Passiontide	Early	1708–12	composing score
630	Heut triumphieret Gottes Sohn	Easter	Early	1708–12	revision copy
632	Herr Jesu Christ, dich zu uns wend	Pentecost	Early	1708–12	fair copy
635	Dies sind die heil'gen zehn Gebot		Early	1708–12	composing score

636	Vater unser im Himmelreich		Early	1708–12	fair copy
637	Durch Adams Fall ist ganz verderbt		Early	1708–12	composing score
638	Es ist das Heil uns kommen her		Early	1708–12	fair copy
599	Nun komm, der Heiden Heiland	Advent	Middle I	1712–13	composing score
600	Gott, durch deine Güte	Advent	Middle I	1712–13	composing score
602	Lob sei dem allmächtigen Gott	Advent	Middle I	1712–13	composing score
607	Vom Himmel kam der Engel Schar	Christmas	Middle I	1712–13	composing score
610	Jesu, meine Freude	Christmas	Middle I	1712–13	fair copy
612	Wir Christenleut	Christmas	Middle I	1712–13	composing score
614	Das alte Jahr vergangen ist	New Year	Middle I	1712–13	revision copy
625	Christ lag in Todesbanden	Easter	Middle I	1712–13	revision copy
626	Jesus Christus, unser Heiland, der den Tod überwand	Easter	Middle I	1712–13	revision copy
627	Christ ist erstanden	Easter	Middle I	1712–13	composing score
628	Erstanden ist der heil'ge Christ	Easter	Middle I	1712–13	composing score
629	Erschienen ist der herrliche Tag	Easter	Middle I	1712–13	composing score
631a	Komm, Gott Schöpfer, Heiliger Geist	Pentecost	Middle I	1712–13	composing score
639	Ich ruf zu dir, Herr Jesu Christ		Middle I	1712–13	fair copy
640	In dich hab ich gehoffet, Herr		Middle I	1712–13	revision copy
641	Wenn wir in höchsten Nöten sein		Middle I	1712–13	composing score

Also listed in Table 1–2 under "proposed entry type" are the composi-
ional categories into which the various autograph entries fall. Some are
clearly composing scores, which contain numerous formative revisions and
have the appearance of first drafts. Others are revision copies, entries in
which Bach appears to have been copying from another source while simultaneously making minor compositional revisions. And some are fair copies,
which contain no compositional revisions and have a calligraphic appearance.[14] But the distinction among the three types is not cut and dried, and
the classifications in the table are therefore by no means absolute. Bach was
a remarkably "clean" worker—he is perhaps second only to Mozart in this
respect—and on a good day he could compose with remarkable assurance.
Hence it is possible that certain entries labelled "revision copy" or "fair
copy" may actually be composing scores.

Let us now look more closely at the genesis of the *Orgelbüchlein,* with an
eye to Bach's changing attitude toward musical style. On the basis of handwriting evidence and the assumption that the initial entry was an Advent
chorale, the first work entered by Bach into the autograph seems to be "Herr
Christ, der ein'ge Gottessohn." Although a melody chorale, by far the most
common chorale type in the *Orgelbüchlein,* this setting is quite uncharacteristic in that it survives in two forms, the well-known version in the autograph
and an early version, not precisely datable, from the Neumeister Collection.[15] These dual versions imply that Bach may initially have planned to
sketch the pieces elsewhere and then enter them into the autograph (but as
far as can be ascertained, most of the works actually set were composed
directly into the autograph). Judging from Bach's working habits as a church
composer, this entry was made sometime in Advent, just as all the *de tempore*
chorales were probably entered during their respective liturgical seasons.

We also see in "Herr Christ" a veritable model for the so-called *Orgelbüchlein*-type, a type of melody chorale invented by Bach in the *Orgelbüchlein.*
As the locution implies, the *Orgelbüchlein*-type is the chorale type that best
defines the collection as a stylistic entity, for it is the most common type of
melody chorale as well as the most common chorale genre altogether in the
collection. The musical traits of the type may be summarized as follows:

(1) the entire chorale tune is stated once in the soprano, in unadorned
    fashion, without interludes;

(2) four-voice texture (except for the addition of voices at the conclusion),
    with obbligato rather than *ad libitum* pedal, is strictly maintained;

No.	Title	Season	Period	Date	
642	Wer nur den lieben Gott lässt walten		Middle I	1712–13	r(
643	Alle Menschen müssen sterben		Middle I	1712–13	c(s(
644	Ach wie nichtig, ach wie flüchtig		Middle I	1712–13	f(
616	Mit Fried und Freud ich fahr dahin	Purification (February 2)	Middle II	1715–16	f(
617	Herr Gott, nun schleuss den Himmel auf	Purification (February 2)	Middle II	1715–16	r(
618	O Lamm Gottes, unschuldig	Passiontide	Middle II	1715–16	r(
619	Christe, du Lamm Gottes	Passiontide	Middle II	1715–16	r(
611	Christum wir sollen loben schon	Christmas	Late	1716–17	r(
615	In dir ist Freude	New Year	Late	1716–17	r(
620a	Christus, der uns selig macht	Passiontide	Late	1716–17	f(
623	Wir danken dir, Herr Jesu Christ, dass du für uns gestorben bist	Passiontide	Late	1716–17	r(
624	Hilf Gott, dass mir's gelinge	Passiontide	Late	1716–17	r(
634	Liebster Jesu, wir sind hier	Pentecost	Late	1716–17	c(s(
633	Liebster Jesu, wir sind hier	Pentecost	Late	1716–17	f(
613	Helft mir Gotts Güte preisen	New Year	Leipzig	after 1726	f(
620	Christus, der uns selig macht	Passiontide	Leipzig	after 1726	r(
631	Komm, Gott Schöpfer, Heiliger Geist	Pentecost	Leipzig	after 1726	r(
Anh. 200	O Traurigkeit, o Herze-leid [fragment]	Passiontide	Leipzig	after 1726	c(s(

(3) the alto and tenor are assigned the same motive(s);

(4) the pedal is either assigned the same motive(s) as the alto and tenor or given its own motive(s).

Most of the works from the early and middle compilation phases either fully exemplify the *Orgelbüchlein*-type or fail to exemplify it only because their bass lines have little motivic material (a number of settings are equipped with a "walking" instead of a motivic bass).

After the opening Advent chorale, Bach next seems to have entered a group of Christmas chorales: "Puer natus in Bethlehem," "Gelobet seist du, Jesu Christ," "Der Tag, der ist so freudenreich," "Vom Himmel hoch, da komm ich her," "In dulci jubilo," and "Lobt Gott, ihr Christen, allzugleich." With the possible exception of "Vom Himmel hoch," these works were composed direct-ly into the autograph, and with the exception of the double canon "In dulci jubilo," they are all melody chorales. "Puer natus," another unambiguous example of the *Orgelbüchlein*-type, is linked to "Herr Christ, der ein'ge Gottessohn," since they are among the few settings to employ unnecessary repeats (in "Herr Christ" there is a repeat of the chorale's *Abgesang*; in "Puer natus" there is a repeat of the entire piece). "Der Tag" and "Vom Himmel hoch" are adjacent in the autograph, have virtually identical handwriting, and contain bass lines that are unusually accompanimental. Not only do these bass lines cadence in every instance with the soprano chorale tune, but they are devoid of motivic content, featuring instead constant eighth-note motion in the manner of a "walking bass" (associated primarily with late Baroque chamber music, a "walking bass" is characterized by steady, stepwise movement in a single note value, usually half as large as that of the main pulse, e.g., an eighth note in common time or a quarter note in $\frac{3}{2}$ time). These two works represent the first of several contiguous entries that may be thought of as "pairs," since they form a double entry with respect to handwriting, liturgical designation, and musical style. It would follow that they were not only entered in direct suc-cession but probably composed at about the same time as well.

In terms of style, "Lobt Gott" obviously belongs with "Der Tag" and "Vom Himmel hoch," since it features a walking bass that cadences with the sopra-no in four of five instances. "Gelobet seist" exemplifies the *Orgelbüchlein*-type, yet its alto and tenor figuration is analogous to that of "Der Tag." Frequently, one of the voices states a ♪. ♪ motive, usually consisting of repeated notes or notes a step apart, while the other voice simultaneously states a ♪ ♪♪ counterrhythmic motive, usually in stepwise motion. Although other *Orgelbüchlein* chorales display material of this ilk, none utilize it so extensively. Furthermore, these are the only two melody chorales in the *Orgelbüchlein*, save "Ich ruf zu dir, Herr Jesu Christ," for which the autograph prescribes performance on two manuals (*à 2 Clav.*).

The Passiontide chorales "O Mensch, bewein dein Sünde gross" and "Da Jesus an dem Kreuze stund," the Easter chorale "Heut triumphieret Gottes Sohn," and the Pentecost chorale "Herr Jesu Christ, dich zu uns wend" conclude the *de tempore* settings from the early compilation phase. "O Mensch" marks the earliest appearance of an ornamental chorale in the *Orgelbüchlein*. "Da Jesus" employs figuration strikingly similar to that of "Vom Himmel hoch," and its syncopated bass line recalls a passage from "Herr Christ, der ein'ge Gottessohn" (see m. 3, tenor). "Heut triumphieret" is a further *Orgelbüchlein*-type that had already been composed in a slightly different but not precisely datable version (BWV 630a) by the time Bach entered it into the autograph.

"Herr Jesu Christ" is a close stylistic match to the Catechism chorale "Dies sind die heil'gen zehn Gebot," also from the early compilation phase. They are the only melody chorales in the collection whose bass lines are clearly derived from the chorale melody, except for the Leipzig entry "Helft mir Gotts Güte preisen." In "Herr Jesu Christ," the bass imitates the soprano for the first three phrases; in "Dies sind," the bass appropriates the opening phrase of the chorale tune as an ostinato of sorts.

Of the remaining *omne tempore* chorales from the early compilation phase, "Durch Adams Fall ist ganz verderbt" and "Es ist das Heil uns kommen her" are back-to-back entries that form a unit on the basis of their handwriting, liturgical designation, and musical style. They are Catechism chorales of a specific type ("Confession, Penitence, and Justification") and perhaps even comprise a unique "antecedent-consequent" pair in which "Es ist das Heil" serves as an "exuberant, assertive answer to the problem of Adam's fall."[16] Moreover, they are both melody chorales whose bass lines cadence exclusively with the soprano. (The lines themselves, though, are rather different: "Durch Adams Fall" has a motivic bass, "Es ist das Heil" a walking bass.) "Es ist das Heil" also survives in an early version (BWV 638a) that is not precisely datable. The final chorale in this group, "Vater unser im Himmelreich," is a further *Orgelbüchlein*-type.

The early stage of the middle compilation phase ("Middle I") encompasses works whose stylistic orientation is analogous to the early compilation phase, with the important difference that the bass lines of the melody chorales are almost exclusively motivic (there is only one walking bass out of fifteen pieces, compared to four out of thirteen pieces in the early compilation phase). The Advent chorale "Nun komm, der Heiden Heiland" exemplifies the *Orgelbüchlein*-type, except for its free voice leading. "Gott, durch deine Güte," a further Advent chorale, stylistically parallels the early Christmas chorale "In dulci jubilo." In both works the chorale tune is set as a canon at the octave between soprano and tenor, and in that order, with the tenor line played on the pedals; the chorale tunes themselves open with essentially the same melodic contour; the canonic voices are exactly a measure apart; and the same time signature ($\frac{3}{2}$) is used.

The Advent chorale "Lob sei dem allmächtigen Gott" and the Christmas chorales "Jesu, meine Freude" and "Wir Christenleut" represent the *Orgelbüchlein*-type. The Christmas chorale "Vom Himmel kam der Engel Schar," a further melody chorale, is stylistically redolent of the two early Christmas chorales "Der Tag" and "Vom Himmel hoch," since it contains a textbook walking bass that cadences throughout with the soprano. Bach returned to the ornamental chorale with the New Year chorale "Das alte Jahr vergangen ist."

The Middle I phase continues with five immediately adjacent Easter chorales, "Christ lag in Todesbanden," "Jesus Christus, unser Heiland," "Christ ist erstanden," "Erstanden ist der heil'ge Christ," and "Erschienen ist der herrliche Tag." The first four reflect the *Orgelbüchlein*-type. With its three verses, "Christ ist erstanden" may be viewed as a group of three such settings. In each verse, somewhat monotonously, Bach assigns the chorale tune to the soprano instead of varying the voice register from verse to verse. The contrast between this rigidity and the relatively free treatment of chorale melodies in later entries is remarkable. In "Erschienen ist," the chorale melody is presented as a canon at the octave between the soprano and bass, in the manner of "Gott, durch deine Güte" and "In dulci jubilo." But in those two works only one manual is used, as opposed to two in "Erschienen ist," with the *dux* of the canon assigned its own manual. This disposition not only allows the canon to be heard more clearly but creates a more variegated organ sonority as well. The latter trait may also be interpreted as a technical means by which Bach freed up the overall style of the *Orgelbüchlein*, since of the six canons from the middle and late compilation phases, four are prescribed for two manuals. The Pentecost chorale "Komm, Gott Schöpfer, Heiliger Geist" (BWV 631a), an additional *Orgelbüchlein*-type, concludes the *de tempore* settings from the early stage of the middle compilation phase. Bach later reworked this setting to form a more extended chorale (BWV 667) for the "Great Eighteen" Chorales.

Turning to the *omne tempore* chorales from the Middle I compilation phase, "Ich ruf zu dir, Herr Jesu Christ" is a unique three-voice setting that may well be some sort of transcription (the version of this work contained in the Neumeister Collection appears to be a corruption rather than an authentic variant version).[17] "In dich hab ich gehoffet, Herr," "Wer nur den lieben Gott lässt walten," "Alle Menschen müssen sterben," and "Ach wie nichtig, ach wie flüchtig" are all specimens of the *Orgelbüchlein*-type. "Wenn wir in höchsten Nöten sein" is the third and final ornamental chorale in the collection (Bach later recast this work as a chorale motet; see "Vor deinen Thron tret ich" from the "Great Eighteen" Chorales.)

It is only with the late stage of the middle compilation phase ("Middle II") that Bach begins to look beyond the compact design of the melody chorale and toward more sophisticated compositional techniques. The relative complexity of the works from this point on seems to have precluded composing them directly into the autograph, which seems to have been Bach's method for most of the earlier entries.

The side-by-side Purification chorales "Mit Fried und Freud ich fahr dahin" and "Herr Gott, nun schleuss den Himmel auf" constitute a pair on the basis of their handwriting and liturgical designation (were these pieces perhaps written for the same worship service?). Stylistically, though, they are quite dissimilar. Whereas "Mit Fried und Freud" is a straightforward *Orgelbüchlein*-type, "Herr Gott" displays traits that are both unusual and progressive. Cast in four-part texture, its bass and tenor are given their own motives to spin out, while the alto is strictly harmonic filler, welded to the rhythm of the soprano chorale tune. The lower two parts furnish interludes between the chorale phrases, foreshadowing the late entry "In dir ist Freude." Furthermore, only in the late entry "Hilf Gott, dass mir's gelinge" is hand-crossing utilized so extensively.

The immediately adjacent Passiontide chorales "O Lamm Gottes, unschuldig" and "Christe, du Lamm Gottes" also comprise a pair, on the basis of their handwriting, liturgical designation, and style. In both works the chorale tune is set canonically, but, unlike previously cited canons, at the relatively difficult interval of the fifth. "Christe, du Lamm Gottes," furthermore, is in five voices instead of four, and both works contain introductory passagework. In only two other chorales from the *Orgelbüchlein* is the opening note of the chorale tune not sounded on the first beat: "Durch Adams Fall," whose prefatory material is rather slight; and "Herr Gott, nun schleuss den Himmel auf," an additional work, just discussed, from the late stage of the middle compilation phase.

The features that distinguish "Herr Gott," "O Lamm Gottes," and "Christe, du Lamm Gottes" are among those that define the works of the late compilation phase as a stylistic phase—and one far removed from the more straightforward melody chorales of the earlier phases. To begin with the Christmas chorale "Christum wir sollen loben schon," here we have the only work in the *Orgelbüchlein*, except for the canonic setting "O Lamm Gottes," where the entire chorale tune is assigned exclusively to a voice (alto) other than the soprano. This piece also contains such progressive traits as chromatic embellishment of the chorale tune, exceedingly wide spacing between voices, and the use of double pedal at the conclusion as a means of thickening the texture (the only instance of this technique in the collection).

The New Year chorale "In dir ist Freude," on the other hand, is the only *Orgelbüchlein* chorale that could be thought of as a fantasia. The chorale tune is stated in its entirety by the soprano, but the individual phrases are fragmented, ornamented, and repeated; there are flashy interludes between phrases; and the chorale tune appears in other voices as well. The part writing is extremely free, often encompassing five voices, and the spacing between voices is unusually wide, as in "Christum wir sollen loben schon." This is a virtuoso showpiece, a setting much more akin to Bach's large organ chorales from the "Great Eighteen" Chorales and *Clavierübung* III (1739) than to other settings from the *Orgelbüchlein*.

The Passiontide chorales "Christus, der uns selig macht" (BWV 620a) and "Wir danken dir, Herr Jesu Christ," conversely, show Bach reverting to earlier models. In "Christus," the chorale tune is set as a canon at the octave between the soprano and bass, in four-voice texture; "Wir danken dir" is an *Orgelbüchlein*-type. But in the next entry, the Passiontide chorale "Hilf Gott, dass mir's gelinge," there is again experimentation with new techniques. This piece begins with a canon on the chorale tune at the fifth between the soprano and alto, in four-voice texture, but for the fifth and sixth phrases the canon is at the fourth. There is no other work in the collection that employs this canonic interval.

The inclination toward canonic writing is also seen in the two Pentecost chorales on "Liebster Jesu, wir sind hier," which, as mentioned earlier, are different versions of the same piece. Bach first penned the composing score BWV 634 and then on the facing page the fair copy BWV 633. As in "Hilf Gott," the chorale tune is stated as a canon at the fifth between the upper two parts. Five voices are maintained from beginning to end, allowing for extraordinarily rich harmonic writing.

In the late compilation phase, then, we see Bach exploring new, more intricate compositional possibilities. He shows a pronounced interest in canon, especially at the fifth between the upper two voices; he often opts for textures thicker than four parts; and he tends to place the chorale melody in voices other than the soprano (largely a by-product of the canonic writing).[18] It is no exaggeration to say that there is more stylistic diversity within these six works than in the nearly forty entered earlier! Without these six works, it would have been disingenuous of Bach to claim, as he does on the title page of the autograph, that the *Orgelbüchlein* shows how to set a chorale "in all kinds of ways."

The relatively small number of works entered during the late compilation phase implies that Bach was losing interest in the *Orgelbüchlein* project, probably because of the monotony of writing so many pieces of the same type. He may simply have overestimated his ability to avoid repetition within the strictly defined type of the melody chorale or to work within the special confines of the preplanned manuscript. In addition, Bach's worsening job situation in Weimar offered him little incentive to finish the *Orgelbüchlein*. On December 1, 1716, Johann Samuel Drese died, leaving vacant the position of Capellmeister. As Konzertmeister, Bach was next in rank and surely felt entitled to the top spot. When the post went instead to Drese's son, a mediocre musician at best, Bach probably took it as a personal insult. This nepotism apparently so disgusted him that he abruptly ceased his cycle of monthly church cantatas for the Weimar court, a project that had been under way for almost three years. The *Orgelbüchlein*, in many ways a counterpart to the cantata cycle, may have been curtailed for the same reason.

For all intents and purposes, Bach's compositional work on the *Orgelbüchlein* was finished by 1717. Late that year he began his duties as Capellmeister at Cöthen, where he was required to supply music for secular occasions; composing organ music was not in his job description. He did see fit at this time, though, to pen the title page of the autograph, which reveals the pedagogical aims behind the collection (see Figure 1–3). One assumes Bach took this step on behalf of his private pupils.

Bach's next and final position was in the city of Leipzig, where he served as Cantor at St. Thomas and municipal director of music from 1723 until his death in 1750. Here he was not expected to supply any organ music either. Still, for reasons we may never know, he momentarily resumed compositional work on the *Orgelbüchlein* during this period. He entered into the autograph two new works, the New Year chorale "Helft mir Gotts Güte preisen" and the fragmentary Passiontide chorale "O Traurigkeit, o Herzeleid," and revised two existing ones, "Christus, der uns selig macht" and "Komm, Gott Schöpfer" (BWV 620 and 631). These portions of the autograph are easily distinguishable from all others because of their black ink (all the other portions are in brown ink).[19] That the same ink was used for the new works and the revisions suggests that all the Leipzig entries originated at about the same time, possibly during the winter and spring (New Year–Pentecost) of the same year.

This black ink also appears to some degree in "Christe, du Lamm Gottes," a piece notated on the recto side of the folio containing "Christus, der uns selig macht." Bach used the black ink to notate brackets in measures 8, 9, and 10 that clarify how the voices are to be distributed between the hands; to complete one such bracket in measure 5; and to draw a diagonal line between the first and second bass notes in measure 5, thereby clarifying the voice leading. All these symbols can be interpreted as performance instructions, suggesting that Bach intended to perform the work himself in Leipzig or to teach it to one of his students there.

The only complete and entirely new work from the Leipzig layer, "Helft mir Gotts Güte preisen," is, significantly, a melody chorale. Bach had reserved only a single page for this title, which meant that his choice of chorale types was limited, but not just to the melody chorale (the ornamental chorale, chorale canon, or chorale fughetta would also have been possible). Thus it is tempting to believe that Bach's choice here of the *Orgelbüchlein*'s most representative type was made out of concern for the collection as a unified entity. Along with the small setting of "Vater unser im Himmelreich" from *Clavierübung* III, "Helft mir" is Bach's last extant melody chorale.

PURPOSE

The *Orgelbüchlein* is simultaneously a compositional treatise, a collection of liturgical organ music, an organ method, and a theological statement. These four identities are so closely intertwined that it is hard to know where one leaves off and another begins.

In terms of composition, the *Orgelbüchlein* may be thought of as an exercise book that allowed Bach to hone his skills as a composer of organ chorales, particularly with respect to the melody chorale, chorale canon, and ornamental chorale. Its significance for Bach as a composer, however, extends well beyond this realm. To begin with, the *Orgelbüchlein* is part of a large body of organ music written by Bach in Weimar, where, according to the obituary of 1754, he authored most of his organ works.[20] The *Orgelbüchlein* is also the first work in which Bach reveals a systematic and "encyclopedic" approach to composition. It gives us our first glimpse of Bach's tendency to write numerous examples of a particular genre within a relatively short period—and to achieve within these narrow confines an incredible level of diversity and individualization. This procedure would lead to such works as the Inventions and Sinfonias, *The Well-Tempered Clavier*, the French and English

Suites, the Sonatas and Partitas for Unaccompanied Violin, the Suites for Unaccompanied Cello, the Leipzig "chorale cantatas," the Six Harpsichord Partitas, the *Art of Fugue*, the *Goldberg Variations* (and the *Goldberg Canons*, BWV 1087), and the *Musical Offering*.

But the *Orgelbüchlein* is also a very pragmatic work, intended to furnish an organist with music for a worship service. Perhaps more than any other Bach keyboard collection, it is *Gebrauchsmusik*. The various ways in which Bach may have utilized the *Orgelbüchlein* need to be understood within the context of religious life at the Weimar court. The court's ruler, Duke Wilhelm Ernst, was a devout if not fanatical orthodox Lutheran. This was, after all, a man who took as his motto "Alles mit Gott" and who preached a sermon at the age of seven.[21] Childless and separated from his wife, Wilhelm's passion was religion, and he demanded a deeply pious lifestyle from those who served him. This meant regular church attendance and strict adherence to the orthodox Lutheran liturgy, not to mention a curfew at eight o'clock in the winter and nine in the summer. The Duke also insisted that all youth in his realm be given a thorough grounding in the Catechism, and he reinstated the Confirmation rite. Anyone so steeped in orthodox Lutheranism would have appreciated the predilection for early Lutheran hymnody that so characterizes the *Orgelbüchlein*, and one cannot rule out the possibility that the Duke was partially responsible for this feature. At all events, the Duke clearly appreciated Bach's organ playing, and his support most probably spurred in Bach "the desire to try every possible artistry in his treatment of the organ," as the abovementioned obituary put it.

It is safe to say that of all the activities at the court of Wilhelm Ernst, none were more important than those related to the chapel, nicknamed the *Himmelsburg*, or "castle of heaven." Exactly what the chapel activities constituted, though, is unclear (far more is known about liturgical custom in such German cities as Leipzig and Halle). For example, the role played by the congregation and choir in hymn singing is uncertain, and next to nothing is known about the congregation's size or makeup. The chapel's hymnal, the *Weimar Gesangbuch*, has survived, but it is representative of Lutheran ritual in general, and sheds no light on the local liturgy of the Weimar court. Although the hymnal is arranged according to the church year, it follows a somewhat different order than the *Orgelbüchlein*; like most hymnals of this era, it contains no music, only texts.

We may surmise from standard Lutheran practice of the time that Bach regularly played the following types of services: the *Hauptgottesdienst* held on the mornings of the Sundays and festivals of the church year; the vigil services that preceded the festivals; the *Vespergottesdienst* held on Sunday afternoon; and daily prayer and preaching services. Bach would also have been expected to play occasional wedding and funeral services.

The different types of services demanded different types of chorales. The *Hauptgottesdienst*, for example, required *de tempore* chorales, while *omne tempore* chorales were appropriate for Vespers. The principal hymn of any *Hauptgottesdienst* was the *de tempore* gradual hymn, sung between the Epistle and Gospel reading. Therefore, any of the first sixty chorale titles inscribed by Bach into the autograph of the *Orgelbüchlein* could have been used as a gradual hymn. In compiling the collection, Bach was surely aware of the primacy of *de tempore* chorales. Of the sixty *de tempore* chorale titles entered, thirty-five were set; of the 104 *omne tempore* titles, only ten were set. (Albert Schweitzer's view that Bach set only those chorales offering good possibilities for text painting is clearly untenable.) Bach seems to have placed particular emphasis on Christmas and Easter, the two main festivals of the year: of the eleven Christmas chorale titles entered into the manuscript, ten were set; all six of the Easter titles were set. These statistics, of course, constitute further evidence of the *Orgelbüchlein*'s function as liturgical organ music.

In view of these numbers, it is hard to explain why Bach set only three of the nine chorales planned for Pentecost, another major festival of the church year. That one of the Pentecost chorales set is "Herr Jesu Christ, dich zu uns wend," however, is entirely expected. Not only was this hymn sung in various churches (including the Weimar court chapel?) during the *Hauptgottesdienst* on most Sundays of the year, which would have made an organ setting of it unusually practical, but its first three stanzas are said to be by Wilhelm Ernst's grandfather, Wilhelm II of Weimar, which would have granted the chorale special significance at the court, even if sung there only at Pentecost.

It would have been customary for an organist at this time to employ organ chorales in a variety of ways, primarily in conjunction with congregational hymns, whether as preludes, interludes, or actual accompaniments. The *Orgelbüchlein* chorales could have fulfilled these functions, including the last one, for of all the chorale types, the melody chorale is undoubtedly the best suited to the actual accompaniment of a congregational hymn: the chorale tune is placed in the most audible part of the texture and is stated without embellishment and without interludes between phrases—just like church hymns today. One factor, however, that speaks against hymn accompaniment is the range of the chorales, for most of them go as high as e″, which today would be considered a very high range for congregational singing. (Unfortunately, the pitch of the organ at the Weimar court chapel—a critical issue in this regard—is unknown.)

We may marvel at how anyone was able to play from such minuscule script, but there can be no question that the surviving autograph is the same

source Bach himself performed from at the organ of the Weimar court chapel.
With its organ registration indications, tempo inscriptions, brackets indicating how the voices are to be distributed between the hands and feet, pedal
cues, and articulation markings, the manuscript seems earmarked as a performer's score. Moreover, all the two-page chorales are laid out in such a way
as to avoid page turns, also a convenience to the player.

No discussion of the *Orgelbüchlein*'s function as liturgical repertory would
be complete without some mention of the organ at the Weimar court church.
Originally built in 1658 by Ludwig Compenius, the organ was rebuilt in
1707–8 by J. Conrad Weishaupt and in 1713–14 by Heinrich Nicolaus Trebs.
Although the instrument has not survived, we have a reasonably accurate idea
of its specifications, at least as of 1737 (see Figure 1–1).[22]

FIGURE 1–1.

*Specifications of the Compenius-Weishaupt-Trebs Organ in the Weimar
court chapel, as described in 1737*

OBER CLAVIER, CD-c'''	UNTER CLAVIER, CD-c'''	PEDAL, C-e'
1. Principal 8', tin*	1. Principal 8', tin	1. Gross Untersatz 32', wood
2. Quintadena 16', metal*	2. Viol di Gamba 8', metal	2. Sub-Bass 16', wood
3. Gemsshorn 8', metal*	3. Gedackt 8', metal*	3. Posaun-Bass 16', wood*
4. Grobgedackt 8', metal	4. Trompete 8', metal*	4. Violon-Bass 16', wood
5. Quintadena 4', metal	5. klein Gedackt 4', metal	5. Principal-Bass 8', metal
6. Octava 4', metal	6. Octava 4', metal	6. Trompeta-Bass 8', metal
7. Mixtur 6 ranks, metal	7. Wald-Flöthe 2', metal*	7. Cornett-Bass 4', metal
8. Cymbel 3 ranks, metal*	8. Sesquialtera 4 ranks "in Octava, aus 3 und 2 Fuss"	
9. A Glockenspiel "und Spiel-Register dazu" ("with stop knob")		

ACCESSORIES
Tremulant for the Hauptwerk
Tremulant for the Unterwerk
Hauptwerk to Pedal coupler
Manual coupler
Cymbel Stern

* From the Compenius organ of 1658.

The instrument was fairly modest in size, with two manuals; its stoplist typifies Thuringian organ building in the early eighteenth century.[23] First and foremost, more than half the stops are eight-foot registers or lower, which would have created an unusually "grave" sonority dominated by fundamental organ tone (writers of the time described this type of organ sound as *gravitätisch*). Specifically Thuringian are the manual string stops—Gemshorn 8' and Viol di Gamba 8'—the pedal Posaun-Bass 16' and Violon-Bass 16', and the Glockenspiel. The instrument's tuning most likely reflected the growing trend in the early eighteenth century toward equal temperament, especially since the leading proponent of equal temperament at the turn of the century, Andreas Werckmeister, was a major influence on both of the principal organists in Weimar: Bach clearly relied on Werckmeister's *Orgelprobe* in testing organs;[24] and Johann Gottfried Walther, organist at the town church, was a pupil of Werckmeister. At any rate, certain *Orgelbüchlein* chorales, most notably "O Mensch" and "Ich ruf zu dir," in the keys of E-flat major and F minor, are incompatible with the meantone tunings used in the seventeenth century.

Easily the most remarkable feature of this organ, though, was its placement in a cupola-shaped, balustraded gallery located at the very top of the building, roughly fifty to sixty feet above ground level, and with an opening at its base of only about nine feet by twelve feet. Both the gallery, nicknamed the *Weg zum Himmel*, or "way to heaven," and the organ itself are visible in the famous painting by Christian Richter of the chapel's interior, ca. 1660 (see Figure 1–2).[25] With the organ separated from the congregation in this way, and with its music filtered down into the rest of the room through such a small orifice, questions have been raised about the degree to which the congregation could hear the instrument and, consequently, how well it could have accompanied congregational singing.

The title page of the autograph, given in Figure 1–3, shows that Bach also thought of the *Orgelbüchlein* as a didactic collection with specific aims. It reads as follows:

Orgel-Büchlein / Worinne einem anfahenden Organisten / Anleitung gegeben wird, auff allerhand / Arth einen *Choral* durchzuführen, an- / bey auch sich im *Pedal studio* zu *habi-* / *litiren*, indem in solchen darinne / befindlichen *Choralen* das *Pedal* / gantz *obligat tractiret* wird. / Dem Höchsten Gott allein' zu Ehren, / Dem Nechsten, draus sich zu belehren. / Autore / Joanne Sebast. Bach / p. t. Capellae Magistri / S.[erenissimi] P.[rincipis] R.[egnantis] Anhaltini- / Cotheniensis.[26]

Figure 1–2. Interior of the Weimar court chapel, painting by Christian Ritter, ca. 1660 (Kunstsammlungen zu Weimar)

Little Organ Book, in which guidance is given to a beginning organist in how to set a chorale in all kinds of ways, and at the same time to
become practiced in the study of pedalling, since in the chorales found
therein the pedal is treated completely obbligato. For the highest God
alone in his honor; for my neighbor, that he may instruct himself from it.
Composed by Johann Sebastian Bach, p. t. [*pleno titulo,* "with full
title"?] Capellmeister to the Serene Reigning Prince of Anhalt-Cöthen.[27]

That the wording may not be entirely original is suggested first of all by
the word *anfahenden* ("beginning") in the second line. By Bach's time, the
verb *anfahen* ("to begin") had been replaced in colloquial German by
anfangen, the former being retained only in poetry.[28] Compared with the rest
of the phraseology, the word sounds both precious and antiquated, and there
is good evidence that it may be borrowed from a sixteenth-century source,
namely, Elias Nikolaus Ammerbach's *Orgel oder Instrument Tabulatur.* The
first edition of Ammerbach's collection, issued in 1571, is subtitled: *Ein
nützlichs Büchlein, in welchem notwendige erklerung der Orgel oder
Instrument Tabulatur . . . zubefinden . . . der Jugend und anfahenden dieser
Kunst zum besten in Druck vorfertiget . . .* ("A useful little book, in which is
to be found a necessary explanation of organ or instrument tablature, issued
in print for the benefit of young people and of beginners in this art"). Its sub-
title aside, Ammerbach's publication is of special significance to Bach and
to the *Orgelbüchlein* in particular, for Bach appears to have owned no fewer
than three copies of the first edition, and the volume represents the first
extant collection of organ chorales. Bach surely recognized the historical
importance of Ammerbach's collection—and hence the historical position of
the *Orgelbüchlein*—and it is conceivable that he chose to express his indebt-
edness to the organ-chorale tradition by appropriating not only the general
scheme and tone of Ammerbach's wording but certain key words as well. In
addition to *anfahenden,* one of these words may be *Büchlein,* even though
this term was commonly used to designate any collection of music (for example, Bach also employs it in the *Clavier-Büchlein vor Wilhelm Friedemann
Bach,* a keyboard manual for his eldest son).

It has been claimed that pedagogical application was not part of the
Orgelbüchlein's original purpose. After all, only the title page reveals didactic intent, and it was penned after most of the works had been composed. Yet,
despite the fact that the *Orgelbüchlein* is hardly a graded organ primer, who
is to say that Bach did not have pedagogy in mind from the outset? He was
already an established private instructor by the time he arrived in Weimar in

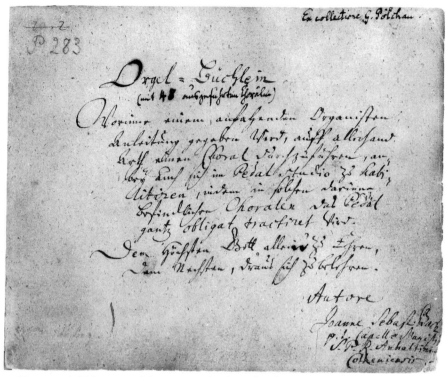

Figure 1–3. Title page of the autograph of the *Orgelbüchlein* (Staatsbibliothek zu Berlin—Preussischer Kulturbesitz, Musikabteilung, Mus. ms. Bach P 283. fol. 1ʳ)

1708, and his teacher's instinct may have been almost as inceptive a force as that of composer or organist.

At any rate, Bach appears to have used the *Orgelbüchlein* as teaching repertory as early as his Weimar period: numerous copies of *Orgelbüchlein* chorales by Bach's Weimar pupil J. T. Krebs have survived. And after Bach left Weimar, his last organ post, the *Orgelbüchlein* seems to have served him *primarily* as teaching repertory. He apparently had organ pupils in Cöthen who he felt could benefit from the collection, and it appears to have served him as pedagogical material for the remainder of his life. (The particular pupils who appear to have studied the *Orgelbüchlein* with Bach himself will be cited in the final chapter.)

It is in Cöthen that we gain our first in-depth look at Bach as a pedagogue, for it was there that he produced his first explicitly didactic works— all of them keyboard collections—such as the Inventions and Sinfonias and Book I of *The Well-Tempered Clavier*. The transformation of the *Orgel-*

büchlein's function from service music to pedagogical material, then, must be viewed against the background of Bach's general inclination towards pedagogy at this time. A most telling comparison is provided by the Inventions and Sinfonias, whose autograph title page expresses strikingly similar didactic goals to that of the *Orgelbüchlein*, using much of the same terminology (*Anleitung, obligaten, durchzuführen*) and phraseology as well:

> Upright instruction wherein the lovers of the clavier, and especially those desirous of learning, are shown a clear way not alone (1) to learn to play clearly in two voices, but also, after further progress, (2) to deal correctly and well with three *obbligato* parts; furthermore, at the same time not alone to have good *inventiones* [ideas], but to develop the same well, and above all to arrive at a singing style in playing and at the same time to acquire a strong foretaste of composition.[29]

In both the *Orgelbüchlein* and the Inventions and Sinfonias, the pupil is to be taught how to compose works of a particular type and, simultaneously, to master aspects of keyboard technique.

The user of the *Orgelbüchlein* is promised two benefits: to become proficient on the pedals and to learn to compose organ chorales "in all kinds of ways." Because the overwhelming majority of *Orgelbüchlein* chorales are of one type (the melody chorale), perhaps this tag (*auff allerhand Arth*) actually refers to different ways of composing within one type rather than in different types. After all, one of the most important compositional lessons to be learned from the collection is that by varying accompanimental figuration,[30] individualization is possible, even within a narrowly defined type like the melody chorale.

By "obbligato" pedal, Bach means that in every one of the *Orgelbüchlein* chorales at least one voice *must* be taken throughout by the feet. This feature may be thought of as a Bachian trademark, since the uncompromising use of pedal distinguishes Bach's organ works as a whole from those of his predecessors and contemporaries. In the context of the organ chorale, it may also have represented an innovation even for Bach, since in many of his earlier organ chorales, such as those from the Neumeister Collection, the pedal is treated in an *ad libitum* manner—these works may be played for the most part on manuals alone or with very little pedal.

But the pedagogical value of the collection is far more comprehensive than what the title page implies. First of all, in addition to learning how to play bass parts on the pedalboard, users of the *Orgelbüchlein* are taught the coordination of hands and feet, arguably the most crucial organ technique of all. They also learn the critical difference between playing on the same manual and on two different manuals. In more general terms, they learn to negotiate a wide range of figuration and textures, to play in over ten major and minor keys, and to handle such matters as phrasing, articulation, registration, and sensitivity to the melody and text of a hymn. In short, they attain the basics of organ playing.

The *Orgelbüchlein*'s highest purpose, however, like that of Bach's music in general, is of a religious nature: service to God and the edification of humankind. It is summed up by the rhyming couplet—essentially a dedication—that concludes the title, and that bears repeating here: *Dem höchsten Gott allein' zu Ehren, Dem Nechsten, draus sich zu belehren* (which Hans David and Arthur Mendel poetically translated as "In Praise of the Almighty's Will, And for my Neighbor's Greater Skill").[31] Like other previously discussed portions, this couplet, too, may have been borrowed from an item in Bach's personal library, the *Gesangbüchlein* of Michael Weisse, published in 1531, which ends with the couplet: *Gott allein zu lob und ehr / Und seinn auserwelten zur leer* ("For the praise and honor of God alone, and for the edification of his chosen ones").[32] Not only do Bach and Weisse express the same message, but they also use the same phraseology and rhyme scheme ("ehr" and "lehr"). And in addition to being a hymnal, Weisse's collection, like Ammerbach's *Tabulatur,* also parallels the *Orgelbüchlein* in its use of the term "Büchlein."

Any connection to Weisse, however, is of secondary significance compared to the couplet's apparent biblical derivation, which would seem to reveal its true meaning. The scriptural source in question is one that has always occupied an important position in Christian liturgy. Known as Christ's "Summary of the Law," it reads: "Thou shalt love the Lord Thy God with all thy heart, and with all thy soul, and with all thy mind. This is the first and great commandment. And the second is like unto it, Thou shalt love thy neighbour as thyself. On these two commandments hang all the law and the prophets" (Matthew 22:37–40). Basically an extension of his more common slogan *Soli Deo Gloria* ("To God Alone the Glory"), Bach's little couplet proclaims that his music has both a divine and worldly purpose, in accordance with Jesus' teachings. Ultimately, then, the *Orgelbüchlein* may be understood as its composer's response to the New Testament.

Chapter 2

COMPOSITIONAL PROCESS

BACKGROUND

The term "compositional process," coined some twenty years ago by Robert Marshall in his pioneering study *The Compositional Process of J. S. Bach*, refers to the manner in which a composition evolves from its original conception to its final, definitive form. Put another way, it involves the means by which a composer produces a finished work. To the extent possible, the researcher imaginatively "becomes" the composer in hopes of explaining the work's genesis—how it was formed "in the beginning." Only through the intensive study of autograph sources, either sketches or compositional drafts, can this line of inquiry be fully realized.

Compositional process in Bach's instrumental music is perforce a little-explored phenomenon. While numerous composing scores (as well as sketches) for his vocal music have survived, few such sources for the instrumental works are extant. Furthermore, there are relatively few extant composing scores of any kind by Bach from the first thirty-five years of his life. Thus the autograph of the *Orgelbüchlein*, which contains not one but evidently over twenty composing scores, is a potentially rich fount of information about Bach's compositional methods.

Specifically, this source offers a rare opportunity to investigate Bach's compositional process in the domain of the organ chorale. His essays in this genre comprise over two-thirds of his approximately 300 organ works, a sizable portion of his compositional output. Yet, excluding the *Orgelbüchlein*, precious few of these works exist in sources that tell us anything about the compositional act. The same may be said of the entire corpus of organ chorales from the seventeenth and early eighteenth centuries, a not insignificant fact considering that the organ chorale is one of the most common of all Baroque genres. The *Orgelbüchlein* autograph, therefore, represents a key to understanding not only how Bach composed his organ chorales but how other Baroque masters might have created theirs.

The only work of any significance on compositional process in the *Orgelbüchlein* is found in the *Kritischer Bericht* of Heinz-Harald Löhlein's edition for the *Neue Bach-Ausgabe*, which lists most of the compositional revisions in the autograph, measure by measure, piece by piece. It is extremely helpful to have this information at hand, and Löhlein is to be credited with having clarified a multitude of seemingly undecipherable passages. The task remains, though, of interpreting the musical significance of these revisions. Simply put: why did Bach revise these passages in particular, and what impact do the revisions have on the work?

PRECOMPOSITION AND THE ORDER OF EVENTS

The earliest point to which we can trace Bach's conception of the *Orgelbüchlein* chorales is his writing of chorale titles into the autograph. As discussed in the previous chapter, since two pages instead of one were reserved for relatively long chorale tunes, it is clear that Bach was thinking of setting melodies in their entirety. This, in turn, has strong implications for the organ-chorale types he had in mind (melody chorale, ornamented chorale, and chorale canon). As an experienced composer of organ chorales, Bach clearly assumed that most of the chorales in bar form (AAB) allotted a single page would not be through-composed. Rather, he envisioned that the repeat of the *Stollen* (the "A" section) would be indicated by repeat signs. This accords with Bach's general practice in setting bar-form chorales.[1]

As a Lutheran and a professional church musician, Bach was well acquainted with the chorales whose titles he penned, and both the tunes and texts of these chorales were undoubtedly important precompositional agents. Because the chorale tune predetermined a work's harmonic as well as melodic design, it is conceivable that before entering a single note, Bach thought through the entire melody in order to realize its harmonic implications, especially at cadences. As concerns the chorale text, it is well known that Baroque composers felt obliged to portray the text of a vocal work in as affective a way as possible, to the degree that the music was considered the text's "servant."[2] While best suited to vocal music, this tenet is also applicable to intrumental genres like the organ chorale, where the text is only implied, and especially applicable to the *Orgelbüchlein*, where the element of textual allusion is unusually pronounced.

No hymnal has been found that uses the same chorale order as the *Orgelbüchlein*, which would seem to demonstrate that Bach drew up the sequence himself. Furthermore, there are often discrepancies between the chorale melodies as notated by Bach in the *Orgelbüchlein* and as notated in contemporary hymnals, suggesting that he was not mechanically copying the tunes from preexisting sources. These discrepancies involve melody, rhythm, and the use of different note values for the basic pulse. Bach uses quarter notes for the basic pulse in most of the duple-meter chorales, whereas half notes are the norm in hymnals of the time, a discrepancy that implies a new instrumental orientation on Bach's part. Given this evidence, and assuming that Bach's knowledge of hymnody was all-encompassing, he probably entered the tunes out of his head.

Based on what is known about Bach's working habits, he would not have relied on sketches or planning drafts in composing works of such modest size and whose principal melodic material (the chorale tune) was predetermined.[3] We may therefore assume that the entries designated in Chapter 1 as "composing scores" contain the earliest music jotted down by Bach for those particular pieces.

The sequence of events that transpired once Bach began notating the music in these composing scores is easy to imagine. In composing the many melody chorales, he most certainly entered the soprano first—for the obvious reason that the chorale tune governs the harmonic structure of the work—then the bass, which serves as the harmonic foundation. Finally, he entered the middle two voices, which fill out the harmony implied by the soprano and bass. Luckily, there is compelling documentary evidence that Bach followed precisely this order in writing melody chorales. For example, in the composing scores of several melody chorales from the *Orgelbüchlein*, there is extreme crowding in the inner voices, implying that these voices were added to a layout initially conceived for soprano and bass parts with fewer notes per measure. Furthermore, as Robert Marshall has shown, Bach adopted the sequence of soprano → bass → middle voices in composing many of the chorale harmonizations that conclude his church cantatas, movements that are analogous to the melody chorales from the *Orgelbüchlein* in their placement of the chorale tune in the top voice, their use of four voices, and their lack of interludes between phrases.[4] As with the melody chorales from the *Orgelbüchlein,* there is little evidence in the autographs of the vocal works whether Bach notated a chorale one phrase at a time or, say, first wrote down the soprano in its entirety, then the complete bass line, and finally the middle voices. C. P. E. Bach's report on his father's teaching methods suggests the latter approach: "His pupils had to begin their studies by learning pure four-part thorough bass. From this he went to chorales; first he added the basses to them himself, and they had to invent the alto and tenor [meaning, of course, that the chorale tune was to be presented in the soprano]. Then he taught them to devise the basses themselves."[5] Several copies of Bach organ chorales by his Weimar pupil J. T. Krebs contain only a soprano melody and figured bass, implying that they are remnants of this practice.[6]

For the other chorale types encountered in the *Orgelbüchlein,* there is less documentation. Because the ornamental chorale is essentially a modified melody chorale, we may assume that Bach employed the same sequence for both types. In composing the nine canons, he surely worked out the canonic voices before the others. Aside from the free canonic parts in "In dulci jubilo," the canonic voices are based on chorale tunes, so again the voices assigned the chorale tune were presumably the first to be composed. (In "In dulci jubilo," it is clear from revisions in the autograph that the chorale canon was entered before the free canon.)

In the case of "Christum wir sollen loben schon," where the alto alone states the entire chorale tune, it would be a logical assumption that the alto was composed first, then the bass, and lastly the soprano and tenor. In creating the fantasy-like "In dir ist Freude," Bach most likely composed the voices simultaneously, rather than in a particular order.

THREE CASE STUDIES

One could easily write a monograph just on the issue of compositional process in the *Orgelbüchlein.* A book of this sort might be organized into case studies of composing scores containing particularly revealing revisions. We will limit ourselves here to three such entries, chosen not only because they are especially rich in terms of compositional revisions but also because they represent three different chorale types and hence illustrate three differ-

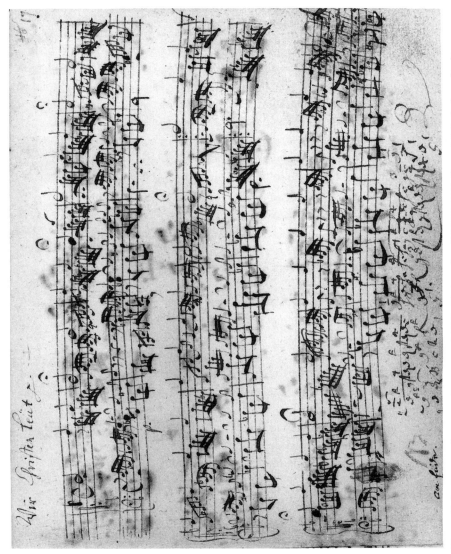

Figure 2–1. Autograph composing score of "Wir Christenleut," BWV 612 (Staatsbibliothek zu Berlin—Preussischer Kulturbesitz, Musikabteilung, Mus. ms. Bach P 283, fol. 10r)

ent compositional procedures. Quite by accident, the latter two works are among the most popular in the collection as well as two of Bach's most beloved organ chorales altogether.

Wir Christenleut, BWV 612

Let us begin with the autograph entry of the Christmas hymn "Wir Christenleut" (Figure 2–1), a representative of the *Orgelbüchlein*-type. This is one of several entries where Bach notated the last bars in German organ tablature in order to fit the entire work onto a single page.[7]

The revisions in this entry imply the general compositional sequence of soprano → bass → middle voices that we have discussed. Observe that all the quarter notes in the soprano lack dots, while all the quarter notes in the lower three parts are dotted. This discrepancy suggests that as Bach entered the soprano, he planned on setting the entire tune in simple duple meter and decided on compound duple (the unnotated $\frac{12}{8}$ time) only upon adding the lower parts. After all, common time is the only meter actually notated, and this meter signature appears to have been entered in both staves before any of the notes.

Corrections in measures 1 and 3 indicate that the bass was entered before the alto and tenor, which already have the appearance of being squeezed onto an existing framework (especially at the end of m. 2, where the voices run across the barline). To begin with, on the third beat of measure 1 and the first beat of measure 3, the first bass note was originally a third higher, g instead of e-flat. In measure 1, the notehead on g was erased, but only partially, and in measure 3 the notehead on g became the very sizable dot of the g dotted quarter note in the tenor. Moreover, the high positioning of the dot for the tenor dotted quarter note on the third beat of measure 1 shows clearly that a bass note on g was already in place before Bach drew the tenor note. The same is evidently true of the first beat of measure 3, where the two voices have the same material as in measure 1. It follows that Bach did not correct the bass note in measure 1 until after he had entered the first beat of measure 3. The musical rationale behind these changes—always the most important issue in these matters—must have had to do with the enrichment of the harmony, for they allow all three pitches of the E-flat major triad—instead of merely g and b-flat—to be sounded simultaneously. Bach may also have been concerned about the harmonic ambiguity of the original readings, which could be taken to represent either G minor or E-flat major.

On the third and fourth beats of measure 3, Bach made alterations to the soprano, demonstrated by the unusually large notehead of the quarter note (and the high placement of the quarter rest on beat four). The rhythm was doubtless a half note originally, since throughout the *Orgelbüchlein* autograph Bach consistently draws much larger noteheads for half notes (and whole notes) than for smaller values. In its original form, then, the second phrase of the chorale tune, which begins on the second beat of measure 2, was rhythmically as well as melodically identical to the first.

It makes no sense that Bach changed the value to relieve the rhythmic monotony of the first five measures of the soprano line, which, in its original form, employed the idea ♩ ♩♩♩ three consecutive times. Nor is it at all plausible that he wished to avoid the voice-crossing between the soprano and alto on the fourth beat, since voice-crossing occurs to a greater degree on the previous beat. Rather, harmonic considerations must have been the reason, specifically, the harsh dissonance generated by the g' on the last eighth note of this bar, where a modulation to the relative major begins. The g' was at odds with the F-major chord formed by the lower three voices, and it severely impeded the modulation by prolonging G minor as the tonic. A similar modulation to C minor begins at the analogous passage on the second beat of measure 2, but in that instance the g' functions as the root of a secondary dominant, causing no harmonic problems.

Far more perplexing is a series of corrections in measures 10 and 11 (see Example 2–1a). The phrase of the chorale tune that concludes on the downbeat of measure 10 is melodically identical to the third phrase, stated in measures 4–5. Bach originally chose not only the same pitches but the same rhythms for the restatement of this phrase in measures 9–10, including a half note on a' on the first beat of measure 10. The phrase that follows in measures 10–11 is melodically identical to these two, and it was initially notated with the same rhythms, a half note on d" on the third beat of measure 10 and a quarter note on c" on the first beat of measure 11 (observe, respectively, the erasure on the top line immediately prior to the c" quarter note on the third beat of m. 10 and the ink smudge between the top two lines on the first beat of m. 11). After entering just the first two notes of this phrase, Bach changed his mind.

The only reasonable explanation for these alterations is that once again the soprano, in its original form, was harmonically incompatible with the lower parts. The alto originally read as in Example 2–1b; the tenor contains two rejected readings, shown in Example 2–1c and Example 2–1d. Example 2–1a, beginning with the second beat of measure 10, is harmonically inconsistent with Examples 2–1b, 2–1c, and 2–1d, so much so that Bach surely never had any intention of combining the rejected soprano reading with the rejected alto reading or with either rejected tenor reading.

Example 2–1. "Wir Christenleut," BWV 612, mm. 10–11: rejected readings

It is possible to envision the following scenario: Bach began notating measures 10–11 with the rejected soprano reading (Example 2–1a) only. After writing the c" on the downbeat of measure 11 (even though he was only midway through the phrase), he returned to the first beat of measure 10 to work out the tenor. He chose for the first beat of measure 10 the accompanimental motive ⁷ 𝄢𝄢𝄢 𝄢 used from the outset, thus continuing the descending sequential statements of this figure begun on the last two beats of the previous measure. He next entered beats 2–4 of Example 2–1c, which continued the downward sequence and, more importantly, gave the tenor the same material presented an octave higher by the alto in measure 9. Perhaps he did not realize until after he had notated the tenor that it was severely dissonant with the soprano. At any rate, he was now forced to redo one of the voices, and he chose the soprano, even though that meant sacrificing the rhythmic regularity of the chorale tune. The counterpoint between the soprano and tenor, as illustrated in Example 2–2a, was now essentially identical to that between the soprano and alto in the previous bar.

Let us continue with the scenario: Bach next entered the original version of the alto line (Example 2–1b). For the first time, measure 10 contained all three parts and read as in Example 2–2a. Whereas the alto was compatible with the soprano, it created three consecutive sevenths with the tenor on the second beat. To remedy this problem, Bach rewrote the tenor line as in Example 2–2b, discarding one motive (⁷ 𝄢𝄢𝄢 𝄢) for another (⁷ 𝄢𝄢 𝄢). The counterpoint was now competent, the harmony correct, but Bach was still not satisfied. He may have found the eighth rest in the alto rhythmically static and the f-sharp' at the end of the first beat oddly unresolved (all the other F-sharp pitches in the piece resolve immediately to G pitches). Whatever the reason, as shown in Example 2–2c, he substituted two sixteenths for the rest and raised the next sixteenth from g' to b-flat'. This was the first instance in the piece of a series of six sixteenth notes—the most consecutive sixteenths prior to this point are four—and Bach would revert to this accelerated motion in the alto voice for

Example 2–2. "Wir Christenleut," BWV 612, m. 10: proposed developmental stages

most of the next bar. The revision to the alto, however, resulted in harmonic and contrapuntal deficiencies on the second eighth note of the second beat: the third of the G-minor chord was doubled, depriving the chord of its root; the two thirds were approached in similar motion; and, worst of all, there were parallel octaves between the alto and tenor. Bach's final step, then, was to rewrite the first two eighth notes of the tenor as in Example 2–2d, restoring the root and allowing for pleasing contrary motion. The contrary motion is enhanced by the extremely wide spacing between the alto and tenor (two octaves plus a third), which represents by far the largest interval between these parts anywhere in the composition. In effect, Bach had made "the faulty good, the good better, and the better perfect."[8]

Measures 10–11 are by far the most heavily revised passage in the work and, ostensibly, the most difficult for Bach to compose. Might this explain why the bass is missing? It is otherwise completely absent only in the preceding bar, where, granted, the downward stems and relatively low notes of the tenor would have made the notation of a bass voice problematic at best. But in measures 10–11, the addition of a bass part, at some point in the compositional process, would not have been all that difficult. It is at least within the realm of possibility that Bach opted against a bass voice in measures 10–11 because of the considerable problems he was having with the other three parts. As if to compensate for the missing bass voice, he increased the rhythmic activity in the alto precisely at measures 10–11. One ingredient is added where another is missing—the composer's way of ensuring continuous musical interest.

O Mensch, bewein dein Sünde gross, BWV 622

Bach's composing score of this famous Passiontide chorale (Figure 2–2) reveals that much of the decorative figuration was added after the chorale tune had been penned in a relatively unadorned form. In no instance was a reading in the soprano—or any other voice—simplified. This is hardly a surprising state of affairs, since the inclination to embellish is basic to Bach's compositional process. And just as Bach tended to add rather than subtract notes while revising, he tended to lengthen rather than shorten a work. For example, there are two *Orgelbüchlein* chorales ("Herr Christ, der ein'ge Gottessohn" and "Heut triumphieret Gottes Sohn") in which there is a discrepancy in length between early and revised versions, and in both cases the revised version is slightly longer.

In the first phrase of "O Mensch," it is clear that the first two beats of the soprano in measure 1 originally read as two quarter notes, representing the second and third notes of the chorale tune (did Bach originally conceive of this most celebrated of all ornamental chorales as a melody chorale?). The noteheads of the thirty-second notes are minuscule compared to those of the quarter notes, while on the first two beats of measure 2, where basically the same material is used, transposed up a third, the thirty-seconds are the same size as the quarters. This implies that Bach added the thirty-second notes on the first two beats of measure 1 (or at least knew that he would eventually add them) before notating the first two beats of measure 2.

Bach initially conceived the tenor line in slower values, too. In measure 1, it contains two half notes, and the tied quarter notes in the tenor in measure 3, beats 2–3, represent a half note as well. Half notes, which are the slowest rhythm in "O Mensch," appear nowhere else in this work. They render these two measures among the least contrapuntally interesting in the piece, and it cannot be happenstance that they occur only at the beginning. Bach needed a few measures before he consistently used faster rhythms in the lower voices, thereby creating greater polyphonic substance.

On the last beat of measure 3, the soprano must originally have concluded with two sixteenths. This is attested to by the high placement of the dot and, more significantly, the even spacing between the two notes (the second note should be farther to the right). The low placement of the dot at the corresponding spot on the next beat strongly suggests that the same revision took place there; the spacing between notes is appropriately uneven, but this is probably due only to the natural sign on a'. To judge from this evidence, beginning with the third beat of measure 3, Bach originally notated three statements of the rhythm ♩♫♫♩ . Most likely, he chose to sharpen the rhythm of just the second and third statements because only they are melodically sequential (they form the first sequence in the piece; the first statement has a slightly different contour). The revisions give to the sequence its own rhythmic and melodic identity.

We should also consider a change made to the bass on the second beat of measure 3. The spacing between the notes indicates that the b-flat, which should be farther to the right, was entered after the g and a-flat, both of which were originally eighth notes. This change allowed for three successive statements of the ♩ ♫ motive presented first by the soprano on the last beat of the previous bar and next by the alto on the first beat of measure 3. It also allowed for motivic interplay between the bass and the upper voices,

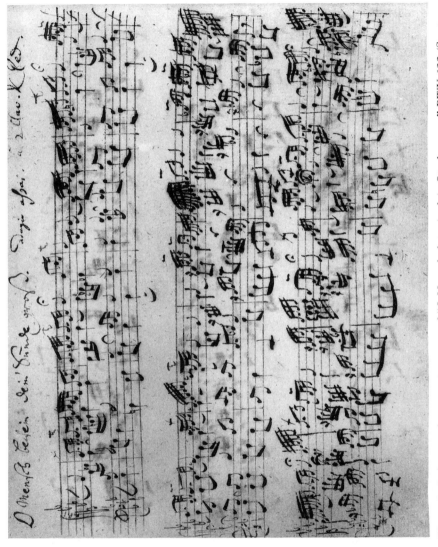

Figure 2–2. Autograph composing score of "O Mensch, bewein dein Sünde gross," BWV 622 (Staatsbibliothek zu Berlin—Preussischer Kulturbesitz, Musikabteilung, Mus. ms. Bach P 283, fol. 15ᵛ)

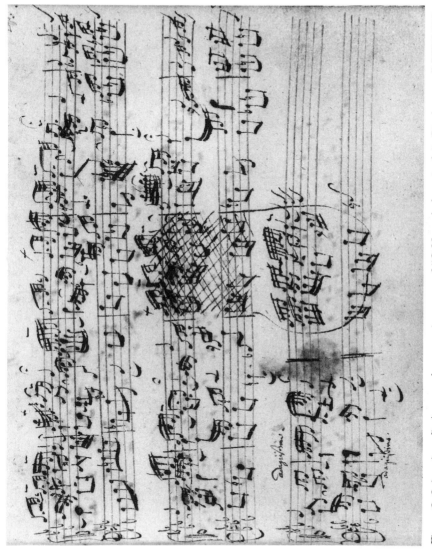

Figure 2-2 *(continued)*. Autograph composing score of "O Mensch, bewein dein Sünde gross," BWV 622 (Staatsbibliothek zu Berlin—Preussischer Kulturbesitz, Musikabteilung, Mus. ms. Bach P 283, fol. 16ʳ)

which happens nowhere else in the work, and gave the passage in general a heightened sense of motivic unity. A similar revision was made to the tenor on the first beat of measure 6, but the harmonic context there is different, with the b-flat functioning as a passing tone instead of a harmonic tone.

The third beat of measure 6 marks the end of the *Stollen,* so this would normally have been the place for Bach to draw repeat signs indicating its restatement. But since two pages instead of one had been allotted for this long chorale tune, Bach had sufficient space to compose a varied reprise of the *Stollen,* a rare opportunity of which he took full advantage. (The only other instance of this sort of varied reprise in the *Orgelbüchlein* occurs in "Helft mir Gotts Güte preisen.") Judging from the large notehead on f' on the second beat of measure 7, the original soprano notation of the reprise was identical to that of the initial statement: three quarter notes in the order e-flat'- e-flat' - f'.

An arresting feature of the first page is the frequency with which the soprano runs across the barline. It may well be that in some of these instances ornamental figuration was tacked onto an existing part, but there is no clear proof of this.[9] A more plausible explanation is that Bach drew barlines for sizable portions of the page before entering any music and that by the time he reached the second page, he realized that he had more than enough space to notate the few remaining phrases of the chorale tune. As a result, the symbols in general are larger, there are fewer measures per system, and the soprano is guilty of encroachment only in measures 17–18.

The most tangible evidence of the creative process may be viewed at the very end of the entry, where, after notating the final measure, Bach crossed out all of measure 21 and entered a different rendition of it directly beneath. The rejected version of measure 21 is given in Example 2–3.[10] One sees that Bach retained the bass line and the fundamental harmony, but changed certain harmonic inflections. The revision was most likely made because of the prosaic character of the original reading, which was transformed into an exceptional passage. There is nothing at all "wrong" with the original reading, and probably were it not for the blank space left over on the bottom system, the revision would never have been made (this is the only occurrence in the whole autograph of the *Orgelbüchlein* of an entire bar being crossed out and rewritten). Here was a rare instance in which the layout of the autograph made wholesale recomposition convenient, and Bach capitalized on it.

In doing so, he produced an extraordinary revision. Most importantly, the first two beats of the revised reading are texturally unique, representing the

Example 2–3. "O Mensch, bewein dein Sünde gross," BWV 622, m. 21: original reading.

most pronounced instance of parallel motion among the upper three voices in the work. Furthermore, the string of eight thirty-second notes on the third beat of the new version is otherwise found only three times in the work, while the soprano motives for the second and third beats of the rejected reading (♩ ♫ , ♫♫♫) are employed in practically every previous bar. Bach achieved harmonic variety through the exotic-sounding ninth chord on the third beat (which replaces the plain triad in the rejected reading), highlighted by the placement of the ninth in the soprano and the high tessitura in general. More subtle differences involve the voice leading between the alto and tenor on the third and fourth beats: in the revised reading, the writing is not nearly as chordal as in the original.

In dulci jubilo, BWV 608

The equally famous setting of "In dulci jubilo" (see Figure 2–3) is a rare specimen of a double canon. The chorale tune is set as a canon at the octave between the soprano and tenor, and for the first twenty-four bars it is accompanied by a second, free canon at the octave between the alto and bass. It would appear that Bach first worked out the canon on the chorale melody (see discussion below); this is hardly a surprise, given the primacy of the chorale tune in any chorale setting. Since in both canons the upper voice serves as the *dux*, or leader, the voices were probably composed in the order soprano → tenor → alto → bass.

There is notational as well as musical evidence that the chorale canon was the first to be composed: for much of the autograph entry the barlines used for the bottom staff are noticeably thicker than those in the upper staff and frequently positioned to the right (see mm. 4–6, 10, 16, and 19–21).

Figure 2–3. Autograph composing score of "In dulci jubilo," BWV 608 (Staatsbibliothek zu Berlin—Preussischer Kulturbesitz, Musikabteilung, Mus. ms. Bach P 283, fol. 7ᵛ)

Figure 2–3 (*continued*). Autograph composing score of "In dulci jubilo," BWV 608 (Staatsbibliothek zu Berlin—Preussischer Kulturbesitz, Musikabteilung, Mus. ms. Bach P 283, fol. 8ʳ)

Notice that the first occurrence of these discrepancies is in measures 4–6, precisely the first instance where both the soprano and tenor are notated for consecutive measures exclusively on the upper staff. Bach had no need to supply barlines for the bottom staff here, as he had done in measures 1–3, and it would seem that he did not draw them until he had entered the free canon, at some later point in the compositional process. It would appear that as Bach continued to work out the chorale canon beyond measure 6, he also continued for the most part to draw barlines for the upper staff, since this is where the soprano is consistently notated, but frequently to omit barlines for the bottom staff, since the tenor is notated there only about half the time. Following this line of reasoning, we can theorize that as Bach was notating the bass voice of the free canon, he regularly encountered areas that lacked barlines. Without these borders, he often slightly exceeded the length of the bar already marked off in the upper staff, which is entirely understandable since the free canon contains many more notes per measure than the chorale canon. This is the only reasonable explanation as to why many of the bottom barlines tend to be to the right of the upper ones. As for the relative thickness of the bottom barlines, we may assume that by the time they were drawn, the tip of Bach's quill had become so blunt that it could no longer consistently draw razor-sharp lines.

To judge from revisions made to the soprano in measures 14 and 22, the chorale canon was notated in its entirety, or at least through measure 22, before the free canon was entered. In these two measures, which contain the same music in all parts, we find in the soprano voice the only instance in this entry where tied half notes (instead of a single whole note) are used; in both measures Bach wrote very different symbols for the two half notes, suggesting that they were not entered in direct succession. Furthermore, in this work Bach tends to draw whole notes larger than half notes, so the relatively large noteheads of the first half notes in both measures also imply that they originated as whole notes. In their original form, both measures obviously contained a whole note on c-sharp" and a half note on b', instead of vice versa.

In its original version, the soprano created dissonance with the tenor in these passages. But the dissonance—a major ninth from b to c-sharp"—is negligible: it is approached through oblique motion, occurs on a weak beat, and resolves quickly on the next beat. If this major ninth bothered Bach, why did he wait until he had notated it twice to change it? Moreover, if a dissonance as trifling as this necessitated a revision, it is hard to see how Bach could have abided the major seventh between these two parts on the last beats of measures 11 and 19, which is stronger because it is reached through parallel motion. One can more successfully explain the changes by considering the harmony between the two canons. In its original reading, the soprano c-sharp" clashed with the B-minor seventh chord that is the underlying harmony of the second beat. The change to b' alleviated the dissonance but resulted in a less strict canon between the soprano and tenor. Bach, therefore, was willing to sacrifice contrapuntal integrity for the sake of smooth harmonic progressions.

Additional evidence that a large segment of the chorale canon was in place before the free canon was begun is supplied by revisions in measures 12–13 and 20–21. Here, the shape and size of the soprano half notes on a' on the first beats of measures 12 and 20 indicate that these notes were originally whole notes; the same goes for the tenor half note on a on the first beat of measure 13. The tenor half note on a on the first beat of measure 21 does not have the obvious physical appearance of originally having been a whole note—the notehead is basically the size used for half notes in this entry—but the phrases of the chorale melody set in these two passages are melodically identical, and it stands to reason that Bach originally concluded both of them with whole notes, as he had done for every other phrase of the tune through measure 21. (The rhythmic discrepancies between the first measures of these phrases—a whole note versus two half notes—probably led Bach erroneously to enter a further half note instead of a whole note on e" on the downbeat of m. 18.) Again, the only plausible reason for these revisions involves the harmony between the two canons, for the whole notes pose no problems within the chorale canon itself. (The dissonance within the chorale canon produced by the whole notes is analogous to the weak dissonance discussed above in connection with mm. 14 and 22.) When superimposed onto the free canon, the whole notes generate a disagreeable tonic-dominant sonority.

The free canon was also revised in a number of places. In measures 2–3 and 6–7, for example, it is apparent that Bach originally drew natural signs for all four G pitches, although the naturals are barely visible due to erasures. Sounding simultaneously with A, C-sharp, and E pitches, the G pitches transform the tonic A-major triads into secondary dominant sevenths to the subdominant, D major. However, they also created cross relations between the alto and bass in measures 2 and 6, and this was obviously the reason for the change. Although there were no false relations in measures 3 and 7, Bach erased the natural signs there as well to maintain consistency within the canonic writing.

Beyond measure 7, the majority of the revisions made to the free canon are found in the alto voice, hardly a surprise, since it was in this voice that

Bach first composed the free melody. The many revisions made to the melody in measures 10–15, for instance, are found only in the alto; the bass that follows it is completely free of corrections. This obviously suggests that Bach revised the alto in this passage before he had entered a single note of the bass. But in measures 15–16, it would seem that the same revisions made between the second and third notes of the alto were made between the second and third notes of the bass in the next bar, since erasures appear at analogous places in both passages. Unfortunately, the original readings are so thoroughly effaced that they cannot be reconstructed with any certainty.

This statement applies to some but by no means all of the alto revisions in measures 10–15. Judging from the relatively large size of the first alto quarter note on the third beat of measure 11, the reading here was originally a half note on e'. The passing tone on e-sharp' adds chromatic spice to an otherwise diatonic melody and creates a secondary diminished seventh to the F-sharp–minor chord that follows on the first beat of measure 12, giving the passage greater harmonic drive. In measure 12, the large notehead for the first alto note indicates that this note, too, was originally a half note. In both measure 11 and measure 12, then, the original readings are more homophonic than what was ultimately notated (this same sort of revision also occurs in the bass on the third beat of m. 32).

Both of these revisions involve a note equal to the basic pulse whose pitch remains the same but whose rhythmic value is diminished. This type of revision to an accompanimental voice happens to be the most common of all the compositional revisions encountered in the autograph of the *Orgelbüchlein*.[11] With their stark chordal texture, the original readings of this ilk often so disrupt the rhythmic flow of the accompanimental voices that one wonders whether Bach ever thought of them as entirely legitimate. He may have considered them all along as nothing more than a harmonic framework on which he would later construct the "real" music.

Ironically, the alto and bass gave Bach the most problems once the work thinned from a double to a single canon. The free canon ends in measure 24. By far the messiest passage in the entry occurs at measures 23–27, due to revisions in the alto and bass. The revisions in the alto at measure 23 may well be corrections of scribal errors, for all Bach had to do—and all that he chose to do in the end—was to enter the same music he had composed for measure 15 (mm. 15 and 23 are analogous, since the portions of the chorale canon set are melodically identical).

This cannot be said, though, for the alto revisions in measure 24. Assuming that the chorale canon was already in place on the middle system of the second page, Bach knew that measure 25 was to be a pivotal point in the work: it breaks the repetitive phrase structure of the chorale canon and initiates a phrase requiring (because of its scalar motion) a doubled distance between canonic voices. To maintain the free canon, Bach could not merely reuse old material, as he had done in measures 5–8 and 17–24. In addition to inventing a new melody, he also had to decide whether the distance between the voices should stay at one measure or conform to the new two-measure spacing of the chorale canon begun in measure 25. It is tempting to believe, in view of the heavy revision, that Bach originally attempted to continue the double canon through this juncture but that this became an overly problematic proposition. As to what he originally notated here we will never know, for the original readings are largely undecipherable.

Once he was through this thicket, Bach was more or less "home free." He was now faced only with the decision of how to conclude the piece satisfactorily. There were two options: either to end in measure 33 or measure 34, at the conclusion of the chorale canon proper, or to sustain the final note of the chorale melody in the tenor for a few measures beyond this point, which would have been a typical concluding gesture for a Baroque organ chorale. Because he had the space—and only because he had the space, probably—Bach took the latter course, a further example of how the layout of the *Orgelbüchlein*'s autograph affected the outcome of the individual works. At five measures, this is the longest such passage in any *Orgelbüchlein* chorale. Observe also how the passage begins in the subdominant; in the context of a concluding pedal point, this is for Bach a trademark.

COMPOSITIONAL PROCESS AND THE PURSUIT OF PERFECTION

At the beginning of this chapter, we used words such as "final," "finished," and "definitive" to describe the work that is the end result of compositional process. This may be useful language in formulating general definitions, but when applied to Bach, it requires some qualification, for a fundamental aspect of Bach's compositional process is its open-endedness. Christoph Wolff has said it well:

> Ultimately for Bach, the process of composition was an unending one. Dynamic markings and indications would be inserted as he looked

through the parts; he would revise and improve a work when he was copying it out, and when giving further performances would make fresh alterations and improvements. He also inserted corrections in works already in print. Throughout his life Bach was his own severest critic. Even in works which went through two or three different versions…the 'final' version does not represent a definitive one but merely a further state in the search for perfection—the central and ultimate concern of Bach's method of composition.[12]

In composing sacred vocal works, Bach normally faced the pressure of an impending deadline—in many cases he could have had no longer than two or three days for the actual composition of a complete church cantata. In composing instrumental music, however, he often labored under no such constraints and could compose at a more leisurely pace. Of time constraints for Bach's composition of the *Orgelbüchlein* chorales—and organ chorales in general—we can only guess. If we accept the premise that he wrote the *Orgelbüchlein* chorales for services in Weimar, there would have been a compositional deadline for the *de tempore* settings. But given the diminutive size of the *Orgelbüchlein* chorales, this cannot have been much of a factor.

Unfortunately, there is no way of knowing to what degree Bach might have utilized a keyboard instrument in composing the *Orgelbüchlein* chorales, an important concern because playing the music could have exposed flaws in the music that the composer's "inner ear" alone might not have detected, allowing him to achieve a higher degree of perfection. According to C. P. E. Bach, his father generally composed away from the keyboard but tested the results at the keyboard afterwards.[13] Only by means of such testing could Bach have known the extent to which a keyboard work was appropriately idiomatic. It is thus tempting to believe that many of the compositional revisions in the *Orgelbüchlein* chorales were not made until after Bach had played the works through at the keyboard.

In any case, the layout of the autograph severely limited possibilities for revision. As we have noted, Bach normally allotted only one tiny page per work. This format obviously precluded the expansion or reworking of entire sections—both standard revisional practices for Bach in other composing scores. In these types of revision—usually made after the entire work had been notated—Bach crossed out passages and then expanded or completely reworked them in blank spaces at the bottoms of pages. The closest he ever got to this in the autograph of the *Orgelbüchlein* was the cross-out and rewrite of one measure in "O Mensch."

The one-page limit also made changes of detail—the only type of revision that was generally feasible in the autograph of the *Orgelbüchlein*—more troublesome than would ordinarily have been the case. If Bach entered all four voices of the *Stollen* and was dissatisfied with the result, he did not have the luxury of crossing out the passage and recomposing it in a blank space. His only recourse was to erase the passage and rework it in the same space. If all four voices were to be revised, this would have been messy business and a rather delicate operation, especially if the reverse side of the paper already contained a fully notated work (for he might have torn a hole in the paper and defaced both pieces). If Bach wished to maintain the autograph as a permanent, legible volume from which he could perform and teach, these mundane concerns must have run through his mind.

If the layout of the autograph discouraged thorough-going revision, it must be seen as a hindrance to Bach's quest for perfection. Would it be unreasonable to suggest that Bach found certain passages in the autograph deficient but left them unrevised simply because the autograph's layout made revision unusually difficult? Just think of "O Mensch," "Puer natus in Bethlehem," and "Dies sind die heil'gen zehn Gebot," whose opening measures are far more homophonic than the remainder of the work. If the *Orgelbüchlein* chorales are not as perfect as Bach could have made them—a bold thing to say—the reason could be the limiting format.

Of course, Bach could have revised the *Orgelbüchlein* chorales by other means. As he had his pupils copy out the collection, he could have instructed them by word of mouth to amend passages left "uncorrected" in the autograph. This is precisely how he appears to have revised such didactic collections as the Inventions and Sinfonias, *The Well-Tempered Clavier*, and the French Suites, where the pupils' copies often preserve readings of greater refinement than the autograph. With respect to the *Orgelbüchlein*, however, there is virtually no evidence of this sort of oral revision; almost without exception, the student copies transmit only the readings of the autograph.

One important aspect of all the manuscript copies of the *Orgelbüchlein* made during Bach's lifetime is that they almost never preserve a reading from the autograph in its *ante correcturam* state. Practically the only exceptions to this procedure appear in copies of "Christus, der uns selig macht" or "Komm, Gott Schöpfer," the two settings in which Bach notated a revised version of the complete work (BWV 620 and 631) directly on top of the original version several years after making the initial entries. This circumstance strongly suggests that the compositional revisions in the *Orgelbüchlein* chorales were made shortly after their initial composition rather than over an extended period. It would also seem to lend credence to the notion that many of the revisions were made immediately after Bach had tried out the pieces at the keyboard.

Whether these little organ chorales are in any sense "perfect" is a moot issue. For even where Bach chose not to refine his handiwork, he reached a level of achievement unsurpassed by any of his contemporaries. In the end, it is the pursuit of perfection that counts: the multitude of compositional revisions in the autograph stand as a lasting testament to this quest.

Chapter 3

THE MUSIC IN ITS HISTORICAL CONTEXT

SIGNIFICANCE

Over the years, the music of the *Orgelbüchlein* has meant different things to different people, everything from impassioned speech to refined part-writing. To the earliest commentators on the collection, writing in the late nineteenth and early twentieth centuries, it was Bach's expressive representation of the chorale texts that gave the music its special quality. Witness the following encomium, addressed specifically to the *Orgelbüchlein*, written in 1873 by the Bach biographer Philipp Spitta:

> A further step towards perfecting this form [the organ chorale] was taken by Bach when he made the contrapuntal elements in his music a means of reflecting certain emotional aspects of the words. Pachelbel had not attempted this; he lacked the fervid feeling which would have enabled him thus to enter into his subject. And it is entering into it, and not a mere depicting of it. For, once more be it said, in every vital movement of the world external to us we behold the image of a movement within us; and every such image must react on us to produce the corresponding emotion in that inner world of feeling.[1]

Spitta's ruminations were echoed some thirty years later by Albert Schweitzer, who in his 1905 monograph *Jean-Sébastien Bach, le musicien-poète* praised the *Orgelbüchlein* as "one of the greatest achievements in music." As the title of his study implies, Schweitzer saw in the affective representation of sacred texts the true nature of Bach's art, and he viewed the *Orgelbüchlein* as a watershed in the development of this phenomenon, a work in which Bach's style emerges "complete and perfect at once" and one that serves, consequently, as a "key to the understanding of his music as a whole." Schweitzer could thus write:

> Never before had [composers of organ chorales] expressed the texts in pure tone in this way; no one afterwards undertook to do so with such simple means. At the same time the essence of Bach's art comes clearly into view for the first time in this work. He is not satisfied with formal perfection and fullness of sound—otherwise he would have continued to work with the forms and formulae of his teachers in the chorale prelude. He aims at more than this; he aspires after the plastic expression of ideas, and so creates a tone-speech of his own. The elements of such a speech already exist in the *Orgelbüchlein*: the characteristic motives of the various chorales correspond to many of Bach's later emotional and pictorial tone-symbols. The *Orgelbüchlein* is thus the lexicon of Bach's musical speech. This must be our starting-point if we would understand what he is striving to express in the themes of the cantatas and the Passions. Until the significance of the *Orgelbüchlein* was perceived, the fundamental character of Bach's art remained, almost down to the present day, obscure and disputable.[2]

Schweitzer was prone to exaggerate. Yet it cannot be denied that one of the most distinguishing and enduring qualities of the *Orgelbüchlein* chorales is the very expressivity he describes. And this attribute resides not, Spitta and Schweitzer are saying, in the harmonization or melodic treatment of the chorale tune but in the use of accompanimental motives that somehow mirror the emotional content or theological symbolism of the chorale text. To cite the most obvious example, the descending diminished-seventh pedal motive in "Durch Adams Fall" depicts Adam's fall from grace. One might add that it is not only the motives themselves that accomplish this mirroring but the manner in which they are woven into the contrapuntal fabric. For instance, in the Ten Commandments chorale "Dies sind die heil'gen zehn Gebot," the primary accompanimental motive is often used as a point of imitation to symbolize obedience to divine law (that is, man "following" God); in the Easter chorale "Erstanden ist der heil'ge Christ," the original presentation of one motive takes the form of an ascending, two-octave sequence, no doubt an allusion to the Resurrection (see Example 3–4 on p. 68). As Robert Marshall has maintained, it is as if "the chorale text, silent but implied by the traditional melody, is presented simultaneously with its exegesis by the counter-voices."[3] This expressivity has even led to not-so-farfetched comparisons with the nineteenth-century *Lied* and character piece for piano.

So convinced was Schweitzer of the importance of affective figures in Bach's music that he classified motives used by Bach according to particular emotions. Within this scheme, the rhythm ♩♪♪♪ ♪♪ invariably signifies joy; the appoggiatura "sigh" motive ⌒⌒⌒ invariably depicts grief. Such categories may be Procrustean, but they are not without historical precedent. Baroque theorists, for instance, identified the descending diminished seventh, because of its dissonance, only with sorrow, even if the erudite name they gave the interval—*saltus duriusculus* ("harsh leap")—is a rhetorical term bearing little hint of affective connotation.

Modern scholars have discovered that many of the accompanimental motives used by Bach in the *Orgelbüchlein* are the same as those codified in Baroque music treatises according to rhetorical terminology. Primarily for this reason, it has become fashionable to see in these organ chorales a rhetorical as well as expressive musical language. The rhetorical analogy raises intriguing but unanswerable questions. To consider one of the most interesting: was Bach consciously emulating rhetorical practice? He probably was at least aware of the parallels to rhetoric offered by his Weimar colleague Johann Gottfried Walther in his *Praecepta der musicalischen Composition,* the composition treatise Walther wrote in 1708 for his pupil Prince Johann Ernst. In the *Praecepta,* Walther describes, through the use of rhetorical jargon, several of the accompanimental motives found in the *Orgelbüchlein.*

Whether Bach intentionally derived the motives from the chorale melodies themselves has also been an issue in recent years. In only a few works ("Helft mir Gotts Güte preisen," "Herr Jesu Christ, dich zu uns wend," "Dies sind die heil'gen zehn Gebot," and "Wenn wir in höchsten Nöten sein") is this obviously the case. In almost all the *Orgelbüchlein* settings it is easy to discern—with or without the aid of a computer[4]—subtle melodic links between an accompanimental motive and the chorale tune. But since these correspondences often involve nothing more specific than, say, similar stepwise motion, one should not read too much into them. Such contrivances scarcely weaken the traditional view that the accompanimental figuration of the *Orgelbüchlein* chorales is mostly independent of the chorale tune.

The great amount of attention paid to accompanimental figuration in the *Orgelbüchlein* chorales has obscured other aspects of the works' general significance. First of all, as examples of contrapuntal writing, those chorales represent a substantial improvement over earlier keyboard works by Bach, such as the Neumeister Chorales, the "Arnstadt Congregational Chorales," the chorale partitas, and various free organ works. They may well reflect his initial success at writing sophisticated counterpoint in four real voices in an instrumental composition. One might even claim that on the basis of its craftsmanship, the *Orgelbüchlein* is Bach's first unequivocal "masterpiece" in the realm of instrumental music.

The notion of a masterpiece *en miniature* is also worth considering, since the *Orgelbüchlein* chorales are among the shortest works Bach ever wrote. As Robert Clark and John David Peterson describe in the preface to their edition of the *Orgelbüchlein*: "Just as the most intimate thoughts of a painter, as well as the depth of his technique, are often best observed in sketches and other small works, so the intensity of expression required in a short composition often shows the greatest dimension of a composer's technique and ingenuity."[5] Spitta so much as said this a century earlier, when he wrote apropos the *Orgelbüchlein*: "The narrower the circle in which Bach had to turn, the deeper he went." Has any other composer ever achieved such profundity of expression in eight or nine measures of textless music?

CHORALE TYPES AND MUSICAL STYLE

The *Orgelbüchlein* represents a musical culmination: preexisting chorale types are elevated to their highest possible artistic level. Bach draws from existing models but surpasses them in technique and imagination. At the same time, there is great innovation, both in the use of novel chorale types and in the application of new techniques to old types. Let us examine these themes one chorale type at a time, beginning with the most common in the collection.

The Melody Chorale

In a "melody chorale,"[6] the entire chorale tune is presented in the uppermost voice, in more or less continuous fashion and basically without embellishment. The presentation of the chorale melody is in the most audible part and in essentially the same melodic and rhythmic design as would have been used in congregational singing; the result is not only the most intimate of all organ-chorale types but the most vocally inspired as well.

The melody chorale has its roots in the late sixteenth- and early seven-teenth-century vocal collections known as cantionales. A typical cantionale chorale setting displays four-part, homophonic texture, with the chorale tune sung by the soprano. This type of chorale harmonization flourished through-out the Baroque era, reaching its apex with Bach, and it lives on in the church hymns of today. Thuringian organ composers from the second half of the sev-enteenth century—Johann Pachelbel, Johann Christoph Bach, and Johann Michael Bach, in particular—elaborated on the cantionale model to produce the first melody chorales for organ, whether as independent compositions or movements from chorale partitas (sets of variations on a chorale tune).

Several features distinguish these two strains of Thuringian melody chorales. The independent melody chorales usually contain interludes of one to two measures between the phrases of the chorale tune; the accompanying voices may harmonize the chorale tune homorhythmically, in the manner of a cantionale setting, or be derived from specific motives. Accompanimental parts based throughout on the same motive are virtually unknown. The num-ber of accompanimental voices and the nature of the accompanimental tex-ture (whether homophonic or polyphonic) may vary from piece to piece or even from phrase to phrase within the same piece (the use of varying textures in a single piece is a trademark of Johann Michael Bach's organ chorales from the Neumeister Collection). The greatest number of voices tends to be reserved for chordal textures; when the accompaniment is motivic, the tex-ture is often pared down to three or even two parts. Since practically the entire repertoire is playable *manualiter,* the use of pedal is normally at the performer's discretion.

In Thuringian partitas, the melody-chorale is usually represented by an opening movement in cantionale style and by variations that employ accom-panimental figuration consistently borrowed from the same motive. A differ-ent texture or figuration is used for each variation. Neither the opening movement, which follows the cantionale model, nor any of the variations contain interludes. The variations are often in three voices, with the chorale tune in the soprano; one of the two lower voices harmonizes the chorale tune, using essentially the same rhythms as the soprano; and the remaining voice, either the middle or bottom voice, spins out motivic figuration. Another com-mon approach—and one that more clearly anticipates the *Orgelbüchlein*—calls for three voices derived from a single motive. In Pachelbel's partitas, the motive is often used to embellish the soprano chorale tune as well (see Example 3–1, m. 2). (This type of melody chorale is also found in partitas by Walther, who probably inherited the design from his teacher Johann

Example 3–1. Johann Pachelbel, Partita on "Was Gott tut, das ist wohlgetan," Partita 1

Heinrich Buttstedt, a student of Pachelbel.) The movements that employ motivic figuration never have more than three voices. As with the independent melody chorales, the use of pedal is normally *ad libitum*.

Bach hewed closely to these designs in writing his first independent melody chorales, such as those from the Neumeister Collection. But in isolated works, we find progressive techniques that clearly adumbrate the *Orgelbüchlein*-type of melody chorale (as we defined it in Chapter 1). Take, for instance, the setting of "Als Jesus Christus in der Nacht" from the Neumeister Collection, a partita-like work with two "variations" (see Example 3–2). Throughout the first variation and for most of the second, Bach manipulates a single motivic idea in all the accompanimental voices, within the context of strict, four-part writing. At odds with the *Orgelbüchlein*-type, though, are the regular interludes between phrases, the use of *ad libitum* rather than obbligato pedal, and the comparatively homophonic texture. Practically all these traits are present as well in the fragmentary setting of "Wie schön leuchtet der Morgenstern," BWV 764, preserved in an autograph from around 1705, except that a new accompanimental motive is introduced to begin the restatement of the *Stollen*, at which point the work breaks off. A further example is the beautiful setting of "Herzlich tut mich verlangen," BWV 727, which features four-part texture, obbligato pedal, and no interludes whatever. The lack of figuration in the lower three parts, though, obviously distances the work from the *Orgelbüchlein*-type, as does the quasi-ornamental presentation of the *Stollen*.

Example 3–2. J. S. Bach, "Als Jesus Christus in der Nacht," BWV 1108
(Neumeister Collection). ©1985 Bärenreiter, Kassel. Used by permission.

Bach's chorale partitas afford similar insights. These works, all of which
were presumably composed after the Neumeister Chorales but before the
Orgelbüchlein, contain melody-chorale variations in the style of Pachelbel. But
in the second and sixth variations (numbering after the NBA) of the partita on
"Sei gegrüsset, Jesu gütig," BWV 768, probably the last of the four partitas to
be composed, one can observe a definite move toward the *Orgelbüchlein*-type
(see Example 3–3). Not only is the accompaniment in both variations derived
throughout from a single motive, but there is constant movement in all the
accompanimental voices, even when the voices are not stating the common
motive. The latter trait makes for a far more polyphonic texture than that in
"Als Jesus Christus" or "Wie schön leuchtet," works whose accompanimental
figuration consists largely of half notes. In measures 3 and 10 of Variatio VI,
the accompanimental motive, stated in the alto, necessitates an interruption of
the chorale tune, something encountered in over half the *Orgelbüchlein*

Example 3–3. J. S. Bach, Partita on "Sei gegrüsset, Jesu gütig," BWV 768, Variatio VI

chorales. Also in agreement with the *Orgelbüchlein*-type is the total absence of interludes in both variations. Yet no one would mistake either variation for an *Orgelbüchlein* chorale. Neither requires pedal, and the accompanimental motives in both invade the soprano (à la Pachelbel) to a greater extent than ever occurs in the *Orgelbüchlein*. Moreover, Bach is not quite able to sustain four-voice texture, a shortcoming also observable in his early keyboard fugues.[7] In both movements, the writing freely alternates between three and four voices.

In all four of these pieces, Bach seems to be experimenting with textures and techniques that he will later perfect in the *Orgelbüchlein*. But he is still a great distance from the fully blown *Orgelbüchlein*-type, a design so original that one is tempted to think of Bach—as in the case of the harpsichord concerto, the trio sonata with obbligato harpsichord, and the chorale-paraphrase cantata—as creator rather than culminator. The concision of the design sharply differentiates the *Orgelbüchlein*-type from earlier independent melody chorales: there are no interludes. Bach presents the chorale tune in a way previously seen only in chorale partitas, thereby creating the shortest independent melody chorales ever written for the organ.

Beneath this continuous chorale melody he places unified motivic material in two to three voices (the number varies depending on whether the pedal is assigned a different motive from the manual parts). The motives themselves, especially those in the inner parts, are quite similar to the succinct, idiomatic figures that had been used by keyboard composers since the sixteenth century, beginning with the English virginalists. These figures normally vary in length from one beat to one measure and tend to proceed in the rhythm one-fourth the value of the main pulse (in common time, a sixteenth note; in $\frac{3}{2}$ time, an eighth note), with an off-the-beat beginning (because of the last feature, most *Orgelbüchlein* chorales begin with the initial note of the chorale tune only).

The most common motive is three off-the-beat sixteenth notes or eighth notes followed by a fourth note of equal or greater value. Regardless of contour, the motive was referred to by Baroque theorists as a *suspirans*, since it begins with a rest or "suspiration." The motive is extremely common in Baroque keyboard music, and its most frequent melodic guise is stepwise motion. We have already seen the stepwise *suspirans* in Examples 3–1 and 3–2. Example 3–4 contains further specimens as illustrated by Walther in his *Musikalisches Lexikon* (1732) and as found in the *Orgelbüchlein* setting of "Erstanden ist der heil'ge Christ."

In achieving motivic unification, Bach relied on several of the same techniques employed in melody-chorale variations from earlier Thuringian chorale partitas, except that in the *Orgelbüchlein*-type three instead of two voices are often involved. The motive may be stated in only one voice at a time or in two voices simultaneously, in parallel thirds or sixths; it may also serve as a point of imitation. It is a given that most of the motives are melodically variable, a phenomenon that encompasses slight intervallic adjustments for particular harmonic and contrapuntal situations, more substantial alterations to adapt a motive to the pedal, and statements of entire motives in inversion. Any rhythmic changes are usually negligible by comparison.

In most of the *Orgelbüchlein* chorales (as in many partita variations), the constancy of the motivic statements results in rapid, continuous motion in the rhythm one-fourth the value of the main pulse. In addition to complementing the slow-moving chorale tune in a rhythmically cohesive way, this trait is one of the hallmarks of late Baroque music, epitomized by the concertos of Antonio

Example 3–4. The stepwise *suspirans* in theory and practice: the *figura suspirans* from J. G. Walther's *Musikalisches Lexikon,* Table X and Bach's *Orgelbüchlein* setting of "Erstanden ist der heil'ge Christ," BWV 628

Vivaldi. It provides a rhythmic thrust—forward momentum—both compelling and mechanical in its regularity. Bach clearly placed a great premium on this feature, since he often revised works—including numerous *Orgelbüchlein* chorales—to ensure that this sort of motion was strictly maintained.

Bach completed the design of the *Orgelbüchlein*-type with the boldest stroke of all: an obbligato pedal part, which was evidently so novel in Thuringian organ chorales that he mentioned it on the title page of the autograph. Consequently, the *Orgelbüchlein*-type represents one of the ideals of Bach's organ technique: the close coordination of hands and feet. Bach, however, was not satisfied with a merely mandatory pedal; he wrote pedal parts that are almost as figural as the accompanying manual voices. Unlike his predecessors, he refused to compensate for thick textures with chordal writing, which would have eased both performing and compositional burdens. The combination of four-voice texture and figuration in two manual voices and pedal renders the *Orgelbüchlein* chorales some of the most technically demanding, if not virtuosic, in the Baroque chorale literature. Moreover, the coupling of performing and compositional virtuosity that is central to the *Orgelbüchlein* reveals the essential Bach. It is a further indication that the collection constitutes a microcosm of his musical style. Because the pedal parts involve a different division of the organ than the manual voices, they can also serve to create a richer, more variegated organ sonority.

With the addition of a pedal part, Bach created the first melody chorales, independent or otherwise, with motivic accompaniment and in four truly contrapuntal voices. The fourth voice increases the complexity of the counterpoint—something we almost expect from Bach—and, because it is played with the feet, bears strong implications for figuration. For often the motive that Bach found appropriate for the manual voices is either impossible or extremely difficult to pedal; in these instances he assigned the pedal a different motive. For technical reasons, these pedal motives tend to move in slower rhythms than the manual motives and, by virtue of their novelty, exhibit a high level of originality. With respect to figuration, then, the obbligato pedal serves to produce compositional diversity within a narrowly defined type.

It is the dense motivic work within the *Orgelbüchlein*-type, however, that also temporarily breaks the chorale tune; in no other organ chorales, by Bach or anyone else, does this occur to such a great degree. This happens especially when the soprano is sustaining a long cadential note in a low register, effectively reducing the amount of space available for the lower three voices, and the alto and tenor become unusually active (to compensate for the inertia in the soprano voice). The alto often sounds the same pitch as the soprano, or pitches a second above or below, which, if sounded simultaneously with the soprano note, creates a jarring dissonance. In other instances, the alto is more than a second higher than the soprano, effectively obscuring the chorale tune and diminishing the work's profile as a melody chorale. Had Bach chosen to revert to chordal texture in these passages, writing whole notes, half notes, or even quarter notes for the alto, he more easily could have kept the part below the soprano.

But the constant presence of active accompanimental figuration is a sine qua non of the *Orgelbüchlein*-type. Bach could have averted the problem by temporarily reducing the number of voices to three, which would have allowed him to maintain the figuration in the alto by moving it into the tenor register (indeed, this often happens in three-voice, figural melody chorales, in which the chorale tune is almost never interrupted.) With only one part

lower than the alto, there would have been plenty of room. Bach was not
about to abandon four-voice writing for the sake of a more audible chorale
tune, though. His unflagging adherence to a rigorous figural and contrapuntal design—his refusal to compromise his artistic standards—made either of
these solutions impossible.

Precisely how these passsages ought to be played is one of the more vex-
ing performance-practice issues raised by the *Orgelbüchlein* melody chorales.
To some extent, the solution depends on the amount of dissonance that results
in a given room and on a given organ. One principle seems to obtain: namely, that whenever there is a common tone between a sustained soprano note
and a moving alto line, the soprano should be broken. Otherwise, the unifying
rhythmic motion provided by the alto would be impaired.

The specific performance problems inherent in such passages are well
illustrated by the excerpt from "Mit Fried und Freud ich fahr dahin" given in
Example 3–5. On the last beat of measure 8 and the first beat of measure 9,
there are common tones of the sort just described; in both cases the soprano
eighth notes are best played as sixteenths, followed by sixteenth rests. More
problematic are the third and fourth beats of measure 9, where the soprano
is sustained for two full beats at an unusually low soprano pitch (c'). On the
third beat, the soprano should be played as a sixteenth note, followed by six-
teenth- and eighth-note rests. On the fourth beat, there are two possibilities:
either bring back the soprano note for the entire beat or replace it with a
quarter rest. Most players take the latter course, since a soprano quarter note
on c' here creates considerable dissonance with the D's and B's in the alto
and tenor, especially at the beginning of the second half of the beat, where
this dissonance occurs at a metrically strong juncture and coincides with
relatively large note values (sixteenths instead of thirty-seconds) in the inner
voices.[8] It also seems pointless to reinstate the soprano note on the fourth
beat when it is essentially hidden by the higher alto line. What is more, the
note's reentry here can give the unfortunate illusion of an extra note in this
segment of the chorale tune.

The Ornamental Chorale

In the ornamental chorale, the complete hymn tune appears in the soprano
in a highly embellished form. The chorale phrases either occur one after the
other or are separated by short, modest interludes (works of this type are
sometimes referred to as "short" ornamental chorales in order to distinguish
them from ornamental chorales containing lengthy, structurally significant

Example 3–5. "Mit Fried und Freud ich fahr dahin," BWV 616, with a possible realization of the soprano voice

interludes, such as those found in the "Great Eighteen" Chorales). Only three *Orgelbüchlein* chorales match this description: "Das alte Jahr vergangen ist," "O Mensch, bewein dein Sünde gross," and "Wenn wir in höchsten Nöten sein." Bach uses four-part texture in all three of these works, as he does in the melody chorales from the *Orgelbüchlein*.

Despite the similarities to the Thuringian melody chorale, the three ornamental chorales in the *Orgelbüchlein* seem oriented more toward North Germany. We find the specific model in the ornamental chorales of Dieterich Buxtehude, who left behind more such works (over thirty) than anyone else. It is well known that Bach traveled to Lübeck in late 1705 to study under Buxtehude, and there can be no question that the Lübeck organist's influence permeates Bach's early organ works, free as well as chorale-based. Buxtehude's ornamental chorales differ from those in the *Orgelbüchlein* chiefly through their use of interludes between chorale phrases. (Earlier ornamental chorales by Bach, such as "Ach Herr, mich armen Sünder," BWV 742, and "Herr Jesu Christ, dich zu uns wend," BWV 709, also contain interludes.) As with the independent Thuringian melody chorale, Bach seems to have taken the North German ornamental chorale and excised its interludes to produce a more concise design. The ornamental chorales in the *Orgelbüchlein* are the first examples of this chorale type without interludes.

It can be no coincidence that Bach calls for two manuals in all three ornamental chorale settings from the *Orgelbüchlein*, while in the thirty-one melody chorales from the collection he does so only in three pieces: clearly, he was bowing to the long-standing tradition of performing ornamental organ chorales "à due clav.", with the soprano chorale tune played by the right hand on one keyboard, and the other manual voices played by the left hand on a different keyboard. This technique was especially prevalent in North Germany, where composers such as Buxtehude wrote for *Werkprinzip* organs with spatially separated divisions. Most North German instruments built in the late seventeenth and early eighteenth centuries were equipped with a *Rückpositiv*, a manual division situated behind the player. Because in most churches this division was also the closest to the congregation, it was considered ideal for the presentation of a chorale tune. To exploit the stereophonic capabilities of North German instruments, Buxtehude and his colleagues often called for two manuals and pedal in their ornamental chorales. In Thuringian organs, the *Positiv* was often represented by a *Brustpositiv* or an *Oberwerk*, both located in the main case. Nevertheless, contrasting colors could be created by using a bold stop for the chorale melody.

The distribution of the hands on two keyboards bears strong implications for figuration. With the right hand unable to assist the left hand in playing the alto part, the left hand must take both the alto and tenor lines *in toto*. The middle two parts therefore cannot be assigned the sort of rapid contrapuntal figuration characteristic of the *Orgelbüchlein*-type. Instead, they must contain slower rhythms that often border on the homophonic ("O Mensch," from the *Orgelbüchlein*, is a particularly good example). Embellishment is concentrated in the soprano, which, with its profusion of ornaments, either written out in full or indicated through symbols, makes up for the slow rhythmic motion in the alto and tenor.

With respect to the embellishment, the roles played by the soprano and the alto-tenor unit in the ornamental chorale are the opposite of what they are in the melody chorale; that is, where the motivic figuration in the melody chorale is centered in the middle parts, in the ornamental chorale the decorative function belongs exclusively to the soprano. Another aspect of this role reversal involves the chorale tune per se, for in the ornamental chorale it is sometimes decorated almost beyond recognition. The appeal of the ornamental chorale, then, lies not in the straightforward audibility of the chorale tune but in its extreme elaboration. It is the ornamentation of the tune that it is important, and the ornamentation is given all the more prominence by its placement in the uppermost part and its timbral separation from all other voices.

The Chorale Canon

The lone criterion for this type is that the entire chorale tune be set canonically. With so general a description, and considering the popularity of canon as a compositional technique in the Renaissance and Baroque, one might expect that by the turn of the eighteenth century there was already a large repertoire of chorale canons and that the nine chorale canons in the *Orgelbüchlein* represent the culmination of a time-honored practice. In truth, though, these nine works are among the earliest surviving specimens of this approach to the organ chorale. As Peter Williams has pointed out, there are many seventeenth-century organ chorales with canonic accompanimental parts but virtually none in which the chorale tune itself is set as a canon.[9]

In retrospect, it seems only natural that a master contrapuntist like Bach would have turned to canon as a means of treating a chorale tune in an organ composition, whether he had models or not. The miscellaneous setting of "Ach Gott und Herr," BWV 714, suggests that he may have adopted this technique at a very early date, before the compilation of the *Orgelbüchlein*. In this work, the chorale melody is set as a canon at the octave between the soprano and tenor, as happens in two *Orgelbüchlein* chorales. But the canon "is less strict than the ingenuity demonstrated in the *Orgelbüchlein* canons could have made it."[10]

On the basis of the surviving repertory, the only other composer who seems to have been writing chorale canons in the early eighteenth century was Bach's distant kinsman and Weimar colleague, J. G. Walther. Walther left behind ten chorale canons, and it is possible that they are contemporaneous with or even earlier than the *Orgelbüchlein* (Walther's keyboard music is not precisely datable). Indeed, in three instances Walther and Bach chose the same chorale tunes for canonic elaboration. Considering the novelty of this chorale type at this time, this suggests a collaboration, or perhaps friendly competition, of the type seen with the two composers' organ concerto arrangements.

Whatever the circumstances, Bach's *Orgelbüchlein* canons greatly surpass Walther's in terms of contrapuntal skill and contrapuntal variety. Walther wrote canons at the octave exclusively, while Bach was just as likely to choose the more challenging interval of the fifth. Similarly, Walther worked with a relatively small number of voice combinations, soprano and bass being his favorite, whereas Bach wrote canons for an inner and an outer voice just as easily as a canon for two outer voices. In one work ("O Lamm Gottes, unschuldig"), he even composed a canon for two interior voices, something Walther never attempted. Bach's canons are also, on the whole, more complex, resulting from thicker textures and canonic or quasi-canonic accompanimental parts (see the double canon "In dulci jubilo"). Walther tended to write long interludes between phrases, which relieved him of having to overlap the end of a *comes* phrase with the beginning of a *dux* phrase. Furthermore, he sometimes reversed the voices representing the *dux* and *comes* midway through the piece. Bach's canons are stricter and more systematic, with minimal use of interludes and a relatively constant overlapping of canonic parts. In short, they are "real" canons.

Miscellaneous Forms

There are two *Orgelbüchlein* chorales that defy classification among the organ-chorale types we have proposed. In "Christum wir sollen loben schon," the entire, unornamented chorale tune is stated in continuous fashion, as in the melody chorale—but it appears in the alto instead of the soprano. Played on the same manual as the soprano and tenor, and in the midst of motivic writing in four voices, the tune is barely audible. In chorale partitas from the late seventeenth and early eighteenth century, it is not uncommon to find a variation or two in which the chorale tune is stated in an interior voice; for the sake of variety, the tune sometimes migrates between variations from an outer to an inner voice. Independent organ chorales from this period with the chorale melody in an interior voice, on the other hand, are quite rare. Except for Telemann's "Schmücke dich, o liebe Seele"[11] and Johann Michael Bach's "Nun komm, der Heiden Heiland" (Neumeister Collection), there would appear to be only four other specimens, all by J. S. Bach: "Von Gott will ich nicht lassen," BWV 658, and "Allein Gott in der Höh sei Ehr," BWV 663, both from the "Great Eighteen" Chorales; and the miscellaneous settings of "Christ lag in Todesbanden," BWV 695, and "Nun freut euch, lieben Christen g'mein," BWV 734.

The fantasy-like "In dir ist Freude" is also sui generis. In no other *Orgel-büchlein* setting is the chorale melody treated so freely. The tune is passed between voices, and individual phrases are repeated—both hallmarks of the seventeenth-century North German chorale fantasy. Yet the work is not to be confused with a "miniature" North German chorale fantasy or even an approximation thereof, because most of the traits associated with that chorale type—fragmentation of the chorale phrases, bravura passagework, meter changes, "echo" effects, and manual changes—are absent. If Bach had a specific model for this rousing piece, its identity remains elusive.

Chapter 4

THE EARLY CHORALES

*L*et us now take a closer look at the music of the *Orgelbüchlein,* examining each chorale in approximate chronological sequence. Although the chronological approach is one that historians take as a matter of course, it has never been applied to the *Orgelbüchlein* because the order in which the works were composed has only recently been clarified. Our purpose here is twofold: to illuminate various features of the individual pieces, and to reveal in more detail than in Chapter 1 how the *Orgelbüchlein* evolved stylistically.

The fifteen works in this chapter represent the collection's early compilation phase. Included are thirteen melody chorales, one chorale canon, and one ornamental chorale. Of the thirteen melody chorales, nine exemplify the *Orgelbüchlein*-type; the other four contain "walking" basses.

HERR CHRIST, DER EIN'GE GOTTESSOHN ("*LORD CHRIST, THE ONLY SON OF GOD*"), BWV 601

Fittingly, what appears to be the initial entry in the autograph, the Advent chorale "Herr Christ, der ein'ge Gottessohn," is a clear-cut example of the *Orgelbüchlein*-type. The title in the autograph, *Herr Christ, der ein'ge Gottes Sohn. oder Herr Gott, nun sey gepreiset,* indicates that the chorale tune could also be sung to the text "Herr Gott, nun sei gepreiset," a *post prandium* prayer (grace after meals). The organ setting does not seem to refer specifically to either text, but its ebullient mood accords with the general affect of both: in "Herr Christ," eager anticipation of Christ's coming; in "Herr Gott," joyful thanksgiving for daily bread.[1]

Bach realizes the *Orgelbüchlein*-type here by means of the *suspirans*. He weaves the motive throughout all three accompanimental voices; in the bass, the motive is extended to five notes, set to the rhythm ♪♫♫ (see Example 4–1). (J. G. Walther adopted the same motivic scheme in his setting of this chorale, except that his work is in three voices and contains no pedal part.) Three of the bass statements are lengthened to four beats and altered to straight sixteenths; by means of this rhythmic acceleration, Bach energizes the final cadence of both the *Stollen* and *Abgesang* (identical passages).

Owing to its pronounced disjunct motion, the bass figure in this chorale is one of the more prominent accompanimental motives in the entire *Orgelbüchlein*. It is doubtless one of the more familiar, too, for by 1700 it belonged to the lingua franca of German organ composers, both as a manual and pedal figure. Easily playable with alternate feet, the motive is idiomatically suited to a pedalboard. Indeed, it is perhaps best known from the introductory pedal solos of Dieterich Buxtehude's Praeludium in C Major,

Example 4–1. "Herr Christ, der ein'ge Gottessohn," BWV 601

BuxWV 137 (the so-called Prelude, Fugue, and Chaconne), and Georg Böhm's Praeludium in the same key. Bach employed it in several of his early keyboard works (the Capriccio in E Major, BWV 993, for instance) as well as the aria "Wer bist du?" from his Weimar cantata *Bereitet die Wege, bereitet die Bahn!* BWV 132. In short, the figure seems less expressive than generic, despite its classification by Albert Schweitzer as a motive of "beatific peace."[2] Curiously, Bach prescribes a repeat of the *Abgesang*, resulting in a binary form (AABB) characteristic of Baroque dance movements. His reasons for departing from the bar form (AAB) of the chorale are by no means clear. It was highly irregular at this time to repeat sections of chorales where the text does not dictate a repeat, although Bach did just this in four other *Orgelbüchlein* settings: "Puer natus in Bethlehem," "Wir Christenleut," "Herr Jesu Christ, dich zu uns wend," and "Liebster Jesu, wir sind hier." Might this reflect Bach's desire to lengthen the music of these short pieces at any (liturgical) cost?

Puer natus in Bethlehem
("A boy is born in Bethlehem"), BWV 603

Bach could easily have set this Christmas chorale as a canon, as Walther did, for the melody lends itself well to canonic elaboration. Instead, he wrote a further specimen of the *Orgelbüchlein*-type, in which the bass sounds its own motive (♩♩ ♩♩♩). The inner voices weave a triple-*suspirans* figure (♪ ♫♫♫♫♫♫|♪). Both motives are the subject of intense, rising sequences that progress from two statements (mm. 1–5) to three (mm. 7–9) and finally to four (mm. 11–14). This buildup is matched by increasingly imitative writing in the inner parts.

The conclusion of "Puer natus" is puzzling. In the autograph, there is no conclusion per se, merely a direct or custos indicating that the tenor is to proceed to b (whether b-flat or b-natural is not specified) and a segno indicating a repeat. Since the first tenor note in the work is b-flat, and since there is no corresponding segno, it seems that Bach meant for a repeat of the entire piece. Most editions of the *Orgelbüchlein*, including those by Novello, Peters, and Albert Riemenschneider, call for no repeat of any kind. But the two most recent editions—the NBA and the Concordia edition—print a repeat with a first ending identical to the last bar of the autograph, which is only two beats long, and a second ending that contains a half note on g for the alto and tenor (see Example 4–2). In these two editions, therefore, the

Riemenschneider edition

Neue Bach-Ausgabe

Example 4–2. "Puer natus in Bethlehem," BWV 603

piece concludes with a fragmentary measure and with G's in all four voices. Devotees of the earlier editions cited above may find this conclusion deficient, for the earlier editions add a third beat containing an enriched (five-voice) G-major triad. A measure of two beats here is proper, however, since it complements the one-beat anacrusis at the beginning of the work. In addition, a unison ending, though atypical for a tonal work, parallels the conclusion of "Vom Himmel hoch," also from the early compilation phase of the *Orgelbüchlein*. Players who cannot abide a unison ending might add a half note on b-natural (Picardy third) on the *second* beat.

Gelobet seist du, Jesu Christ ("*Praise to you, Jesus Christ*"), BWV 604

Although this Christmas chorale represents the *Orgelbüchlein*-type, its opening two phrases are ornamented to a degree unusual for a melody chorale. According to the autograph, the chorale melody is to be played on a separate manual, a practice that also evokes the ornamental chorale.

"Gelobet seist" is notated in G major without a sharp because of the mixolydian nature of the chorale tune, which leads to a vacillation in the organ setting between F and F-sharp as the seventh degree of the scale and between G major and C major as the tonality. As its modal character suggests, the melody is derived from plainchant: the first stanza of the text originated in the fourteenth century as a *Leise*, a German medieval sacred song concluding with the acclamation "Kyrie eleison," sometimes contracted to "kirleis" or "leis."

Robert Clark and John David Peterson have remarked that the inner parts of the *Orgelbüchlein* setting function rhythmically as a single voice comprised of continuous sixteenths.[3] Bach achieves this effect by integrating two concise and nondescript motives: ⌐♩, usually set to stepwise motion or repeated notes; and ♪ ⌐♩ , usually in stepwise motion (see Example 4–3). Whenever this figuration ceases, the bass presents a *suspirans* motive, ensuring steady sixteenth-note motion.

The type of figuration found in the inner voices is common in German Baroque keyboard music. Bach himself employed it in many early keyboard works, most extensively in the Neumeister Chorales. In virtually all these pieces, each motive is confined to a single voice, a technique that can become tiresome if the figuration ranges over large sections, as in the Prelude in A Minor, BWV 922. "Gelobet seist" avoids this pitfall by stating each motive, more or less equally, in both the alto and tenor.

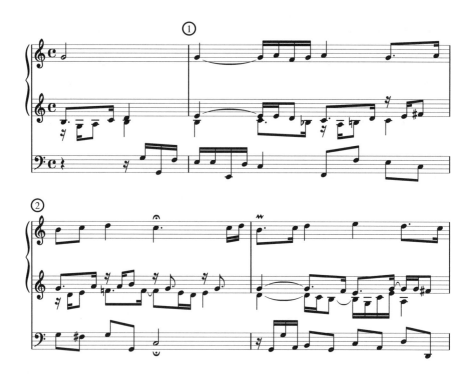

Example 4–3. "Gelobet seist du, Jesu Christ," BWV 604

DER TAG, DER IST SO FREUDENREICH
("THE DAY IS SO FULL OF JOY"), BWV 605

Bach also prescribes two manuals for this Christmas chorale and employs the same type of "integrated" figuration as in the previous work. Yet there is no mistaking that "Der Tag" is an altogether simpler work. It features a walking rather than a motivic bass and a far greater percentage of strictly diatonic harmonies. Just compare the first two bars: "Gelobet seist" contains a concentration of secondary dominants and secondary leading-tone chords, while "Der Tag" is devoid of any chromaticism.

Bach's rigid handling of the inner voices also bespeaks a relatively simple style. At first blush, it might seem that he integrates the ♪⎯♩ and ♪♩♩ motives with greater variety than in "Gelobet seist," since so many statements of the latter motive are ornamented as ♪ ♫♩ . But actually every *other* statement is embellished in this way, resulting in a pattern that tends to slacken only at cadences (see Example 4–4). Moreover, Bach confines each motive to a single voice (the ♪⎯♩ motive to the tenor, the ♪ ♫ motive to the alto)

Example 4–4. "Der Tag, der ist so freudenreich," BWV 605

and sets almost half the statements of the ♪. ♩ motive to repeated notes. By the end of this long work—about twice the size of "Gelobet seist"—the figuration becomes rather monotonous.

All unfavorable comparisons aside, this remains a popular piece—and an excellent exercise for the left hand. The animated thirty-second notes have suggested to commentators since Philipp Spitta a rhythmic vitality expressive of Christmas joy.[4]

VOM HIMMEL HOCH, DA KOMM ICH HER ("FROM HEAVEN ON HIGH I COME HERE"), BWV 606

The *Orgelbüchlein* setting of this Christmas chorale also contains a walking bass and utilizes in the inner voices the stepwise form of the *suspirans*. As Schweitzer noted, Bach's use of the motive here creates a "charming maze" of ascending and descending scales, perhaps symbolic of the angels at the Nativity.

The treatment of the chorale tune is of special interest in this work, for the melody is set to an unexpected rhythm and is liberally embellished with the motive used for the inner parts. Each line of the chorale text is in iambic tetrameter—eight syllables in the order weak-strong, weak-strong, weak-strong, weak-strong—the most common verse prosody in the German language and the most common of all chorale verse types, especially for initial lines. Bach normally set such verse to the rhythm ♩ |♩ ♩ ♩ ♩ |♩ ♩ ♩. For example, this is the rhythm of all the chorale phrases of the *Orgelbüchlein* settings of "Lob sei dem allmächtigen Gott" and "Vater unser im Himmelreich," two other hymns that employ iambic tetrameter exclusively. Furthermore, in all of Bach's choral settings of "Vom Himmel hoch," including those from the *Christmas Oratorio*, this is the rhythm of all four phrases. The rhythm also obtains in the organ settings of "Vom Himmel hoch" by J. G. Walther, Johann Pachelbel, and Johann Bernhard Bach (1676–1749). Rhythmized in this logical and natural way, the unaccented syllables fall on weak beats and the accented syllables on strong beats. In the *Orgelbüchlein* setting of "Vom Himmel hoch," however, each phrase begins on a strong beat (either beat one or three), set to the faltering rhythm ♩ ♩♩|♩ ♩ ♩ ♩|♩ (see Example 4–5).

Example 4–5. "Vom Himmel hoch, da komm ich her," BWV 606

Thus the weak initial syllables are not only placed on a strong beat but are given a note twice as long as that for the strong syllable that immediately follows. Curiously, Bach adopted this "unmetrical" rhythm in all of his organ compositions on this melody, from early miscellaneous settings (BWV 700, 701, and 738) to the very late "Canonic Variations," BWV 769.

Just as this soprano rhythm undermines the poetic meter of the chorale text, the frequent incorporation of the *suspirans* into the soprano part obscures the chorale melody. In no other *Orgelbüchlein* chorale is the latter device used so often ("Mit Fried und Freud" runs a distant second); the motive appears in the soprano at least once every phrase. In this respect, "Vom Himmel hoch" is the *Orgelbüchlein* chorale most indebted to Pachelbel, who used this technique extensively in his chorale partitas.

IN DULCI JUBILO *("IN SWEET JOY"), BWV 608*

This delightful bit of Christmas music (to the tune known in America as "Good Christian Men, Rejoice") exemplifies the chorale canon. It is the only instance in which Bach treats both the chorale tune and accompaniment canonically (see Example 4–6). Indeed, one searches in vain for a second such double canon in the Baroque organ-chorale literature.

Why did Bach conceive of this chorale as a canon? Often, the answer to this question is that the text suggests a "leader-follower" relationship. Take, for instance, "Dies sind die heil'gen zehn Gebot" ("These are the holy Ten Commandments"). To symbolize obedience to divine law—man "following" God—Bach set this hymn as a canon in the opening movement of Cantata 77 (*Du sollst Gott, deinen Herren, lieben*) as well as in an organ chorale from *Clavierübung* III (BWV 678). In the case of "In dulci jubilo," though, it is by no means clear that the text was a factor, despite such a suggestive phrase in stanza 2 as "Draw me to thee."[5]

At any rate, the text was surely less of an agent than the chorale tune, which is tailor-made for canonic writing. Except for the last two phrases, the melody may easily be sung as a round, since all the downbeat pitches are from the tonic triad and all the phrases are four bars long. The tune is also very repetitive for one not in bar form, which makes setting it as a canon easier still (as in the free canon, phrase 2 restates phrase 1, and phrases 5–6 restate phrases 3–4). As Hermann Keller noted, composers began to realize the canonic potential of the melody as early as the sixteenth century, and the tradition has persisted to the present.[6] The tune was set canonically for organ

Example 4–6. "In dulci jubilo," BWV 608

by J. G. Walther and Fridolin Sicher (1490–1546), and for voices by Michael Praetorius (1571–1621). There must be more canons on this chorale than on any other.

The accompanimental canon is every bit as strict as that on the chorale melody. Yet in addition to contrapuntal artifice, it also provides supporting figuration in continuous, rapid motion—a hallmark of *Orgelbüchlein* style. Indeed, once the free canon ends in measure 24, its triplet figuration—which Bach incorrectly notated with eighths instead of quarters—continues until the end. The figuration suggested to Schweitzer a "direct and naïve joy."

Like the chorale tune, the free melody tends to contain pitches from the tonic triad on downbeats, and it too uses four-bar phrases exclusively. The free melody also echoes the repeated A's at the beginning of the chorale tune with repeated A's in measures 3–4 and 7–8. Williams has conjectured that these repeated notes are a simulation of a bagpipe drone, a pastoral effect employed in a great deal of Christmas music from this period, including J. M. Bach's organ setting of "In dulci jubilo" from the Neumeister

Collection (formerly BWV 751).[7] The implied drone, triplet figuration, dance-like phrase structure, and major mode produce an atmosphere somehow evocative of the Christmas season (which many organists enhance with the *Zimbelstern*). There is no piece in the *Orgelbüchlein* that sounds so much like "Christmas" music.

Of all the issues raised by this ingenious piece, none has been discussed more than performance practice. To begin with, Bach notated the desired pitches for the tenor voice but not how to achieve them. The *Ped.* inscription in front of the first note labels the tenor as a pedal part, but it frequently rises to f-sharp', while the pedalboard of the Weimar court church extended only to e' (see Chapter 1). Not all of these pitches are available even on modern pedalboards, and when they are, playing this high on the pedals is awkward at best. The most common solution today is to play the part down an octave, on a four-foot stop. As Spitta and others have maintained, this is presumably what Bach did himself, on his four-foot Cornett-Bass.

A far more contentious matter is the performance of passages where the beat is divided simultaneously into quarter-note duplets in one voice and eighth-note triplets in another. Does one assimilate the duplets to triplet rhythm by performing them ♩ ♪ , or play two-against-three? Several writers claim to have "resolved" this problem, but the evidence is inconclusive.[8] Had Bach consistently positioned the second quarter note of each pair between the second and third triplets or directly in line with the third triplet, a persuasive argument might be made one way or the other. In this composing score, however, note spacing and alignment are anything but consistent. One theory is that the quarters should be played evenly only when they are repeated notes, and the use of even rhythms for the repeated A's in measures 3–8 does better approximate a drone. It is hard to reconcile this view, though, with Bach's notation in measures 25–28 of the rhythm ♩ ♪ , which he set to repeated notes as well as notes a second and a third apart. Unfortunately, this passage is not analogous to any others and therefore should not be taken as a model. Perhaps its greatest significance resides simply in the rarity of the ♩ ♪ rhythm in Baroque music notation; duplets set to triplet rhythm were normally notated ♪♩ .

Finally, "In dulci jubilo" is one of the most technically challenging works in the *Orgelbüchlein*—and one of the most difficult of Bach's organ works altogether. The fast triplets frequently involve leaps of an octave or more, and the three-sharp key poses considerable difficulties of its own. Despite the piece's infectious charm, most organists are too timid to play it.

LOBT GOTT, IHR CHRISTEN, ALLZUGLEICH *("PRAISE GOD, YOU CHRISTIANS, ALL TOGETHER"), BWV 609*

As a melody chorale with a walking bass, this Christmas chorale is quite representative of early *Orgelbüchlein* style. In other respects, though, "Lobt Gott" is hardly a standardized work.

The motivic construction of the inner voices, for example, implies a certain randomness (such as one might expect from a composing score). Indeed, the primary motive—ostensibly four sixteenths, beginning on the beat—appears in as many as fourteen different melodic forms, representing perhaps the most extreme case of melodic variability of an accompanimental motive in the *Orgelbüchlein*. Notice too that the figure is absent in measure 3, where the inner voices lapse into the integrated motivic figuration of "Der Tag" and "Gelobet seist." Bach seems to have had little concern about the melodic profile of the motive, or whether it was constantly present, as long as sixteenth-note motion was maintained. Schweitzer interpreted this motion as a metaphor for joy.

Remarkably, the bass line traverses the entire pedalboard. Within the span of ten bars, all the pitches of the G-major scale from D to d' are played at least twice. The two-octave range is at its most conspicuous in measures 4–8, where the bass twice climbs from D to d', with the two ascents separated by a jolting, two-octave downward leap (see Example 4–7). It is conceivable that the all-inclusive nature of the line symbolizes *allzugleich* ("all together"). According to Clark and Peterson, the increasingly wide intervals between the pedal and the soprano in the first two bars—beginning with an octave and progressing to a fifteenth—may portray the phrase "who today *opens* his heavenly kingdom" in the first stanza.

DA JESUS AN DEM KREUZE STUND *("AS JESUS HUNG UPON THE CROSS"), BWV 621*

In contrast to most of the chorales set in the *Orgelbüchlein*, this Passiontide hymn—a contemplation on the Seven Last Words of Christ—appears in Bach's oeuvre only in this instance. As Williams notes, the melody seems to have been rarely set outside of southern Germany.

The figuration of "Da Jesus" is extraordinarily dense. There are four accompanimental motives altogether (including two in the tenor) and, once all the voices have entered, no rests at all. Still, Bach manages to express the chorale text by means of a drooping, syncopated motive in the bass that surely symbolizes Christ's languishing on the cross (see Example 4–8).[9] The figure also constantly forms suspensions against the upper three parts, giving

Example 4–7. "Lobt Gott, ihr Christen, allzugleich," BWV 609

the piece an overall dissonance appropriate to the tragic subject matter. As Spitta observed, the work has a "wonderfully true aesthetic feeling."

O MENSCH, BEWEIN DEIN SÜNDE GROSS ("O MAN, BEWAIL YOUR GREAT SINS"), BWV 622

This Passiontide chorale, which Bach set in the *Orgelbüchlein* as an ornamental chorale, is probably the most beloved piece in the collection—and one of Bach's most acclaimed organ chorales altogether. Widor is said to have found it "the finest piece of instrumental music written."[10]

"O Mensch" owes its exalted status, first of all, to Bach's vivid depiction of the melancholy chorale text, as one can see in the appoggiatura "sigh" figures in measures 12 and 21 and, especially, in the chromaticism in measures 18–19 and 22–24. Most striking is the C-flat-major chord at the end of the penultimate measure (see Example 4–9). As Williams points out, Bach used the same chord at the very same juncture in his setting of "O Mensch" in the 1725 version of the *St. John Passion* (Bach later recycled the movement in the *St. Matthew Passion*).

Example 4–8. "Da Jesus an dem Kreuze stund," BWV 621

Bach accompanies this chord with an *adagissimo* marking, slowing the tempo from *adagio assai*. The marking coincides with the word *lange* ("*long upon the cross*") in the first stanza and, since the notes become "longer," must refer specifically to it. We almost expect this of Bach, given his general penchant for depicting "long" words such as *lang* ("long"), *Verlangen* ("longing"), and *ewig* ("eternal") with long notes. But rarely in the *Orgelbüchlein* does Bach portray a specific word, as he does here. The passage is, to quote Spitta, "full of imagination and powerful feeling."

Example 4–9. "O Mensch, bewein dein Sünde gross," BWV 622

Certain other features of "O Mensch" are also responsible for its renown. The work must have the largest harmonic vocabulary of any *Orgelbüchlein* chorale, evidenced not only by the chromaticism cited above but also by the many diminished- and dominant-seventh chords. There is even, on the third beat of measure 21, a major-ninth chord, which coincides with the word *Sünde* ("sins") in the first stanza. In this chord, as in many of the seventh chords, the top note is placed in the soprano, heightening the already piquant flavor. Just observe how often a soprano d-flat" constitutes the seventh of a dominant- or diminished-seventh chord.

No one would deny, however, that the most aesthetically pleasing element in "O Mensch" is its ravishing coloratura. Like the chorale tune itself, the part is unusually lyrical, tending toward unified motivic work and large intervals.[11] Except for the major seventh, every interval from the unison to the octave is stated at least once, and the range covers two full octaves—easily surpassing that of the other two ornamental chorales in the *Orgelbüchlein*. These two factors create a sumptuous melodic palette.

The coloratura part is a veritable catalogue of Baroque graces, both written out and indicated by symbols. As George Stauffer has observed, the numerous "hooked" appoggiaturas betray the influence of French keyboard music.[12] Yet there are many more unornamented notes than expected, such as the quarter notes in measures 18–19 and 22–23, where the accompanimental figuration is at its most chromatic and intricate (note the stretto writing in the inner voices). The performer certainly has no business adding any ornamentation in these passages, and so specific is Bach's ornamentation throughout that this rule should probably be applied to the whole piece.

HEUT TRIUMPHIERET GOTTES SOHN ("TODAY GOD'S SON TRIUMPHS"), BWV 630/630A

This Easter chorale exemplifies the *Orgelbüchlein*-type, and its inner voices are based on the ubiquitous stepwise *suspirans*. Despite its workaday appearance, though, "Heut triumphieret" is the only *Orgelbüchlein* chorale wrought in the style of a passacaglia.

The accompanimental voices in the *Orgelbüchlein* are typically based on a motive that lasts only a beat or two, and material other than the motive itself is often used as well. In contrast to this paradigm, the bass line of "Heut triumphieret" consists almost entirely of six consecutive statements of a melody that lasts four bars, the standard length of an ostinato bass (see Example 4–10). Other traits of the passacaglia in this work are triple meter and the minor mode.

Example 4–10. "Heut triumphieret Gottes Sohn," BWV 630

Because the final chorale phrase is half as long as the others, Bach abandons the passacaglia scheme for the last three bars, opting instead for accelerated motion in the feet and, in the last measure, an additional voice in the hands. Both devices effectively illustrate the Easter acclamation of "Hallelujah" found at this point in every stanza of the text.

HERR JESU CHRIST, DICH ZU UNS WEND ("LORD JESUS CHRIST, TURN TO US"), BWV 632

Although this chorale is found in the Pentecost section of the *Orgelbüchlein* and is appropriate to that season—the text twice refers to the Holy Ghost—in Leipzig and elsewhere it was sung on most Sundays of the year as a response to the pastor's pulpit greeting and call to prayer. The numerous organ settings by Bach and others probably reflect the hymn's weekly use.

Like the previous work, the *Orgelbüchlein* setting of "Herr Jesu Christ" is a melody chorale with a unique bass line that, in this case, imitates the soprano phrase by phrase, in diminution. Other anomalies include an accompanimental motive clearly borrowed from the chorale tune, an unnecessary repeat of the last two phrases, and a style-brisé ending reminiscent of harpsichord music.

As Keller maintained, it may have been the ending of the first stanza of the chorale text ("And *lead* us along the path of truth"), with its imagery of divine guidance, that gave Bach the idea of quasi-canonic style. Certainly, the chorale tune was no factor, as it staunchly resists strict canonic technique at every turn. Thus canonic writing is more implied than realized.[13]

Throughout the work, the inner voices state a triadic form of the *suspirans* whose first three notes are identical to those of the chorale tune (see Example 4–11). Walther used the same motive in Variation 6 of his partita on this melody. Schweitzer maintained that the constant repetition of these notes underscores the initial three syllables of the text ("Herr Jesu") throughout the work. Such an effect seems very appropriate for a "prayer-chorale."

At the end of the chorale, arpeggiation is used to increase the number of voices from four to eight, and the appearance of the arpeggiation recalls the allemandes of Bach's French and English Suites. These dance movements share a number of features with "Herr Jesu Christ": common time; an

Example 4–11. "Herr Jesu Christ, dich zu uns wend," BWV 632

anacrusis; imitative texture; binary form, with a repeat of each half (in the organ chorale, only the second half is repeated); constant sixteenth-note motion; and sixteenth-note arpeggiation at the end of each half that thickens the overall texture. Accordingly, performers of this *Orgelbüchlein* chorale might consider an allemande-like tempo and a registration sufficiently light to simulate harpsichord timbre, perhaps 8' and 4' principals, which would have been the equivalent of Bach's brass-strung harpsichord.

DIES SIND DIE HEIL'GEN ZEHN GEBOT *("THESE ARE THE HOLY TEN COMMANDMENTS"), BWV 635*

Bach set this most "canonic" of chorale texts in the *Orgelbüchlein* not as a chorale canon but as an *Orgelbüchlein*-type. As in "Herr Jesu Christ," the main accompanimental motive is derived from the chorale tune, stating all eight notes of the first phrase in double diminution (see Example 4–12).

Example 4–12. "Dies sind die heil'gen zehn Gebot," BWV 635

Williams points out that the motive appears exactly ten times in its original melodic guise (GGGGGABC).

We see a far greater incidence of repeated notes in this work than in any other *Orgelbüchlein* chorale. The modal chorale tune begins with five repeated notes, and the remainder of the melody contains many more. Since the primary accompanimental motive quotes the opening phrase, repeated notes are a strong presence in the lower three parts as well. These repeated notes, of course, restrict both harmonic and melodic motion—probably the reason Keller found the work "dry." It is, however, Bach's use of half notes for the chorale tune that so drastically decelerates the harmonic rhythm, which is the slowest of any piece in the collection.

Yet in terms of motivic construction, "Dies sind" is a thoroughly engaging work. As Spitta remarked, the main accompanimental motive has "an inherent organic connection with the chorale itself." Moreover, Bach often treats the motive canonically (see the first two statements), which suggests an allusion to the chorale text. Accompanying this figure throughout is a melodically variable sixteenth-note motive (♩♩♩♩). Twice this motive appears in the bass, changing (for the sake of alternate-feet pedalling) beyond all recognition from conjunct to markedly disjunct motion, with intervals as large as a ninth. Nowhere else in the *Orgelbüchlein* is there a more extreme transformation of an accompanimental motive.

VATER UNSER IM HIMMELREICH ("OUR FATHER WHO ART IN HEAVEN"), BWV 636

Like that of the previous chorale, this text is Luther's versification of a central biblical passage (the Lord's Prayer), one fundamental to the Catechism as well as Christian liturgy in general. Like "Herr Christ," the *Orgelbüchlein* setting of "Vater unser" is an example of an *Orgelbüchlein*-type whose accompanimental voices are all based on the same motive; here, however, the concept is strictly realized. The motive is yet another example of a *suspirans*, set to disjunct motion that allows for easy, alternate-feet pedalling (see Example 4–13). Bach took great advantage of this possibility by including on the average one pedal statement per bar. The constancy of statement and the motive's distribution among all three voices make for an extraordinarily unified design.

For the first four phrases, Bach presents the *suspirans* motive in only one voice at a time and tends to reduce the other two accompanimental parts to

Example 4–13. "Vater unser im Himmelreich," BWV 636

harmonic filler, in the form of a quarter note or two eighths. For most of the piece, then, two of the three accompanimental voices merely form chords, an unusually homophonic texture within the *Orgelbüchlein*. No wonder Keller summoned "Vater unser" to show how the *Orgelbüchlein* chorales could have "grown" conceptually from simple, block-chord harmonizations.

Not all performers may realize that, despite instructions given in modern editions, the alto can be easily played throughout by the right hand, something that cannot be said of most melody chorales in the *Orgelbüchlein*. Other factors that contribute to ease of performance are the chordal texture and the easy key. It is hard to think of an *Orgelbüchlein* chorale that falls more naturally under the fingers and feet.

This almost serene work is not without its peculiarities, though. In measure 3, beat 2, the soprano reads B instead of G, the pitch found in all other surviving versions of this melody. And in measure 5, beat 1, Bach uses a chromatic passing tone—exactly what he does at the same place in the small setting of this chorale in *Clavierübung* III.

Durch Adams Fall ist ganz verderbt ("Through Adam's fall is totally spoiled"), BWV 637

A further example of an *Orgelbüchlein*-type, "Durch Adams Fall" is a work of great profundity and originality, especially in terms of textual-musical relationships. There is perhaps no other chorale setting, instrumental or vocal, whose music so clearly and effectively symbolizes its text. Because of this quality, the piece has found a niche in music-history textbooks. Indeed, this may be the only *Orgelbüchlein* chorale as well known to academics as to practitioners.

As Williams notes, the repertory of accompanimental motives is the largest in the entire *Orgelbüchlein*. There are six distinct motives employed throughout, five for the alto and tenor and one for the bass. All tend toward chromaticism, which leads to an abundance of cross-relations.

Spitta was the first to point out that the descending-seventh motive stated in the bass must represent Adam's fall from grace, not only in its descending motion but also in its regular use of the diminished seventh, an interval traditionally associated with grief (see Example 4–14). Whether any other motives have symbolic meaning is debatable, although the five-note figure stated initially by the alto, with its major/minor dualism, might well be a metaphor for corruption. (Keller maintained that the tenor's chromatic scalar figures depict the writhing of the serpent.)

Whatever the case, the true symbolism of the work lies in its unorthodox contrapuntal and harmonic language. Other *Orgelbüchlein* chorales may have as many chromatic notes, but nowhere is the chromaticism handled as boldly. For example, both "Das alte Jahr" and "Christus, der uns selig macht" exhibit more or less constant chromaticism in the accompanimental voices, but it is almost exclusively in smooth, stepwise motion and usually in parallel motion between the voices. Hence the chromatic lines are normally consonant with one another, in the form of parallel thirds or sixths. Any dissonance created by the chromatic notes is introduced and resolved, in textbook fashion, by step. The tonality is never in doubt. In "Durch Adams Fall," on the other hand, chromatically dissonant notes are just as likely to be approached by leap (note the many diminished sevenths and tritones) as by step, and the dissonance is often left unresolved. With the exception of the famous harmonization of "Es ist genug," BWV 60/5, quoted in Berg's Violin Concerto, probably no other chorale setting by Bach approaches this level of chromaticism and dissonance. There is not a single instance of two

Example 4–14. "Durch Adams Fall ist ganz verderbt," BWV 637

chromatic voices in parallel motion, and the tonality is in constant flux. As Wolfgang Budday has pointed out, these unorthodox procedures may be interpreted as a "corruption" of normal practice, symbolizing the depravity of the human race.[14]

The effect is quite different from that of Buxtehude's organ arrangement of this chorale, which is usually cited as one of that composer's most expressive organ chorales, a work, according to Kerala Snyder, "imbued with sorrow."[15] Buxtehude also set the whole tune, but with a varied repeat of the *Stollen*, a feature that allows for unusually precise text-painting. In Buxtehude's setting, too, a descending bass motive undoubtedly portrays Adam's fall, but the motive is stated only during the first phrase (mm. 1–4). When the varied repeat of the *Stollen* begins, the harmony suddenly becomes chromatic, probably a depiction of the word "poison" in the third line ("The same poison has been bequeathed to us"). The chromaticism continues through the next phrase and then, like the falling bass motive, disappears. In Bach's *Orgelbüchlein* setting, the reference to Adam's fall and to its dire results remains constant.

Es ist das Heil uns kommen her
("Salvation comes to us"), BWV 638/638a

The text of this chorale may be viewed as a positive response to the conse-
quences of Adam's fall. Its central message—that Christian salvation is
granted not through good deeds but through faith alone—is a basic
Reformation tenet. Accordingly, the chorale was of special doctrinal significance. Like "Durch Adams Fall," it fell into the Catechism category of
"Confession, Penitence, and Justification."

There is also a complementary relationship between the *Orgelbüchlein*
settings of these two chorales. Indeed, with regard to several features, the
Orgelbüchlein setting of "Es ist das Heil" is the perfect foil to "Durch
Adams Fall." Its harmonies are almost exclusively diatonic, there are no
cross-relations, and there is only one accompanimental motive to speak of.
In other words, "Es ist das Heil" lacks the very ingredients that make
"Durch Adams Fall" so provocative.

As in "Vom Himmel hoch," the inner voices are based on the stepwise
suspirans, a walking bass occupies the pedals, and the statements of the
motive often form scales (see Example 4–15). According to Keller, the constant sixteenths and eighths "suffuse the setting with health and strength."

Example 4–15. "Es ist das Heil uns kommen her," BWV 638

Chapter 5

THE MIDDLE CHORALES

*T*he twenty-three works that comprise the middle compilation phase of the *Orgelbüchlein* include seventeen melody chorales, four chorale canons, and two ornamental chorales. As we discussed in Chapter 1, the early stage of this phase is stylistically similar to the early compilation phase, except that virtually all the bass lines of the melody chorales are motivic, as opposed to "walking" basses. Thus the *Orgelbüchlein*-type assumes an even greater role than before. In the late stage of the middle phase, Bach introduces techniques that prefigure the final compilation phase of the collection.

Nun komm, der Heiden Heiland ("Come now, Savior of the heathen"), BWV 599

On the face of it, this Advent chorale is entirely representative of *Orgelbüchlein* style: it both exemplifies the *Orgelbüchlein*-type and derives its inner voices from the *suspirans*. The work's voice leading, however, is quite free. This separates "Nun komm" from all other *Orgelbüchlein* chorales save "In dir ist Freude," a work from the late compilation phase.

For most of the piece, Bach alternates between four and five voices, and the numerous rests throughout in all voices imply an even freer style. In the last phrase, for example, five-part writing suddenly gives way to a lone bass note. Clark and Peterson note that this unexpected shift coincides in the first stanza with the text "All the world is *amazed* that God gave him such a birth."[1]

Other irregularities involve motivic work. As Riemenschneider indicated
in the score of his edition, the *suspirans* is sometimes present *between* voices
rather than within a single voice (see Example 5–1). This particular form of
the *suspirans* adopts a pattern (ascending second - descending fourth - ascending second) commonly employed in Baroque keyboard and lute music for
arpeggiating chords. Although the pattern creates an idiomatic pedal figure,
the pedal part of "Nun komm" consists mostly of a dotted rhythm (♪. ♪) that
leads to occurrences of the integrated motivic figuration found in "Gelobet
seist" and "Der Tag." This is especially the case in measure 4, where the *suspirans* all but disappears.

Bach's handling of the chorale tune is more exceptional still. All four lines
of the chorale text contain seven syllables, implying a uniform, metric rhythm
such as ♩ ♩ ♩ ♩ |♩ ♩ ♩. This is the basic rhythm to which "Nun komm" was
set in early eighteenth-century hymnals and in cantatas by Bach, Buxtehude,
and others. But in the *Orgelbüchlein* chorale, this is the rhythm only of the
interior phrases. The exterior phrases adopt the decidedly unmetrical pattern
of ♩ ♩ ♩|♩ ♩ ♩ |♩ . In both of the exterior phrases, which are melodically
identical, the second note initiates a *suspirans* in the soprano voice. Together

Example 5–1. "Nun komm, der Heiden Heiland," BWV 599

with the metric displacement, this embellishment serves to veil the chorale tune, as if to symbolize the mystery of the Incarnation.

GOTT, DURCH DEINE GÜTE
("GOD, THROUGH YOUR GOODNESS"), BWV 600

Bach gave this setting a dual title (*Gott durch deine Güte oder Gottes Sohn ist kommen*), indicating that the chorale tune could be sung to two different texts. While "Gott, durch deine Güte" is associated primarily with Advent, "Gottes Sohn ist kommen" is a Christmas hymn. Although the work appears in the Advent section of the *Orgelbüchlein*, there is nothing in the music that suggests one text over the other. The canonic treatment of the chorale melody, for example, could have been suggested equally by phrases in either text.

As we mentioned in Chapter 1, the *Orgelbüchlein* setting is a chorale canon along the lines of "In dulci jubilo," except that the latter is for the most part a double canon. Bach set the chorale melody in both works as a canon at the octave and at the distance of one measure between a soprano *dux* and tenor *comes*, with the tenor line notated as an extremely high pedal part (see Example 5–2). Furthermore, the opening two chorales' phrases are practically identical, and both works are in $\frac{3}{2}$ time. Composers such as Walther and his teacher Buttstedt sometimes set "Gott, durch" in duple meter. But all three of Bach's organ chorales on this melody (see also BWV 703 and 724) are in triple meter. The only two extant canonic settings—the present work and a partita movement by Walther—are in triple meter simply because the tune otherwise does not lend itself to canonic writing.

Meanwhile, the accompanimental voices—whose first order of business is to detour the tonality to B-flat—provide harmonic enrichment and continuous motion in two different rhythms. Bach derives the alto from the stepwise *suspirans*, whereas the bass line is a textbook walking bass. Following Schweitzer's lead, Riemenschneider maintained that "the exuberance of the passage work indicates a joyous background."[2]

The issue most often discussed in connection with "Gott, durch" is performance practice, hardly a surprise considering that the work contains the only registration indications in the *Orgelbüchlein*. Bach prescribed that the soprano, alto, and bass voices be played on an eight-foot principal in one of the manual divisions (*man. Princip. 8 f.*) and the tenor on an eight-foot trumpet stop in the pedal (*ped. Tromp. 8 f.*). Both stops were available on the

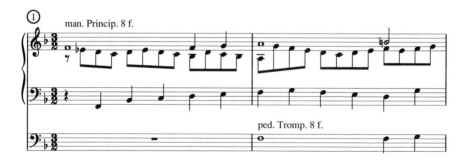

Example 5–2. "Gott, durch deine Güte," BWV 600

Weimar court organ. As in "In dulci jubilo," however, the high pedal line exceeded the compass of the instrument, a problem that Bach probably remedied by playing the tenor down an octave on his Cornett-Bass, a four-foot pedal reed. Accordingly, all that *Tromp. 8 f.* means is that the tenor line is notated at the intended pitch and should be played on a stop of the trumpet family. Of course, pedalboards today typically go as high as f', the highest pitch in the tenor line, allowing modern players to follow Bach's instructions literally. Consistently playing on the upper end of the pedalboard, though, is prohibitively difficult for most performers.

Nor should one feel obliged to use a separate manual for the bass, as indicated in the Riemenschneider edition. There is no instruction in the autograph for two-manual performance, and Bach even drew a bracket around the soprano, alto, and bass at the beginning of the piece, which can only signify that he intended all three parts to be played on the same manual. Moreover, in measure 14 the left hand has to take certain alto notes, due to the large intervals between the soprano and alto. And in measure 7, it is most convenient for the left hand to play the alto c' on the second beat, since the soprano has a trill. With the left hand on a separate manual, the player has to risk "thumbing" these alto notes with the left hand.

LOB SEI DEM ALLMÄCHTIGEN GOTT
("PRAISE BE TO ALMIGHTY GOD"), BWV 602

The melody of this Advent chorale derives from the Gregorian hymn "Conditor alme siderum." Although the original tune is in the phrygian mode, only the final phrase of the *Orgelbüchlein* setting contains "phrygian" harmonies, with a final on A, harmonized as an A-major chord. The second phrase of the tune ends exactly like the last, but the cadence there is in F major. In the opening phrase, Bach disguises the melody's phrygian character by rewriting the two B-flats as B-naturals.

This infrequently played work employs two different *suspirans* motives. A five-note embellished form appears in the alto and tenor, while the conventional four-note version is found in all three accompanimental parts (see Example 5–3). The figuration suggested to Riemenschneider "an atmosphere of dignified praise."

Whereas the chorale tune consists of four phrases, the bass contains only three, each of which descends stepwise for at least an octave. This is the most calculated use of downward motion anywhere in the *Orgelbüchlein* and, as Keller argued, it is most likely a representation of Christ's descent to earth.[3]

Example 5–3. "Lob sei dem allmächtigen Gott," BWV 602

VOM HIMMEL KAM DER ENGEL SCHAR *("FROM HEAVEN CAME THE HOST OF ANGELS"), BWV 607*

The text of this Christmas chorale by Luther is highly reminiscent of his "Vom Himmel hoch," also a Christmas chorale. Indeed, the hymn was frequently sung to the "Vom Himmel hoch" melody. The tune used in the *Orgelbüchlein* setting, on the other hand, was originally published to the text of the Christmas chorale "Puer natus." This is Bach's only known use of the melody.

Technically speaking, "Vom Himmel kam" is a melody chorale with a walking bass, the only such work in the middle compilation phase of the *Orgelbüchlein* and the last example of a walking bass in the collection. Yet this seems all too mundane a description for such a special piece. For one thing, the walking bass here is closely integrated with the inner voices: all three lower parts—especially the tenor—consist of scales, with the pedal proceeding in double augmentation (see Example 5–4). In addition, the tenor voice has a range of over three octaves (F-g''), the largest compass of any voice in the *Orgelbüchlein*. The part is also manifestly symbolic, as its

Example 5–4. "Vom Himmel kam der Engel Schar," BWV 607

mercurial scales unquestionably depict angels fluttering between heaven and earth. As Spitta put it, "Bach's music rushes down and up again like the descending and ascending messengers of heaven."[4]

Although the autograph prescribes neither one manual nor two, some modern editions, including Riemenschneider's, instruct the left hand to play the tenor on a different manual from the soprano and alto. In measure 16, the only bar in which an accompanimental voice rises above the soprano, this approach allows the chorale tune to sound without interruption and facilitates the requisite handcrossing. Otherwise, though, the evidence points to one manual. To begin with, separating the voices between two manuals undermines the cooperation among the three upper parts in the many passages where the tenor joins with the alto or soprano (or both) in forming scales. Secondly, Bach was careful never to allow the inner parts to cross. Whenever the tenor has ideas of going higher than the alto (mm. 5, 12, 14, and 16), the alto simply drops out. The composer would have had relatively little concern about such voice-crossing on two manuals.

On one manual or two, "Vom Himmel kam" can be a scintillating work if played at a sprightly tempo. A four-foot flute in the manual, or a "gapped" registration, supported by an eight-foot flute in the pedal, creates an ethereal sound consistent with the text. A detached articulation for the bass line also lends an appropriately atmospheric quality (as well as allowing for easy, all-toe pedalling). With the exception of Bach's "Wedge" Fugue, organists will find no better scale exercise for the left hand.

JESU, MEINE FREUDE ("JESUS, MY JOY"), BWV 610

Although the text of "Jesu, meine Freude" makes no reference to Christmas, various early hymnals—including that published in Weimar in 1708—designated the chorale for that season. Indeed, we find it in the Christmas section of the *Orgelbüchlein*. The melody is transmitted in two versions, which offer different readings for the second phrase, either (in C minor) G-A-B-G-C-B or G-G-A-B-C-B. While Bach adopted the former reading in his famous chorale-motet (BWV 227) on this melody, he used the latter in the *Orgelbüchlein*. This version of the tune also appears in Bach's other extant keyboard settings (BWV 713, 753, and 1105) as well as in Walther's fine organ partita on the chorale, published in 1713. Of Bach's keyboard settings, only that in the *Orgelbüchlein* is in C minor, the same key used by Walther.

The *Orgelbüchlein* setting of "Jesu, meine Freude" marks a return to the *Orgelbüchlein*-type, with the inner parts mostly paired against the bass. Yet one also finds shared motives among all three accompanimental voices, most notably the two (⁷ ♫♪♪ and ⁷♪♪♫) that supply practically all the bass material (see Example 5–5). These motives are closely related, beginning off the beat and ending with a written-out mordent.

We should not be surprised that Schweitzer heard in this subtle work a "mystic adoration" as opposed to outright worship, for the music is unusually somber. Observe, for instance, the very low range of the soprano (especially in the first and last phrases), which dictates relatively low pitches throughout for all parts. Furthermore, the counterpoint is strikingly dense— in Spitta's words, an "exquisite labyrinth." This maze is the result of nonstop activity within all three accompanimental voices and the compression of these voices caused by the low soprano. An additional factor is the constant use of dissonant harmonies in a minor-mode context. The dissonance is frequently the result of suspensions and occasionally the byproduct of chromaticism, such as the A-flat/F-natural/F-sharp complexes in measures 4, 12, and 13, which intimate augmented-sixth chords. Finally, Bach inscribed in

Example 5–5. "Jesu, meine Freude," BWV 610

the autograph a tempo marking of *Largo,* which allows the player carefully to negotiate the complex motivic and harmonic design.

WIR CHRISTENLEUT
("WE CHRISTIAN PEOPLE"), BWV 612

This Christmas chorale also exemplifies the *Orgelbüchlein*-type. As in "Jesu, meine Freude," Bach works with two related motives. Both begin off the beat with a descent of a fourth, followed by an ascending second. Here, however, the motives are strictly separated between hands and feet (see Example 5–6). The dance-like figure found in the inner voices (♪ ♫♫♪) is perhaps most familiar from Bach's Prelude in C Major, BWV 547, while the striding bass motive (♪♫♫♪) recalls the pedal line of Bach's large setting of "Wir glauben all an einen Gott" from *Clavierübung* III. Schweitzer interpreted the pedal parts of both works as a depiction of unwavering Christian faith. In the first stanza of "Wir Christenleut," this ideal is expressed by the text "whoever trusts in him and firmly believes will not be lost."

This chorale tune is possibly the most repetitive in all of Lutheran hymnody and the most repetitive of any chorale set in the *Orgelbüchlein.* Each of the three musical phrases is restated at least once, resulting in the scheme AABCBBC. Yet except for the unusual repeat of the last three phrases—not indicated in the Riemenschneider edition—Bach assiduously avoids note-for-note repetition in his *Orgelbüchlein* setting: no two statements of any phrase use the same harmonies or rhythms.

Example 5–6. "Wir Christenleut," BWV 612

DAS ALTE JAHR VERGANGEN IST
("THE OLD YEAR HAS PASSED"), BWV 614

Bach set this New Year hymn in the *Orgelbüchlein* as an ornamental chorale—and one shot through with dissonance and chromaticism. As Keller noted, the piece projects a degree of sorrow seemingly unwarranted by the chorale text, which is more a supplication than a lament. Still, the text refers to a number of melancholy subjects, not merely the passing of the old year— and thus the transitory nature of human existence—but also danger and (in stanza 4) "the sins of the old year."

The soprano coloratura of "Das alte Jahr" may not be as lyrical as that of "O Mensch," but it is every bit as intricate rhythmically. The complexity of the accompaniment therefore comes as a surprise. All three parts employ the chromatic, stepwise figure known as the *passus duriusculus* ("dissonant step"), which Bach subjects to constant stretto treatment and, in the first four bars, invertible counterpoint (see Example 5–7).

Three passages stand out. First, in order to achieve contrary motion with the soprano, Bach delays the first statement of the accompanimental motive

Example 5–7. "Das alte Jahr vergangen ist," BWV 614

until after the *second* chorale note, a unique start for an *Orgelbüchlein* chorale. The monophonic texture, which coincides with identical pitches and rhythms for the first two chorale notes, makes for an extraordinarily stark beginning.

At the beginning of the second phrase, all the accompanimental voices drop out for a beat, during a soprano melisma that bridges the first two phrases in a particularly fluid way. As Clark and Peterson observe, the writing is reminiscent of Bach's "Arnstadt Congregational Chorales," in which such solo figuration regularly occurs between phrases of the hymn tune.

Equally remarkable is the work's conclusion, where the bass and tenor rest on harmonic tones while the soprano and alto rise in parallel motion by means of appoggiatura "sighs." The texture and melodies drastically slow the harmonic rhythm and—for the first time in the piece—thoroughly hide the chorale tune.

CHRIST LAG IN TODESBANDEN ("CHRIST LAY IN THE BONDS OF DEATH"), BWV 625

The *Orgelbüchlein* setting of this Easter hymn is closely tied to the three Easter chorales that follow it in the autograph. Not only do the settings succeed one another without break, but all four adopt the *Orgelbüchlein*-type.

As in "Das alte Jahr," the accompanimental voices are unified by a single motive, which in this case is nothing more than two sixteenth notes in ascending, stepwise motion. The motive is usually the subject of double or quadruple statements that form a descending, stepwise sequence, tailor-made to alternate-feet pedalling (see Example 5–8).

This downward motion suggested to Marcel Dupré the "descent by the holy women, step by step, down to the tomb," a fanciful interpretation, to be

Example 5–8. "Christ lag in Todesbanden," BWV 625

sure, since none of the seven stanzas of the text refer to this act.[5] Dupré also heard in this work the "last moment of sorrow before the world beheld the Resurrection," a notion diametrically opposed to Luther's celebratory poetry. If understood within the context of the modern French organ school, though, such views are understandable, for there was a tradition among French organists of the late nineteenth and early twentieth centuries of playing this piece in an introspective, almost melancholy vein. Dupré's teacher Guilmant, for example, played the work softly and slowly.[6] Organists today, however, tend to perform "Christ lag" in full Easter dress, with a big registration and fast tempo, in accordance with the festivity of the Easter season.[7]

JESUS CHRISTUS, UNSER HEILAND, DER DEN TOD ÜBERWAND *("JESUS CHRIST, OUR SAVIOR, WHO OVERCAME DEATH"), BWV 626*

This Easter chorale by Luther should not be confused with the Communion hymn "Jesus Christus, unser Heiland, der von uns den Gotteszorn wandt," set by Bach in the "Great Eighteen" Chorales and *Clavierübung* III. Like "Christ lag," this *Orgelbüchlein* setting has a "monothematic" accompaniment, in this instance based on a syncopated motive (♪♩♪♪♪) that Riemenschneider construed as a "Resurrection theme" (see Example 5–9). Williams points out that the motive is of a type known from compound-time variations in Baroque chorale partitas, such as Buxtehude's "Auf meinen lieben Gott" and Bach's "Sei gegrüsset, Jesu gütig."[8]

Above all, what distinguishes this work is its texture, for once all the voices have entered, the writing is the most homophonic in the entire

Example 5–9. "Jesus Christus, unser Heiland, der den Tod überwand," BWV 626

Orgelbüchlein. This results from the many paired statements of the accompanimental motive in the inner parts as well as from Bach's tendency to conform the rhythm of the accompanimental voices to that of the soprano. Because of its chordal texture, "Jesus Christus" is one of the easiest *Orgelbüchlein* chorales to play, and is typically among the first *Orgelbüchlein* chorales that an organist learns.

Christ ist erstanden
("Christ is risen"), BWV 627

This Easter chorale was particularly cherished by early Protestants, including Luther himself. The hymn is unusual—and unique among the chorales set in the *Orgelbüchlein*—since each of its three stanzas uses a different poetic meter and, consequently, a different tune. The form of the *Orgelbüchlein* setting is also unique within the collection, consisting of three movements (called "verses" in the autograph) that have the outward appearance of a miniature chorale partita. Bach is the only composer known to have set all three stanzas of the chorale within a single work.

Certain aspects of this setting bespeak an unusually strict musical style. To begin with, the chorale tune appears throughout in the soprano, rather than migrating to a different voice between movements, as frequently occurs in chorale partitas. Furthermore, the harmonies of the first two movements are essentially the same, just as the melodies of these two stanzas of the chorale are very similar. There is even something austere about Bach's use of half notes, instead of the usual quarters, to notate the chorale tune.

As Williams observes, the motivic writing in the first movement is relentless. One motive is present in all the accompanimental voices (γ ♩ ♫), while another confines itself to the inner parts (γ ♫♩) (see Example 5–10a). Both contain a pair of stepwise sixteenths, followed by a longer rhythm. Since both motives are constantly stated, this three-note cell sounds on literally every beat until the penultimate bar.

This doctrinaire style gives way in *Vers* 2 to accompanimental writing that freely admits material other than the primary motive. Here the accompaniment is derived from a figure (γ ♬ ♩ ♩ ♬♪) that is twice as long as any other in the work (see Example 5–10b). Bach frequently states the motive in stretto, as he does in the opening measures. Otherwise, the motive divides into two segments (γ ♬ ♩ ♩ and the *suspirans* figure ♬ ♪), usu-

Example 5–10. "Christ ist erstanden," BWV 627

ally stated simultaneously in two separate voices. The fragmentation is so
regular as to suggest two different motives.

The third movement, in turn, initially reverts to the workaday character
of *Vers 1*, with a *suspirans* accompaniment (see Example 5–10c). As the
movement unfolds, however, the bass line breaks free of the *suspirans* for
measures at a time. Toward the end of the chorale, it speeds up to continu-

ous sixteenths on four consecutive beats, just as the movement as a whole features constant sixteenth-note motion. As Spitta characterized the rhythmic acceleration from one movement to the next, "a fresh vitality as of the rising sun flows with constantly increasing power through all three stanzas."

Erstanden ist der heil'ge Christ ("The Holy Christ is risen"), BWV 628

The opening bars of this Easter chorale—Bach's only setting of this melody—are a vivid depiction of the first line of the text. Both the alto and tenor begin with an ascent of a tenth, in the midst of a sequential statement of the stepwise *suspirans* that rises for two octaves (see Example 5–11). Such pronounced upward motion occurs nowhere else in the piece and is an obvious play on the word *erstanden* ("risen").

This simple yet delightful work—an additional example of the *Orgelbüchlein*-type—projects an exuberance eminently appropriate for the

Example 5–11. "Erstanden ist der heil'ge Christ," BWV 628

Easter season. The constant presentation of the *suspirans* in the alto and tenor suggested to Schweitzer the joy of Easter. The bass, meanwhile, stamps out a two-note motive that, in accordance with the regular phrase structure of the chorale tune, always occurs between the third and first beats. Because most of the statements ascend, Schweitzer interpreted the figure—like the upward surge at the beginning of the piece—as symbolic of the Resurrection.

ERSCHIENEN IST DER HERRLICHE TAG ("*THE SPLENDID DAY HAS APPEARED*"), *BWV 629*

As Keller maintained, the phrase "he *leads* into captivity all his enemies" in the first stanza of this Easter hymn may have suggested to Bach the idea of a canonic setting in the *Orgelbüchlein* (see Example 5–12). Walther also set this chorale as a canon, perhaps for the same reason. At all events, the melody is not an ideal candidate for canonic elaboration. In the *Orgelbüchlein* setting, melodic as well as rhythmic discrepancies exist between the *dux*

Example 5–12. "Erschienen ist der herrliche Tag," BWV 629

and *comes* in most phrases. The third phrase of the *comes* is even a beat shorter than that of the *dux*.

As with "In dulci jubilo" and "Gott, durch deine Güte," Bach set this canon at the octave between a soprano *dux* and a pedal *comes*. But his indication that each canonic voice be assigned its own division of the organ (*á 2 Clav. & Ped.*) casts the work in a very different light. This disposition, which is used for no other chorale canon in the *Orgelbüchlein*, allows the performer to give each canonic voice its own registration and eliminates the possibility of interruptions to the soprano *dux* by a high-rising alto part. (Such interruptions occur in both "In dulci jubilo" and "Gott, durch deine Güte.") The listener is able to comprehend the canon in an unusually clear way.

Because the left hand alone plays the two inner voices, the intervals between these parts never exceed an octave, and the figuration is exceptionally homophonic. Both voices derive from a simple dactyl (♪♪ ♩), roughly half the statements of which are in parallel thirds or sixths. Fast parallel sixths are of course common in Baroque organ music, but they are usually played by two hands. Played by one hand, the wide stretches lead naturally to a somewhat detached articulation.

Performance-practice concerns of a different sort arise in the final phrase. For instance, from measure 17 to the downbeat of measure 18, practically all the alto notes are higher than the soprano, a circumstance that in this type of two-manual scheme results in handcrossings very uncharacteristic of the *Orgelbüchlein*. Even more anamolous are the last five beats of the piece, where the soprano joins with the alto and tenor in an upsurge of parallel statements of the dactyl motive, which may be yet another metaphor for the Resurrection. Riemenschneider's edition instructs that the right hand should change here to the manual used for the inner voices, but the autograph contains no such prescription.

KOMM, GOTT SCHÖPFER, HEILIGER GEIST ("COME, GOD CREATOR, HOLY GHOST"), BWV 631/631A

The Pentecost hymn "Veni creator spiritus" is the basis for some of the most famous items in the organ repertory, including a movement from Nicolas de Grigny's *Livre d'Orgue*—a collection that Bach himself copied out during his early Weimar years—and, more recently, Maurice Duruflé's *Prélude, Adagio et Choral varié sur le thème du "Veni creator."* This *Orgelbüchlein* setting, derived from Luther's paraphrase of the original hymn, represents a relatively modest contribution to this tradition.

Among the most colorful works in the *Orgelbüchlein*, "Komm, Gott" seems to evoke the "spiritual" nature of Pentecost at every turn. First of all, the meter is compound duple, which, at a fast tempo, can give the impression of a gigue (Walther, by contrast, set the chorale in straightforward common time). Furthermore, the minuscule bass motive, which consists merely of two eighth rests followed by an eighth note, produces a jazzy syncopation throughout (see Example 5–13). As Clark and Peterson observe, the motive is especially effective when the bass note coincides with harmonic change in the other voices, as on the first two beats of the first measure. A thoroughly original idea, the motive would seem to portray the position of the Holy Spirit within the Trinity: to depict the third member of the Godhead, the bass sounds on the third eighth note of the beat.

The motivic bass implies a return to the *Orgelbüchlein*-type. This notion is confirmed by the equally motivic alto and tenor parts, which share two primary motives (♪♩♪ and ♪♫♪). Like the bass figure, both of these motives last one beat, allowing for many simultaneous statements of all three motives, especially during the second half of the work. During the first half, the inner voices normally present the same motive in parallel motion. Just as the work's texture becomes increasingly polyphonic, its figuration inclines more toward sixteenths as the piece progresses. One can tell from the more or less continuous sixteenths in the last two bars that, as in "Christ ist erstanden," this acceleration leads to a climactic conclusion. Many of the sixteenths—as well as all the ornaments in the piece—exist only in the revised version, BWV 631.

Example 5–13. "Komm, Gott Schöpfer, Heiliger Geist," BWV 631

Ich ruf zu dir, Herr Jesu Christ
("I call to you, Lord Jesus Christ"), BWV 639

This poignant work initiates a block of six *omne tempore* chorales that will conclude our survey of the early stage of the middle compilation phase. One of the most popular pieces in the *Orgelbüchlein*, "Ich ruf zu dir" abounds in chromatic inflections. These nuances are perfectly suited to the plaintive chorale text, characterized by Clark and Peterson as a "supplication in time of despair."

The work is an anomaly within the *Orgelbüchlein*, primarily because it is the only setting in three voices. But the piece is also an atypical example of a melody chorale, since the chorale tune is highly embellished at the beginning (see Example 5–14). As we will see in Chapter 7, Mendelssohn even referred to the work unqualifiedly as an *ausgeschmückter Choral*. Bach's instruction for the chorale tune to be played on a separate manual contributes further to the impression of an ornamental chorale.

Why does the ornamentation cease beginning in measure 6? As Clark and Peterson relate, one theory is that Bach retracted the ornamentation to symbolize the text of the first stanza at this point ("The true faith, Lord, I aspire to") and that the absence of ornamentation specifically depicts the word *rechten*, which could conceivably be translated as "pure" as well as "true." (Thus a "pure" chorale is one devoid of ornamentation.) Bach, however, wrote an ornament precisely on this word (m. 6, beat 2), which renders this hypothesis dubious at best. It seems much more likely that he intended for ornamentation to continue until the end of the piece, but did not write it out. Certain manuscript copies contain more ornamentation than the autograph from measure 6 on, but for the most part only at cadences.[9]

Example 5–14. "Ich ruf zu dir, Herr Jesu Christ," BWV 639

Meanwhile, the middle and lower parts supply continuous motion in sixteenths and eighths, respectively. The middle voice, which Keller heard as "meekly imploring," contains arpeggios whose notes are slurred together in groups of four—a clear simulation of string writing. (About a century earlier, Samuel Scheidt had labelled such slurred figuration in his organ music *imitatio violistica*.) This has led to speculation that Bach transcribed "Ich ruf zu dir" from a work with an obbligato string part. As Klaus Peter Richter has shown, a particular model is suggested by the third movement of Cantata 180 (*Schmücke dich, o liebe Seele*), a trio for soprano, violoncello piccolo, and continuo in which the soprano sings a chorale in quasi-ornamental style, the violoncello piccolo plays sixteenth-note arpeggios, and the continuo moves in constant eighth notes.[10]

In dich hab ich gehoffet, Herr ("In you have I hoped, Lord"), BWV 640

This text, based on Psalm 31:1–6, was sung to two very different melodies, one in the major, the other in the minor mode. The former is quite famous, owing to Bach's use of it in certain cantatas, most notably Cantata 106 (*Gottes Zeit ist die allerbeste Zeit*), as well as the *St. Matthew Passion* and *Christmas Oratorio*. Walther also used this tune for his setting. The minor-mode version, on the other hand, appears in Bach's oeuvre only in this *Orgelbüchlein* chorale.

A clear example of the *Orgelbüchlein*-type, the setting features an accompaniment based on two related motives, a simple anapest (♪ ♫ ♪) assigned to the middle voices and a bass figure that adds to this motive a concluding eighth note (see Example 5–15). Schweitzer categorized the anapest as a

Example 5–15. "In dich hab ich gehoffet, Herr," BWV 640

"joy" motive, while Keller claimed that it "signifies constancy." Whatever the case, the ongoing statements of the figure are consistent with the central theme of the text: continuous hope in a faithful God.

WENN WIR IN HÖCHSTEN NÖTEN SEIN *("WHEN WE ARE IN THE GREATEST DISTRESS"), BWV 641*

This beautiful work is in two ways a rarity within the *Orgelbüchlein*. It not only exemplifies the ornamental chorale, but it also employs an accompanimental motive (♪♫♪) drawn from the chorale melody (see Example 5–16). This motive, melodically identical to the opening four notes of the chorale tune, furnishes the material for all three accompanimental parts. As Keller maintained, "even the accompanying voices join in prayer with the beginning of the melody."

Except for the ornamental soprano setting of "Allein Gott in der Höh sei Ehr" from the "Great Eighteen" Chorales, no other chorale setting by Bach

Example 5–16. "Wenn wir in höchsten Nöten sein," BWV 641

contains such profuse ornamentation. As Clark and Peterson observe, the common occurrence of the upward-resolving *port de voix* gives the embellishment a distinctly French character. Yet the line is also very lyrical, due to its wide range (a twelfth) and large intervals. The many sixths even impart a certain sweetness, in keeping with the consolatory text. To quote Schweitzer, "the melody flows . . . like a divine song of consolation, and in a wonderful final cadence seems to silence and compose the other parts."

WER NUR DEN LIEBEN GOTT LÄSST WALTEN ("WHOEVER LETS DEAR GOD RULE HIM"), BWV 642

The tune associated with this text was transmitted in triple as well as duple meter. Bach sometimes set the melody in triple meter, but the vast majority of his settings, including that in the *Orgelbüchlein*, are in duple. Walther, Georg Böhm, and Bach's pupil Johann Ludwig Krebs also employed duple meter in their organ settings. To judge from the large number (fourteen) and wide chronological distribution of Bach's settings, the chorale was a personal favorite throughout his life.

Generally speaking, the *Orgelbüchlein* setting represents the *Orgelbüchlein*-type, even if its bass line alternates between motivic figuration and walking-bass patterns. The inner voices, on the other hand, are intensely motivic. They derive from a simple anapest (♪ ♫) that Bach tends to state simultaneously in both parts (see Example 5–17). This figure is closely related to the dactyl (♫ ♪) that serves as the primary bass motive. The combination of these brisk rhythms suggested to Schweitzer a "joyful feeling of confidence in God's goodness."

ALLE MENSCHEN MÜSSEN STERBEN ("ALL MANKIND MUST DIE"), BWV 643

In contrast to "Wer nur," here is an unambiguous specimen of the *Orgelbüchlein*-type. All three of its accompanimental voices derive from a five-note form of the *suspirans* (♪ ♫♫), one of Schweitzer's "beatific peace" motives (see Example 5–18). The degree to which the motive is stated by the inner voices in parallel thirds and sixths is unsurpassed in the *Orgelbüchlein*.

The constant harmonization of the motive in this way makes for a euphony unmatched anywhere in the collection. Whether one likens it to "tender

Example 5–17. "Wer nur den lieben Gott lässt walten," BWV 642

melancholy" (Spitta) or "celestial happiness" (Schweitzer), the mood is utterly serene. Bach, then, is depicting not the harsh inevitability of death, as referred to in the opening line, but death as a blissful release from worldly anxieties—the text's main message.

Against this pacific background, any dissonance or chromaticism stands out in bold relief. This applies not only to the chromatic passing tone in the chorale tune at measure 5, but also to the cross relation between the bass

Example 5–18. "Alle Menschen müssen sterben," BWV 643

and tenor on the first beat of the last bar. This cross relation coincides with the only instance of the *suspirans* in the soprano. Spitta found the passage "indescribably expressive."

Because the interval between the alto and tenor never exceeds an octave, one can play these voices with the left hand alone, freeing up the right hand to play the soprano on a different manual. Even though there is no such prescription in the autograph, this is the customary way of performing the work, presumably because it allows for a highlighted chorale melody and a more variegated organ sonority.

ACH WIE NICHTIG, ACH WIE FLÜCHTIG
("OH, HOW EMPTY, OH, HOW FLEETING"), BWV 644

This work also clearly exemplifies the *Orgelbüchlein*-type. The chorale text compares human life to "a fog that quickly appears and then quickly disappears." Bach captures this sense of transitoriness with running scales in the inner voices and frequent rests in the bass line (see Example 5–19). As Spitta put it, the scales "hurry by like misty ghosts." Bach's setting of this chorale in the first movement of Cantata 26 (*Ach wie flüchtig, ach wie nichtig*) contains precisely this sort of scalar figuration, as does Variation 4 of Georg Böhm's organ partita on this chorale. The parallels between the Böhm movement and the *Orgelbüchlein* setting are close enough to suggest compositional borrowing on Bach's part. Meanwhile, the bass sounds a motive (♪ ♪ ♫) that Keller likened to the "futility of human existence." Walther employed this figure in the pedal line of his partita on "Herr Gott, nun schleuss den Himmel auf."

Example 5–19. "Ach wie nichtig, ach wie flüchtig," BWV 644

Most striking is the absence of the pedal at the end, a feature of only one other *Orgelbüchlein* chorale ("Erstanden ist"). Clark and Peterson are surely correct to find an analogy in the "Esurientes" movement from Bach's Magnificat, which concludes with an "empty" final note after the word *inanes* ("empty"). The effect is also not unlike that of the aria "Wie zittern und wanken" from Bach's Cantata 105, *Herr, gehe nicht ins Gericht*, where the missing continuo part symbolizes the sinner's precarious existence.

MIT FRIED UND FREUD ICH FAHR DAHIN ("WITH PEACE AND JOY I DEPART"), BWV 616

This piece is the first of four adjacent settings in the autograph that constitute the late stage of the *Orgelbüchlein*'s middle compilation phase. Positioned between the New Year and Passiontide chorales, the work's liturgical designation is the Purification of the Virgin (February 2). Bach also set this chorale in two of his Purification cantatas, Nos. 83 and 125. The text, by Luther, is based on the *Nunc dimittis* or "Song of Simeon" (Luke 2:29–32), in which the aged Simeon rejoices upon seeing the infant Jesus. The chorale text's first stanza contains adjectives (*sanft* and *stille*, or "soft" and "still") that suggest a quiet registration—restrained elation.

At first glance, it might seem that Bach realizes the *Orgelbüchlein*-type here with two different accompanimental motives, one for the hands, another for the feet. But all three accompanimental voices actually derive from the same motive, which is merely simplified for the pedal from ♪♪♪♪♪ to ♪♪♪♪ (see Example 5–20).[11] Schweitzer viewed the figure in its unaltered state as representing Simeon's "lively and radiant joy."

Except for the extremely low tessitura of the soprano and the many statements of the accompanimental motive in that voice, the work generally proceeds as expected. But its conclusion is unusually chromatic and dissonant. Having tonicized the subdominant at the end of measure 14, Bach begins the last bar with a G-minor chord, only to change the sonority to G major, and, finally, to a diminished seventh on C-sharp.[12] Sounding at the same time as the D's in the outer voices, the diminished seventh produces great friction, thus intensifying the sense of cadential repose when the harmony finally settles on D major. This cadence type is a veritable trademark of Bach's keyboard music.[13] Two other *Orgelbüchlein* chorales in which it serves as a final cadence are "Christus, der uns selig macht" and "Herr Gott, nun schleuss den Himmel auf," the work that immediately follows "Mit Fried und Freud" in the autograph.

Example 5–20. "Mit Fried und Freud ich fahr dahin," BWV 616

HERR GOTT, NUN SCHLEUSS DEN HIMMEL AUF ("LORD GOD, NOW UNLOCK HEAVEN"), BWV 617

Also a Purification chorale, this hymn likewise derives from the *Nunc dimittis*. Its last stanza even contains an explicit reference to Simeon.

In various respects, "Herr Gott" departs from standard *Orgelbüchlein* style and presages the late compilation phase of the collection. To begin with, it commences not with the initial chorale note but with figuration in the lower two parts (the figuration closely resembles the opening bars of Bach's Third Harpsichord Partita, also in A minor). Bach employs this material in the form of interludes between all the chorale phrases—a clear portent of the late chorale "In dir ist Freude."

This figuration encompasses two utterly different lines. The tenor moves in continuous sixteenths over a range of almost three octaves, allowing for dramatic, sweeping contours (see Example 5–21). Various motives, embedded in a web of scales and arpeggios, are present. Simultaneously, the bass states a syncopated eighth-note figure (𝄽) whose faltering rhythm suggested to Schweitzer the "uncertain steps of a pilgrim who has finished

Example 5–21. "Herr Gott, nun schleuss den Himmel auf," BWV 617

his course and now goes with weary steps to the gate of eternity." This mood of lassitude is far removed from the flamboyance of Bach's setting of this chorale in the Neumeister Collection, where Simeon seems to exit in a blaze of glory, accompanied by bravura passagework.

The alto, in turn, is the most overtly harmonic voice in the whole *Orgelbüchlein*. It adopts the same, slow rhythms as the soprano because the right hand alone obviously has to play both voices, on a different manual from the tenor. (On a single manual, the tenor would interrupt the alto to the point of obliteration.) As we will see in Chapter 6, the late chorale "Hilf Gott, dass mir's gelinge" employs precisely this type of two-manual texture, the same kind of rhythmic layering (quarters and halves in the alto and soprano, sixteenths in the tenor, and eighths in the bass), and the same frequency of hand-crossings. Played on two manuals, with the hands constantly crossed and with lively tenor and bass lines, "Herr Gott" feels rather like the bottom two-thirds of a trio. The tenor constitutes an exacting study for the left hand, complete with leaps of over two octaves.

Bach employed a different type of common time for each accompanimental voice, perhaps to emphasize the independence of the three: $\frac{4}{4}$ for the alto,

$\frac{24}{16}$ for the tenor, and $\frac{12}{8}$ for the bass. Although he wrote even eighths for the alto (and soprano), these notes should no doubt be played to the rhythm ♩ ♪ .

O LAMM GOTTES, UNSCHULDIG *("O LAMB OF GOD, INNOCENTLY SLAUGHTERED"), BWV 618*

This Passiontide chorale and the one that immediately follows it in the autograph ("Christe, du Lamm Gottes") are both canons at the fifth, and the only canons in the *Orgelbüchlein* with introductory passagework. Additional likenesses are the similar textual incipits and the common key. These two chorales represent a paraphrase and translation, respectively, of the Agnus Dei.

Writers have claimed that in setting over half the Passiontide chorales in the *Orgelbüchlein* as canons, Bach was symbolizing such Passion themes as Christ following God's will, the Lamb being led to slaughter, and the carrying of the cross. But it is also possible that in each instance specific phrases in the chorale text suggested canonic technique. As Clark and Peterson observe, the phrase in this case is the line "You have *borne* all sins," found in all three stanzas. The chorale tune itself does not invite canonic treatment.

In terms of canonic writing in the *Orgelbüchlein,* "O Lamm Gottes" breaks new ground in two respects: it is the first canon at an interval other than the octave and the first set exclusively in the inner voices. The unusual canonic interval of the fifth leads to a host of unexpected harmonies, most notably at the phrase endings of the *dux.* For example, the first phrase ends on A minor rather than F major or C major (see Example 5–22), and the last phrase ends on D minor rather than F major. Note also the paucity of root-position chords, even at cadences.

To set the *Abgesang,* Bach turns increasingly to chromatic, dissonant harmonies. See especially the fourth phrase, beginning with the fifth note of the *dux,* where between measures 12 and 13 the pedal has tied notes on middle C. This is no random use of dissonance, for the note in question begins the word *verzagen* ("depair"). Bach also singled out this word for intensely chromatic treatment in his setting of "O Lamm Gottes" from the "Great Eighteen" Chorales.

But the aura of melancholy surrrounding this work is due more to the slurred, falling "sigh" motive (♫♫) on which the noncanonic parts are based. This figure was a time-honored symbol of grief, and Bach often used it to express this affect, most notably in the setting of "O Mensch, bewein

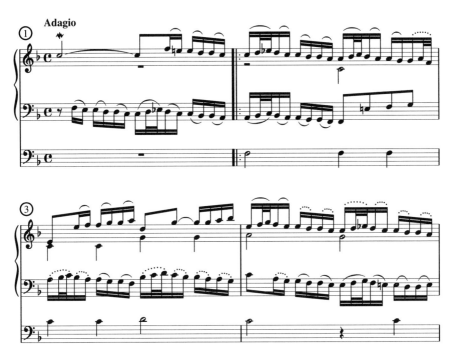

Example 5–22. "O Lamm Gottes, unschuldig," BWV 618

dein Sünde gross" in Part I of the *St. Matthew Passion*. As in that chorus, the
motive here is normally slurred in couplets, in imitation of bowing technique. According to Schweitzer, "the second of the two slurred notes must
always be lightly breathed, making the motive seem like a series of sighs
from the depth of the soul."

The opening mordent raises an unusual performance-practice issue, for
on the repeat of the *Stollen*, its tonal context changes from F major to C
major. One should therefore play b-flat as the auxiliary pitch for the initial
statement, and b-natural for the restatement. This may be a unique instance
in Bach of an ornament that should be performed with different notes on its
restatement than on its initial appearance.

CHRISTE, DU LAMM GOTTES
("CHRIST, YOU LAMB OF GOD"), BWV 619

We conclude our survey of the middle compilation phase with Bach's only
organ setting of this chorale. The chorale tune is the shortest set in the
Orgelbüchlein. In accordance with the melody, the work begins in F major

and ends in G major, constituting the most extreme example of modal shift in the *Orgelbüchlein*. As Clark and Peterson argue, the line "you who *bear* the sins of the world" may have given Bach the idea of a canonic setting, and it is significant that he also set this chorale as a canon in the last movement of Cantata 23, *Du wahrer Gott und Davids Sohn*.

"Christe, du Lamm Gottes" displays innovative stylistic features, too. Like its companion piece, "O Lamm Gottes," it is a canon at the fifth, prefaced by a free introduction. But it is also the first *Orgelbüchlein* chorale scored exclusively in five voices and the only work in the collection scored solely in rhythms no faster than one-half the value of the main pulse: the fastest rhythm is a quarter note. These two traits will resurface in the late entry "Liebster Jesu, wir sind hier." A further connection to this late chorale is Bach's prescription that the soprano and alto be played on a different manual from the two tenor parts.

Bach may have written the three-bar introduction to compensate for the brevity of the chorale melody. The introduction derives from an off-the-beat, descending hexachord (♪ ♪ ♪ ♪ ♪ |♪) that is the basis for the accompaniment throughout the work (see Example 5–23). Riemenschneider interpreted this figure as "the prostrating of the petitioner before his savior," while Keller viewed it as "the descent of Christ from his divinity into human sorrow." The motive is essentially identical to the one that opens Bach's Canonic Variations on "Vom Himmel hoch," and in both works the initial motivic statements are treated similarly: the voices enter in descending order, sequence the motive at the third below, and overlap canonically on the entrance of the second voice. The presence of a tonic pedal point in the midst of this introductory figuration recalls Bach's F-major organ toccata, in which an initial pedal point on F sounds beneath canonic writing at the octave.

Example 5–23. "Christe, du Lamm Gottes," BWV 619

Aside from the tritone between the canonic parts on the downbeat of measure 6, Bach's handling of the hexachord figure is primarily responsible for the work's freely dissonant style (see especially the first beat of m. 5, the first beat of m. 6, the third beat of m. 10, and the second beat of m. 11). Spitta's thoughts on these "peculiar and melancholy harmonies" are probably shared by many: "At first their strangeness strikes us, perhaps even repels us, but by repeated hearing they grow upon us more and more, and we end by finding them unforgettable, so profound and so truly musical is the interpretation they engraft onto the chorale."

Chapter 6

THE LATE CHORALES

$\mathscr{W}$e will now examine the six works from the late Weimar phase of the *Orgelbüchlein*'s compilation as well as the two settings from Bach's Leipzig years. The six Weimar works include one melody chorale, three chorale canons, and two pieces that defy strict classification. They are distinguished from the early and middle chorales not only by a strong inclination toward canonic writing (especially at the fifth between the upper two voices), but also by textures thicker than four parts and by the placement of the chorale tune in voices other than the soprano. These traits suggest that Bach wished to broaden the compositional style of the *Orgelbüchlein*.

CHRISTUM WIR SOLLEN LOBEN SCHON ("WE SHOULD INDEED PRAISE CHRIST"), BWV 611

This Christmas chorale is the only noncanonic setting in the *Orgelbüchlein* that presents the entire chorale tune exclusively in a voice other than the soprano. As we mentioned in Chapter 3, it is also a rare example of a Baroque organ chorale in which the entire chorale tune appears in an inner voice alone. Other innovations of the work include extremely wide spacing between voices, made possible by the very high tessitura of the soprano, chromatic embellishment of the chorale tune, and the sole instance in the *Orgelbüchlein* of double-pedal. The double-pedal ending, which underscores the shift from D minor to A minor on the downbeat of measure 14, recalls the conclusion of Bach's Passacaglia in C Minor, probably composed in Weimar as well.

The chorale text may have inspired some of these features. For example, both the placement of the chorale tune in an interior voice and the use of chromatic passing tones (mm. 5 and 8) serve to "mystify" the melody, just as one of the main messages of the text is the mystery of the Incarnation. Moreover, as Clark and Peterson note, the wide polyphonic spacing effectively depicts a phrase in stanza 1 that reads "the dear sun shines and *reaches to the ends of the whole world.*"[1] The spacing is at its widest in measure 6, where, for the only time in the *Orgelbüchlein*, Bach called for the highest and lowest notes on the Weimar court organ (C and c''') to sound simultaneously. Keller was convinced that the work is the most "ethereal" of any in the collection.[2]

On the other hand, the piece's motivic construction is quite typical of the collection, for all three accompanimental voices derive from the stepwise *suspirans* (see Example 6–1). The motive consistently appears in the bass as part of a larger, five-note figure (♪ ♫♩♪). In the tenor and soprano, it is present in various guises, the most striking of which is the opening double statement in the form of a descending scale. According to Schweitzer, this figuration "entwines the chorale melody in a consummately effective way and embraces a whole world of unutterable joy."[3] Many other *Orgelbüchlein* chorales, of course, contain manual voices based on the stepwise *suspirans*, but since the stepwise motion is generally unidiomatic on a pedalboard, the pedal either states a completely different motive or, as in *Vers* 3 of "Christ ist erstanden," a different form of the *suspirans*. But since Bach prescribed a slow tempo (*Adagio*) for the present work, he could risk assigning the stepwise form to the feet.

Example 6–1. "Christum wir sollen loben schon," BWV 611

Two passages bespeak a relatively free compositional style. First, an opening pedal point such as Bach writes here is a highly unusual occurrence in the *Orgelbüchlein*, encountered elsewhere only in "Christe, du Lamm Gottes." (We normally expect the pedal part of an *Orgelbüchlein* chorale to open with motivic or walking-bass figuration.) It throws the initial soprano b-flat''' into the boldest possible relief, at the distance of nearly four octaves. Second, in measures 11–12, the bass extricates itself from the *suspirans* for two full beats and presents the chorale tune in canon with the alto, while (in m. 11) the soprano and tenor form a canon of their own. Such a shift to chorale-canon style happens in no other *Orgelbüchlein* chorale.

IN DIR IST FREUDE
(*"IN YOU IS JOY"*), BWV 615

Bach's only setting of this New Year chorale has, in keeping with the celebratory text, all the spirit of New Year's Eve. As Keller put it, "here gladness is heightened into exuberance." "In dir ist Freude" is without a doubt the most flamboyant work in the *Orgelbüchlein*, and possibly the most virtuosic as well. It is also an extraordinarily free composition, both in its treatment of the chorale melody and its voice leading. Although the chorale melody appears more or less complete in the soprano, as would happen in a melody chorale, the individual phrases are fractured, ornamented, and unnecessarily repeated. Fragments of the chorale melody appear in various voices. Regular interludes occur between phrases, and those in measures 8 and 25 represent the only pedal solos in the *Orgelbüchlein*. The texture varies from one or two voices during the interludes to four or five voices whenever the chorale tune is stated. Riemenschneider maintained that, for its size, the work is one of the "biggest" in all of music.[4]

Not surprisingly, Bach most often embellishes the chorale tune with the *suspirans*, the same motive that dominates the accompaniment for the duration. Of the many other accompanimental motives, the only one used throughout is the pedal figure stated at the outset (♪ ♪ ♫♫♪ | ♩), characterized by Schweitzer as an "animated theme of joy" (see Example 6–2). The motive's emphasis on tonic and dominant pitches suggests the ringing of a carillon.

Measure 48 contains one of the few pedal trills (complete with turn) in the *Orgelbüchlein* as well as one of the few pedal trills notated by Bach in his

Example 6–2. "In dir ist Freude," BWV 615

organ works. The trill concludes an idea ($\flat$ 🎵🎵🎵🎵♪ ♪ | ₒ) that in measures
44–49 is treated as a fugato, and that leads to the conclusion. Bach's Fantasia
on "Komm, Heiliger Geist" from the "Great Eighteen" Chorales ends similarly.

CHRISTUS, DER UNS SELIG MACHT ("CHRIST, WHO MAKES US BLESSED"), BWV 620/620A

The text of this Passiontide chorale graphically relates the events leading up
to the Crucifixion as well as the Crucifixion itself. The intensely chromatic
and dissonant style of the *Orgelbüchlein* setting is consistent with the harsh
tone of the text. Keller ventured that the work possesses "almost an excess of
expressiveness." As in "Das alte Jahr," Bach achieves this idiom by means
of a chromatic, stepwise motive—a traditional symbol of grief (see Example
6–3). But in this case the figure accompanies a canon on the chorale tune,
at the octave between the soprano and bass. Clark and Peterson conjecture

Example 6–3. "Christus, der uns selig macht," BWV 620

that the phrase "*led* before godless people" in stanza 1 may have suggested the idea of a chorale canon. As numerous discrepancies between the *dux* and *comes* evince, the chorale melody is not an ideal candidate for canonic treatment.

In Leipzig, Bach revised the Weimar version (BWV 620a) by inserting sixteenth notes into the accompaniment or dotted rhythms into the canon in practically every measure. These revisions transform a rhythmically prosaic work into one of genuine rhythmic excitement. Just consider the rewriting of the accompanimental motive stated at the outset from ♪ ♫♫♫ |♩ to ♪♩ ♫♫♫♫ |♩ . Instead of straightforward eighth notes, the revised reading begins with a syncopated quarter note and ends with a flurry of sixteenths.

This powerful work also has organological significance, for, as Williams points out, in measures 10 and 21 occur the only instances in the *Orgelbüchlein* of a pedal C-sharp.[5] This note was normally absent from organ pedalboards, but it was available on the organ at the Weimar court. And so Bach exploited the pitch here, amidst a chorale canon.

WIR DANKEN DIR, HERR JESU CHRIST, DASS DU FÜR UNS GESTORBEN BIST ("WE THANK YOU, LORD JESUS CHRIST, THAT YOU DIED FOR US"), BWV 623

Just when it appears that Bach has abandoned the melody chorale for good, we encounter a textbook example of the *Orgelbüchlein*-type. "Wir danken dir" is also a work whose mood is positively ebullient but whose liturgical designation is the solemn season of Passiontide. The music may depict only the first three words of the chorale text, which as a whole represents less a thanksgiving than a plea for salvation.

In addition to such factors as a major key and jaunty accompanimental motives, the piece derives it buoyancy from a combination of triple meter and regular phrase structure. Save the extension of the last phrase, all four phrases are four bars long, as in dance music. Why, for the only time in the *Orgelbüchlein*, Bach chose $\frac{3}{4}$ instead of $\frac{3}{2}$ as a triple-meter time signature surely has to do with chronology, for this is apparently the very last of the triple-meter works in the collection. One also sees this chronological shift from $\frac{3}{2}$ to $\frac{3}{4}$ among Bach's organ chorales in general. For example, in his triple-meter organ chorales that clearly predate the *Orgelbüchlein* (such as the Neumeister Chorales), he used $\frac{3}{2}$ almost exclusively, while in such works that definitely or presumably postdate the *Orgelbüchlein* (such as the chorales from *Clavierübung* III and the "Great Eighteen" Chorales, respectively), $\frac{3}{4}$ is the rule. The shift probably reflects Bach's growing interest at the time in modern Italian instrumental music, most notably the concertos of Vivaldi.

The work's accompaniment is unified merely by a stepwise anapest (♩♩ ♪), which appears in the bass as the incipit of a much longer motive (♪ ♫♫ ♫) (see Example 6–4). As Clark and Peterson note, the figure can begin on the second as well as the first beat, evidence of the subtlety with which Bach treats motives in the *Orgelbüchlein*. Both the motive itself and its type of additive construction are strongly reminiscent of the bass figure in "Herr Christ, der ein'ge Gottessohn."

Owing to the large interval between its fifth and sixth notes, usually an octave, the bass motive is easily the most distinctive feature of the whole work. It is particularly prominent on the downbeat of measures 4 and 16,

Example 6–4. "Wir danken dir, Herr Jesu Christ, dass du für uns gestorben bist," BWV 623

where the concluding interval is a seventh, with the lowered seventh degree of the scale in the bass (f-natural) coinciding with a cadential tonic pitch in the soprano (g'). Thus the first and last chorale phrases end initially not with the expected root-position triads but with secondary dominant-seventh chords (V^7/IV). Rather than undermining any sense of thanksgiving, these unstable sonorities simply add to the work's effervescence.

HILF GOTT, DASS MIR'S GELINGE
("HELP ME, GOD, THAT I MAY SUCCEED"), BWV 624

In this exquisitely wrought Passiontide chorale, Bach set the chorale tune as a canon, mostly at the interval of a fifth, between the upper two voices. For the fifth and sixth phrases, though, the canon is of necessity at the fourth, the only instance of this canonic interval in the *Orgelbüchlein*. This vacillation between canonic intervals, encountered nowhere else in the *Orgelbüchlein*, is only one indication that this is by far the freest canon in the collection, for the canonic writing within individual phrases is also very free, both rhythmically and intervallically. Simply put, Bach has taken an uncanonic melody and forced it into a canonic mold, just as the first stanza of the text reads "that I may succeed . . . in *forcing* these syllables into rhyme."[6]

Against this Procrustean backdrop flows a tenor line of nonstop sixteenth-note triplets (see Example 6–5). Keller interpreted the perpetual motion as "constant endeavor." Except for the tenor line of "Vom Himmel kam," the part is the widest-ranging—over three octaves—in the entire *Orgelbüchlein*. Bach grants it special prominence by assigning it a separate manual. It frequently rises above the upper two voices in spectacular arabesques, serving to overshadow the canon (and making the canon seem almost incidental). As Spitta remarked, "only an outline of the chorale melody falls upon our consciousness—a silhouette, like the shadow thrown behind a solid body."[7]

Meanwhile, to quote Schweitzer, "the bass staggers wearily along," primarily in stepwise eighth notes or syncopated octave leaps (♪ ♩). In measures 11 and 12, the bass presents pairs of sixteenths against sixteenth-note triplets in the tenor, as does the alto in measures 13 and 16. The performer may either assimilate these duplets to triplets according to the rhythm ♪ ♪ or play three-against-two. There is no harmonic, contrapuntal, or notational reason for choosing one approach over the other.

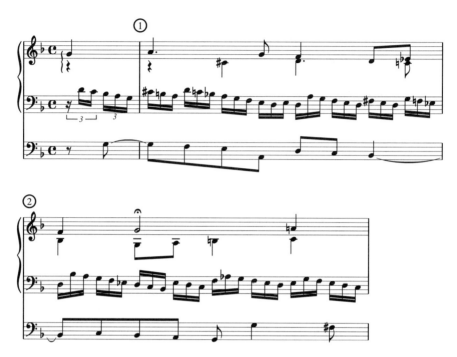

Example 6–5. "Hilf Gott, dass mir's gelinge," BWV 624

The harmonic style of "Hilf Gott" is remarkably intricate and highly chromatic. But certain harmonies are so dissonant that one wonders whether Bach was not testing the rules of counterpoint as understood at the time. On the second beat of measure 13, for example, G-minor and D-major sonorities are pitted against one another. Two beats later, the pitches c-sharp' and c" sound simultaneously.

LIEBSTER JESU, WIR SIND HIER ("DEAREST JESUS, WE ARE HERE"), BWV 633/634

Although they carry separate BWV numbers, the *Orgelbüchlein* settings of this Pentecost hymn are two versions of the same work. In preparing the *Orgelbüchlein* autograph, Bach had reserved two settings for this chorale, on two consecutive pages. He first entered a composing score of the original version BWV 634, then, on the next page, a fair copy of the revised version BWV 633.[8]

As in "Hilf Gott," Bach set the chorale tune as a canon at the fifth between the upper two voices, and assigned the canonic parts their own manual (see Example 6–6). But the canon here (at least in BWV 633) is entirely strict, since the melody is ideally suited to canonic writing at this interval. Another factor that may have suggested canonic elaboration, as Keller observed, is the phrase "so that our hearts become completely *drawn* from earth to you" in stanza 1 of the chorale text. Accompanying the canon throughout is figuration based on an augmented form of the stepwise *suspirans* (). There are four more statements of the motive in the revised version than in the original, which enriches not only the work's motivic construction but its harmonic scheme as well.

Except for "Christe, du Lamm Gottes," this is the only *Orgelbüchlein* chorale consistently scored in five voices and featuring continuous motion in the rhythm one-half rather than one-quarter the value of the main pulse. The thick texture allows for unusually piquant harmonies, while the slow rhythm projects an atmosphere of utter tranquility—and possibly receptiveness to the Holy Spirit as well. Notice, for example, the constant minor-seventh and dominant-seventh chords, which impart to the music an overall sweetness possibly symbolic of the "sweet teachings of heaven" cited in stanza 1. Highly dissonant chords occur as well—especially, in BWV 633, on the second eighth note of measure 6—but exclusively off the beat.

Perhaps the most saccharine element in "Liebster Jesu" is the chorale tune itself, one of the sweetest sounding in all of Lutheran hymnody. It begins on the "sweet" third degree of the major scale—a unique circumstance among the chorale tunes set in the *Orgelbüchlein* and a highly unusual beginning for any chorale melody—and employs this pitch as the climax of the second and fourth phrases. No doubt Riemenschneider had this quality in mind when he described the pair as "beautiful settings of a beautiful chorale."

Example 6–6. "Liebster Jesu, wir sind hier," BWV 633

The melody also tends to repeat itself. Its phrase structure is ABABCB, and its B and C phrases begin with four repeated notes. This, however, did not deter Bach from unnecessarily repeating the *Abgesang* (as Walther also did in his partita on this chorale), or from using the same material whenever a phrase is restated, or from employing identical pedal lines for the A and C phrases. In various respects, then, "Liebster Jesu" is an extraordinarily repetitive—and extraordinarily beautiful—piece.

HELFT MIR GOTTS GÜTE PREISEN
("*HELP ME TO PRAISE GOD'S GOODNESS*"), *BWV 613*

This New Year chorale is the only complete and entirely new setting from the Leipzig layer of the autograph. As an example of the *Orgelbüchlein*-type, the piece signals a return, after many years, to the collection's most common chorale type. Despite its late date, "Helft mir" does not exhibit any compositional techniques not already seen in the Weimar settings.

As in "Wenn wir in höchsten Nöten sein," the primary accompanimental motive comes from the first four notes of the chorale melody. According to Keller, "the counterpoint . . . thus 'helps,' unceasingly, 'to praise God's goodness.'" The motive in both chorales also begins off the beat, with four eighth notes in the order tonic-tonic-supertonic-mediant. In "Helft mir," Bach follows these notes with a descending sixteenth-note scale, resulting in an unusually long motive by *Orgelbüchlein* standards (see Example 6–7). Williams maintains that, as in "Ach wie nichtig," the appearance of the scale throughout reflects "the passing of time." For the first ten bars, the two halves of the motive are stated in stretto. Within the *Orgelbüchlein*, only *Vers* 2 of "Christ ist erstanden" places a greater emphasis on this technique.

Example 6–7. "Helft mir Gotts Güte preisen," BWV 613

In measures 11 and 13, Bach saw fit to pedal the scale—the only occurrences in the *Orgelbüchlein* of a pedal scale in rhythms faster than eighth notes. His avoidance of the scale in the pedal for the first ten bars is understandable, since, as Williams implies, a fast scalar figure like this is extremely unidiomatic on a pedalboard. There had been numerous opportunities for pedal statements earlier—following the many pedal statements of the head motive—but in every instance four eighth notes were used instead. Bach's "St. Anne" prelude (also composed in Leipzig) also contains a descending scale motive with a syncopated beginning (the theme is initially stated in m. 71). But when the theme finally appears in the pedals (mm. 135–44), it is drastically rewritten to accommodate the feet.

Both pedal scales in "Helft mir" are paired with a rising chromatic figure in the alto, which is introduced by the pedal much earlier (m. 5). As Williams observes, Bach states the chromatic idea in measure 11 at the same time that stanza 1 of the text refers to the passing of the old year.

O Traurigkeit, o Herzeleid
("*O sadness, o heartache*"), *BWV Anh. 200*

This fragment of one-and-one-half bars also stems from Bach's Leipzig years. The autograph entry, obviously a composing score, shows that the soprano chorale tune originally contained no embellishment, merely three half notes in the order c" - a-flat' - f'. Bach subsequently filled in these pitches with eighth-note passing tones and various ornaments, reaching a level of embellishment suggestive of an ornamental chorale (see Example 6–8). Perhaps the triadic contour of the first three chorale pitches led to the predominantly triadic figuration in the accompaniment. The *Molt'adagio* tempo inscription seems eminently appropriate for a Passiontide chorale and

Example 6–8. "O Traurigkeit, o Herzeleid," BWV Anh. 200

is analogous to the slow tempo markings in two other Passiontide chorales from the *Orgelbüchlein*, "O Mensch" and "O Lamm Gottes."

Despite the hint of ornamentation in "O Traurigkeit," one assumes that if Bach had completed the piece, he would have created yet another example of a melody chorale, the most common chorale type in the *Orgelbüchlein*. And as we have just seen, the latest entries in the collection do indeed include two complete specimens of the melody chorale ("Wir danken dir" and "Helft mir"). Still, most of the late settings show the composer looking beyond the narrow confines of this chorale type and toward freer, more complex musical styles. This trend first emerges in the late stage of the middle compilation phase, where, for example, the melody chorale "Herr Gott, nun schleuss den Himmel auf" contains interludes between the phrases of the hymn tune and an introduction, to boot. Of the thirty-four works that had been composed prior to this juncture, no fewer than twenty-eight were cast in the melody-chorale mold. The last twelve works, on the other hand, show remarkable variety. This variety is present in virtually all aspects of the music, from texture and form to counterpoint and rhythm.

One must conclude, then, that monotony was one of the main reasons why Bach never finished the *Orgelbüchlein*. As he laid out the autograph, he probably envisioned that the vast majority of the projected 164 chorales would be melody chorales. During the first two compilation phases of the collection, while his interest was still high, he worked diligently toward this end, writing almost thirty melody chorales and achieving within these pieces an admirable level of individualization. Having exhausted the compositional possibilities of the melody chorale, Bach turned increasingly to other chorale types (such as the chorale canon) as well as to novel compositional techniques. Yet he entered relatively few works in the new style, perhaps because constraints of space limited his ability to realize more ambitious designs. By the time Bach left Weimar, the *Orgelbüchlein* project had lost its appeal.

Chapter 7

RECEPTION

THE EIGHTEENTH CENTURY

The reception of the *Orgelbüchlein* begins with Bach himself, because he was the chief catalyst in the collection's early transmission. He accomplished this role by instructing his private keyboard pupils to copy the chorales and by allowing colleagues to make copies as well.

As is well known, Bach taught his own works to his keyboard pupils, and the pupils prepared manuscript copies of these works during the period of instruction; these pupils, in turn, taught these same works to *their* pupils, who subsequently taught the works to *their* pupils, and so forth. It was primarily by means of this "pupils-of-pupils" legacy that Bach's keyboard music was disseminated in the eighteenth century, and the *Orgelbüchlein* was no exception. For instance, Bach's pupil Johann Christian Kittel prepared a copy of the *Orgelbüchlein* presumably while studying under Bach, and there are extant copies by three of Kittel's pupils: Johann Andreas Dröbs, Johann Wilhelm Hässler, and Johann Nikolaus Gebhardi. This particular line of transmission, centered around Erfurt, ends in 1846 with one of the first complete publications of the *Orgelbüchlein*, edited by Gebhardi's pupil Gotthilf Wilhelm Körner (see Table 7–1 on pages 154–55).[1]

One can only speculate about the extent to which Bach taught the *Orgelbüchlein*. The paucity of surviving copies by Bach's students suggests that he did not teach it as regularly as such collections as the Inventions and Sinfonias or *The Well-Tempered Clavier*.[2] Also in contrast to these two collec-

145

tions as well as the French Suites, the student copies of the *Orgelbüchlein* do not, as discussed in Chapter 2, preserve readings that improve on those in the autograph. If Bach regularly used the *Orgelbüchlein* as pedagogical repertory, why did he break from his practice of revising the music as he taught it?

The appearance of the autograph carries similar implications. As opposed to the calligraphic, fair-copy autographs of these other three collections, the *Orgelbüchlein* autograph is for the most part a composing score and contains many passages that are largely illegible due to compositional revisions. Moreover, a number of passages are in organ tablature, a notational system that by the turn of the eighteenth century was considered impractical and out-moded, and one that must have been rather unfamiliar to Bach's young charges. If Bach regularly taught the *Orgelbüchlein,* why did he not make a perfectly clean and legible master copy, notated entirely in score, from which his students could easily prepare their copies?

These nagging questions notwithstanding, it does appear that Bach taught the *Orgelbüchlein* over many years' time, if only on an intermittent basis, for the three extant student copies of the collection, all presumably made during the period of instruction with Bach, are by students from various periods of Bach's life: J. T. Krebs, who studied under Bach in Weimar from 1714 to 1717; Christian Gottlob Meissner, who was a Bach pupil in Leipzig between 1723 and 1729; and Johann Gottfried Müthel, who studied with Bach just a few months before the master's death in 1750. (The afore-mentioned copy of the *Orgelbüchlein* by Bach's pupil Kittel, which is lost, also presumably dates from very late in Bach's life, as Kittel studied with Bach between 1748 and 1750.)

There is also the obvious possibility that many of the student copies are lost, a notion supported by evidence of various kinds. To begin with, several of Bach's pupils composed organ chorales that contain elements of *Orgel-büchlein* style, suggesting that these pupils studied the collection with him, regardless of whether any copies of the *Orgelbüchlein* by these pupils have survived. For example, Johann Ludwig Krebs's setting of "Ich ruf zu dir, Herr Jesu Christ"[3] satisfies all the criteria for the *Orgelbüchlein*-type, and his rendering of "Es ist gewisslich an der Zeit"[4] would satisfy the same cri-teria were it not for its unmotivic pedal (see Examples 7–1 and 7–2). The inner voices of the latter work, moreover, are based on the stepwise form of the *suspirans,* and the constancy of statement results in continuous six-teenth-note motion except at phrase endings. Johann Caspar Vogler's setting of "Jesu Leiden, Pein und Not"[5] takes as its model a specific *Orgelbüchlein*

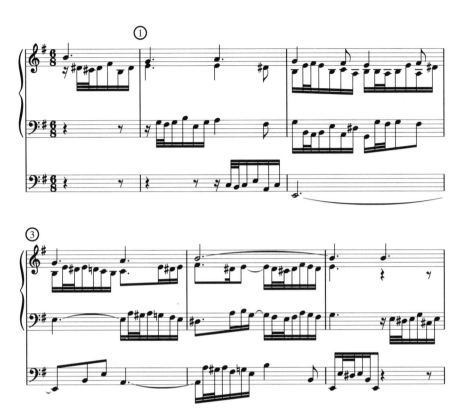

Example 7–1. Johann Ludwig Krebs, "Ich ruf zu dir, Herr Jesu Christ"

chorale, the ornamental setting "O Mensch, bewein dein Sünde gross" (see Example 7–3). Vogler imitates his teacher here in virtually every respect, even concluding with an ultra-chromatic passage marked *adagissime*. Again, it is significant that Bach taught these students at different periods of his life: Krebs was one of Bach's Leipzig pupils in the late 1720s and early 1730s; Vogler studied under Bach in Weimar between 1710 and 1715 (and also in Arnstadt around 1706).

Although the evidence is far more circumstantial, another pupil who may have studied the *Orgelbüchlein* with Bach is Johann Gotthilf Ziegler. Ziegler was one of Bach's organ pupils in Weimar, probably between 1710 and 1712,[6] during which time, presumbly, Bach was compiling the *Orgelbüchlein*. Many years later Ziegler recalled that "As concerns the playing of chorales, I was instructed by my teacher, Capellmeister Bach . . . not to play the songs merely offhand but according to the sense (*Affect*) of the words."[7]

Example 7–2. Johann Ludwig Krebs, "Es ist gewisslich an der Zeit"

Considering the dates of Ziegler's instruction and the strong element of textual allusion in the *Orgelbüchlein*, it is conceivable that Ziegler studied certain *Orgelbüchlein* chorales with Bach and that he is obliquely referring to them here.

As for Bach's colleagues who contributed to the *Orgelbüchlein*'s early transmission, none seems to have copied more of the chorales than Johann Gottfried Walther in Weimar. Certain works were also disseminated within the circles of the Gräfenroda organist Johann Peter Kellner (1705–72) and the Weimar-area organists Johann Nicolaus Mempell (1713–47) and Johann Gottlieb Preller (1717–85). Kellner was a friend of Bach's and possibly a pupil as well. There is no proof that Mempell or Preller was personally acquainted with Bach, but they obviously had close ties to the Bach circle; Mempell may have been a pupil of Kellner, and Preller may have been a pupil of J. T. Krebs. Thanks to this network of pupils, colleagues, friends, and devotees, the *Orgelbüchlein* was circulated throughout central Germany even during Bach's lifetime.

Example 7–3. Johann Caspar Vogler, "Jesu Leiden, Pein und Not"

With Bach's death, the *Orgelbüchlein* became known in other parts of Germany as well, due to the inheritance of the autograph by Bach's son C. P. E. Bach, who at the time worked in Berlin as court harpsichordist to Frederick the Great. Since Frederick discouraged religious music of any kind, Emanuel Bach could not have had much professional use for the manuscript, and perhaps we should not dissaprove of his attempt to sell it.[8] Still, he appears to have played a significant role in the *Orgelbüchlein*'s dissemination. It was most likely Emanuel, for example, who introduced the *Orgelbüchlein* to the Berlin theorist Friedrich Wilhelm Marpurg, whose treatise *Abhandlung von der Fuge* (1753) contains the incipits of four *Orgelbüchlein* chorales: "Liebster Jesu, wir sind hier" (BWV 633), "Herr Christ, der ein'ge Gottessohn," "Jesus Christus, unser Heiland," and "Wir danken dir, Herr Jesu Christ." These excerpts, chosen to illustrate various contrapuntal procedures, represent the beginnings of the *Orgelbüchlein*'s publication history.[9] Similarly, one suspects that the copies of the *Orgelbüchlein* from the Berlin circle of Johann Philipp Kirnberger are the result of Emanuel's having placed the autograph at Kirnberger's disposal. By the same token, though, Kirnberger had been one of Sebastian Bach's keyboard pupils, and during the period of instruction he might have prepared his own copy of the *Orgelbüchlein*, which could have served as the exemplar for the copies by his Berlin scribes. Once Emanuel Bach left Berlin in 1768 to become Kantor in Hamburg, his Hamburg scribes copied the *Orgelbüchlein* from the autograph, which stayed in Emanuel's possession until his death in 1788.

Two manuscripts from Emanuel Bach's Hamburg circle contain an arrangement for organ solo, presumably by Emanuel himself, of the *Orgelbüchlein* setting of "Ich ruf zu dir," listed in the Schmieder catalogue as BWV Anh. 73. For a complete score of this arrangement, heretofore available only in facsimile,[10] see Appendix 1. In one manuscript, Emanuel is given as the composer (the other contains the attribution "Bach"). The *empfindsam* style of the added material and the overall skillfulness of the adaptation are consistent with Emanuel's style.

Like other eighteenth-century adaptations of Bach's organ chorales,[11] the arranger of "Ich ruf zu dir" has expanded his model (by more than ten bars) through the addition of an introduction, interludes between phrases, and a codetta. Since the longest of these added passages (the introduction, the interlude at mm. 9–10, and the codetta) are thematically identical, and since two of them occur at the beginning and end, the arrangement can be analyzed in terms of ritornello form. The "ritornello" is stated in its entirety only

at the beginning. As is clear from the repeated bass notes as well as the contour of the top voice, the ritornello is heavily indebted to the accompanimental figuration of the model. The four interludes independent of the
ritornello (mm. 5–6, 12–13, 15–16, 18–19) are in a sense not interludes at
all, because they coincide not with rests in the chorale-tune voice but with
cadential notes that the arranger has lengthened from one to five beats. All
the interludes maintain the continuous sixteenth-note motion present in the
left-hand part of the model, though never in one voice alone. There are no
interludes between any of the last four phrases (beginning at m. 19), presumably for two reasons: the sixth, seventh, and eighth phrases of the model
already end with elongated cadential notes (either a half note or a dotted half
note, as opposed to a quarter note); and the seventh and eighth phrases of
the model are quite short, perhaps too short for interludes.

In addition to the obvious musical expertise of the arranger—who can be
criticized only for the overly repetitive interlude at measures 5–6—the
arrangement is successful because it heightens rather than debases the
model's affect, which, in agreement with the chorale text, is a longing for
divine grace. Through the addition of chromatic harmonies (especially in the
second measure of the ritornello), "sigh" figures (mm. 8, 15, 18–19), and a
slow tempo marking, this sense of yearning is considerably enhanced.

Still, certain passages are bound to raise eyebrows, and none more so
than measure 8, beat 2, where the arranger has added a flat to the pedal g,
creating an unexpected Neapolitan-sixth harmony. In both sources this passage is notated twice (it returns, in the written-out repeat of the *Stollen*, in m.
15) with the flat, so there can be no question as to the intended pitch. The
arranger may well have been influenced by the g-flats in the left-hand part
of the model in the preceding measure.

This alteration, in turn, most likely prompted a change on the same beat
to the chorale-tune voice, wherein an ornamental figure in the model
(⌢♩♩♩♩) is simplified to an appoggiatura sigh (⌢ ♩♩♩♩). Two beats
later, on beat 4, there occurs at the beginning of an added interlude the most
extreme example of handcrossing in the arrangement (the interlude at mm.
18–19 also involves handcrossings). In this respect the arranger adds an element of performing technique to his model, as the model requires no hand-
crossings whatever.

The only disappointing feature of the arrangement, really, is the lack of
added ornamentation to the chorale melody. Although cadential ornaments
have been added in four places (mm. 5, 12, 18, and 27), they do little to

redress the imbalance in the model between the profusion of ornamentation in the *Stollen* and the general lack thereof in the *Abgesang*. Furthermore, the repeat of the *Stollen*, which is fully written out rather than indicated by repeat marks, is identical to the initial statement. If Emanuel Bach, the greatest proponent of varied reprise in the eighteenth century, is the arranger, why did he not make use of the technique here?

A more fundamental question is the aesthetic intent behind the added material. When Emanuel Bach offered the autograph of the *Orgelbüchlein* for sale, he remarked that "most of [the chorales] are only short settings,"[12] a caveat that could be taken as a criticism of the concise design of the melody chorale. In addition to finding the model too compact, the arranger may have felt the constant presentation of the chorale melody in the model to be somewhat severe. The added material, of course, rectifies both "defects," resulting in a form at once more expansive and more flexible. Hence, the arrangement may be interpreted as an act of criticism.

A further manuscript from Emanuel Bach's Hamburg circle (SBB: *P 778*) preserves an arrangement of the *Orgelbüchlein* chorale "Christe, du Lamm Gottes." The model is unchanged except for the redistribution of the five voices on four staves, as opposed to only two staves in the autograph. The upper of the two canonic voices is assigned the top staff; the two accompanimental voices, which in the model are manual parts, occupy the second highest staff; the staff below is given to the lower canonic voice, notated in tenor clef; and the bottom staff, marked *Ped.*, contains the pedal part of the model and is obviously to be played on the organ pedals. Like Emanuel's own setting of "Jesu, meines Lebens Leben," H. 639,[13] this arrangement is probably for organ and oboe (which would take the top part).

Two additional late eighteenth-century arrangements of *Orgelbüchlein* chorales deserve to be mentioned as well, even if they have less musical integrity than the two adaptations from Emanuel Bach's circle. They are solo-organ arrangements of "In dir ist Freude" and "O Mensch." Their only source, in the hand of an anonymous scribe, stems from the circle of the Nuremberg organist Leonard Scholz (1720–98).[14] The provenance of the manuscript verifies the *Orgelbüchlein*'s early dissemination in South Germany. The two arrangements do not enhance their models; on the contrary, the arranger tends to excise or alter material in order to make it easier to play. The result in both instances is a crude simplification lacking crucial elements of the original version. Scholz copied out many of Bach's organ works in abridged or simplified versions, presumably to compensate for his weak performing technique.[15] He is probably also the arranger here.

The Nineteenth Century

By the turn of the nineteenth century, the *Orgelbüchlein* had spread throughout Germany, though almost exclusively in manuscript form. Aside from the
excerpts printed by Marpurg, only one of the chorales—the early version of
"Heut triumphieret Gottes Sohn" (BWV 630a)—was published in the eighteenth century, in an anthology of organ chorales published around 1784 by
Breitkopf. But as Bach's music became increasingly popular in the early
nineteenth century, publications of his works began to proliferate, and by
1845 no fewer than sixteen *Orgelbüchlein* chorales had appeared in print, as
either organ compositions or piano transcriptions. This trend culminated in
1845–46 with the appearance of the first complete editions of the collection.
These editions, of course, guaranteed a much speedier and wider dissemination of the music than had previously been possible, and they effectively
ended the manuscript transmission of the *Orgelbüchlein* that had flourished
for well over a century.

   Most of these early publications (see Table 7–1) presented the music without editorial markings, even though they do display such modern amenities as
a separate pedal staff and the notation of the top staff in treble rather than
soprano clef. Indeed, some of the editors proudly proclaim that the music is
reproduced "from the original manuscripts," essentially as Bach himself wrote
it down. While this *Urtext* style of editing is laudable in scholarly terms, a
reception historian might wish instead for a text laden with editorial additions
(fingerings, tempo and dynamic markings, and the like), since such a text
would be enlightening about early nineteenth-century performance practice of
the *Orgelbüchlein*. Furthermore, when these early publications contain editorial commentary it tends to involve only historical and text-critical matters; a
reception historian might prefer a commentary of a more aesthetic nature.

   In view of this, the edition of the Easter chorale "Erschienen ist der herrliche Tag," BWV 629, in August Gottfried Ritter's 1844 organ method *Die
Kunst des Orgelspiels*, is doubly noteworthy (see Example 7–4). Ritter seems
to have included the work in his treatise primarily to illustrate how a chorale
tune can be set canonically (its title reads *Cantus firmus in Canone*). But he
must also have found particularly apropos for pedagogical purposes the difficult and unusual left-hand part, which, as discussed in Chapter 5, consists
largely of fast parallel sixths. Ritter provides detailed fingerings for the left
hand, and occasionally even finger substitutions. Of greater historical interest are the letters "l" and "r" in the pedal line (abbreviations for *link* and
recht, or "left" and "right"), which indicate which foot should play a partic-

ular note. According to these letters, Ritter's pedalling often requires foot crossings, even at the bottom end of the pedalboard (m. 12), and therefore seems designed for the toes of alternate feet, evidently the basic pedal technique in organ playing prior to the nineteenth century. Two registration possibilities are given: full organ, with the hands on separate manuals (as prescribed in Bach's autograph); or full organ on one manual. Ritter also furnishes a brief and quintessentially Romantic commentary: "The whole piece expresses lively, vigorously confident emotion: the upper and lower voices recount the joyous event of the Lord's Resurrection. Therefore all the stops of the various keyboards should be engaged."[16] Most players today register the work accordingly.

TABLE 7–1.
The Publication History of the Orgelbüchlein *to 1846*

TITLE OF PUBLICATION	EDITOR (OR AUTHOR OF TREATISE)	DATE AND PLACE OF PUBLICATION	TITLE AND BWV NO. OF *ORGELBÜCHLEIN* CHORALE(S) PUBLISHED
Abhandlung von der Fuge, Part 1	F. W. Marpurg	1753, Berlin	Incipits of "Liebster Jesu, wir sind hier," BWV 633; "Herr Christ, der ein'ge Gottessohn," BWV 601; "Jesus Christus, unser Heiland," BWV 626; "Wir danken dir, Herr Jesu Christ," BWV 623
Sammlung von Praeludien, Fugen, ausgefuehrten Choraelen etc. fuer die Orgel, von beruehmten aelteren Meistern, Vol. 1	Marian Stecher	ca. 1784, Leipzig	"Heut triumphieret Gottes Sohn," BWV 630a
Johann Sebastian Bach's Choralvorspiele für die Orgel mit einem oder zwei Clavieren und Pedal	J. G. Schicht	1803–6, Leipzig	"Liebster Jesu, wir sind hier," BWV 633 and 634; "Das alte Jahr vergangen ist," BWV 614
Var. Choraele fürs Pf. zu 4 Haenden eingerichtet	J. N. Schelble (d. 1837)	n. d., Frankfurt/ Main	"Christus, der uns selig macht" 620a; "Das alte Jahr vergangen ist," BWV 614; "O Mensch, bewein dein Sünde gross," BWV 622
Orgel-Archiv	C. F. Becker and A. G. Ritter	1835–36, Leipzig	"Vom Himmel hoch, da komm ich her," BWV 606; "Christ lag in Todesbanden," BWV 625

Sammlung der besten Meisterwerke des 17. und 18. Jahrhunderts für die Orgel	Franz Commer	1839, Berlin	"Wenn wir in höchsten Nöten sein," BWV 641
Neue Zeitschrift für Musik, Vols. 8, 10, 16	Robert Schumann	1839–41, Leipzig	"Ich ruf zu dir, Herr Jesu Christ," BWV 639; "Das alte Jahr vergangen ist," BWV 614; "Durch Adams Fall ist ganz verderbt," BWV 637; "O Mensch, bewein dein Sünde gross," BWV 622
Der Orgelfreund	G. W. Körner and A. G. Ritter	1841–47, Leipzig	"Vom Himmel hoch, da komm ich her," BWV 606
Caecilia, eine Zeitschrift für die musikalische Welt, Vol. 22	S. W. Dehn	1843, Mainz	"Es ist das Heil uns kommen her," BWV 638; "Vom Himmel hoch, da komm ich her," BWV 606; "Lobt Gott, ihr Christen, allzugleich," BWV 609; "O Lamm Gottes, unschuldig," BWV 618; "Helft mir Gotts Güte preisen," BWV 613; "Durch Adams Fall ist ganz verderbt," BWV 637
Auswahl aus Sebastian Bach's Kompositionen, zur ersten Bekanntschaft mit dem Meister am Pianoforte, veranstaltet von Adolph Bernhard Marx	A. B. Marx	1844, Berlin	"Das alte Jahr vergangen ist," BWV 614; "Christe, du Lamm Gottes," BWV 619
Die Kunst des Orgelspiels	A. G. Ritter	1844, Erfurt	"Erschienen ist der herrliche Tag," BWV 629
Der Orgelvirtuos	G. W. Körner	1845–46, Erfurt	"Nun komm, der Heiden Heiland," BWV 599
John Sebastian Bach's Organ Compositions on Corales [sic] (Psalm Tunes,) Edited from the Original Manuscripts	Felix Mendelssohn	1845, London	complete collection
44 kleine Choralvorspiele für die Orgel von Johann Sebastian Bach	Felix Mendelssohn	1845, Leipzig	complete collection
Johann Sebastian Bach's Kompositionen für die Orgel, Vol. 5	F. C. Griepenkerl and Ferdinand Roitzsch	1846, Leipzig	complete collection
Der anfahende Organist. Orgelbüchlein.	G. W. Körner	1846, Erfurt	complete collection

Of the early devotees of the *Orgelbüchlein,* none was more influential than Felix Mendelssohn, the greatest champion of Bach's music in the early nineteenth century. Mendelssohn promoted the *Orgelbüchlein* both as a performer and an editor, and in 1845 he published the first complete edition of the collection. His encounter with the work began in the summer of 1832.

Example 7–4. "Erschienen ist der herrliche Tag," BWV 629, as edited by August Gottfried Ritter

On September 4 of that year he sent a letter from Berlin to his Parisian friend Marie Kiéné, including a music excerpt (Figure 7–1), about which he wrote:

> As I am still unable today to send you, by way of atonement, something I am working on myself, old Bach will have to be my shield and refuge; and so, on the next page, I'm writing down a little piece that I got to know here by accident fourteen days ago . . . The upper voice is an ornamented chorale and should be played on the organ with somewhat strong registers; on the piano it must be played in octaves; or it would be best, I believe, if Mr. Baillot would "sing" the upper voice on his violin, in which case the piano would properly proceed beneath.[17]

The "little piece" is none other than the *Orgelbüchlein* setting of "Ich ruf zu dir," written by Mendelssohn in modern three-staff organ notation, with readings virtually identical to those in Bach's autograph.

The quoted passage is intriguing in a number of respects. First of all, assuming that Mendelssohn had just gotten acquainted not merely with this setting but with the entire *Orgelbüchlein*, his citation of "Ich ruf zu dir" suggests that the piece was one of his favorites in the collection, or at least one that he felt would have particularly pleased Madame Kiéné. Mendelssohn's categorical description of the upper voice as an "ornamented" chorale is also noteworthy, since only the first five bars contain any embellishment. Does this mean perhaps that in performance Mendelssohn added his own ornamentation from measure 6 on?

Clearly, though, the most fascinating aspects of the passage have to do with instrumentation. Not only does Mendelssohn suggest three different instrumentations, but he refers or alludes to such diverse matters of performance practice as organ registration, piano technique, and a *cantabile* style of string playing. His casual attitude toward instrumentation may strike us as cavalier, but it is typical of an era when transcription was a far more common practice than it is today and when musicians were eager to play and hear Bach's music for the first time, using whatever instrumentation was convenient.

Mendelssohn's remarks also need to be understood within the context of Parisian musical life in the early 1830s, at which time salons instead of concert halls were the typical venue for performances. He had first-hand knowledge of these gatherings, having spent the winter of 1831–32 in the French capital and having performed regularly at the homes of both the letter's addressee and the violinist mentioned in the quoted passage, Pierre Baillot. (Madame Kiéné's daughter had given Mendelssohn a few music lessons when he was a boy; Baillot and Mendelssohn had been chamber-music part-

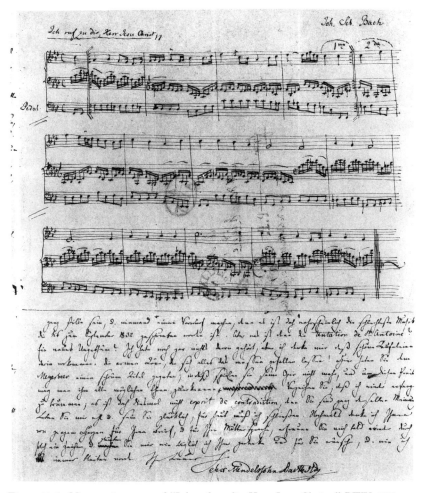

Figure 7–1. Manuscript copy of "Ich ruf zu dir, Herr Jesu Christ," BWV 639,
in the hand of Felix Mendelssohn, contained in a letter from Mendelssohn to
Marie Kiéné, dated September 4, 1832 (Universitätsbibliothek Basel, Autogr.-
Slg. Geigy-Hagenbach Nr. 1727)

ners, and together they had played everything from Mozart concertos to Bach
sonatas.) Thus Mendelssohn's choice of violin and piano as the "best"
instrumentation for "Ich ruf zu dir" is probably not an indication of his own
absolute preference but rather what he felt would be the most appropriate
instrumentation in a salon of one of his Parisian friends.

With regard to solo organ, Mendelssohn's recommendation of "strong"
registers for the right-hand part is noteworthy in light of the long-standing
tradition today of playing the part on a soft solo stop, usually a reed. His

rationale for a relatively big sound is far from obvious—assuming that his objective was more than just the audibility of the chorale tune—especially when the thin texture and subjective text imply intimacy and introspection.

As a pianist, Mendelssohn realized that an idiomatic alteration in a piano transcription was to play the right-hand part in octaves, obviously minus the trills and duplicated at the upper octave. In addition to rendering the work more pianistic in technique and sonority, the octave duplication approximates Mendelssohn's suggested organ registration, which presumably would have included at least one four-foot stop. Octave doublings of either the top or bottom voice, incidentally, are commonly found in nineteenth- and twentieth-century piano transcriptions of *Orgelbüchlein* chorales, including those of "Ich ruf zu dir" (see Appendix 2). One of these transcribers (Stuart Duncan) states in his preface that the doublings are meant to simulate four-foot or sixteen-foot organ stops.

Finally, as a chamber musician, Mendelssohn realized the effectiveness of a violin melody with piano accompaniment. His metaphorical use of the verb "sing" vis-à-vis string playing may point to nothing more specific than a lyrical style of playing, but it also implies the liberal use of vibrato, in imitation of vocal practice (might the metaphor also have been inspired by the word "call" in the opening line of the text?). Another possibility, of course, is that Pierre Baillot's violin playing was known particularly for its "singing" style and that Mendelssohn is making a somewhat frivolous reference to this quality.

We can only assume that Mendelssohn continued to promote the *Orgelbüchlein* throughout the 1830s. His interest in the collection was apparently rekindled at the end of the decade, in 1839, upon his acquisition of what he believed to be Bach's autograph, but what was in fact the copy by Bach's pupil Christian Gottlob Meissner. Mendelssohn would eventually base his edition of the *Orgelbüchlein* on this source. It was one of two manuscripts of Bach's organ music given to Mendelssohn that year by the Frankfurt Capellmeister Carl Wilhelm Ferdinand Guhr; the other was the putative double-autograph of the Passacaglia in C Minor and the *Fugue on a Theme by Legrenzi*. On June 18, 1839, Mendelssohn wrote from Frankfurt to his sister Fanny about his newly obtained Bach manuscripts:

> I take much greater pleasure in the organ preludes, because they begin with the "old year," because other big favorites [of mine] are among them, and because the passacaglia and the fugue are already printed.[18]

Mendelssohn here expresses his enthusiasm for the *Orgelbüchlein* in general and for "Das alte Jahr vergangen ist" in particular. Lest there be any doubt that "old year" refers to this chorale, it should be pointed out that Meissner's copy does indeed begin with this setting. (The manuscript was a torso when Mendelssohn received it, and he mutilated it further by removing two leaves for his wife and a third for Clara Schumann.) What is unclear is whether Mendelssohn is revealing his preference for the chorale per se (i.e., the chorale tune and chorale text) or the *Orgelbüchlein* setting of it. Judging from the familiarity of the reference, this hymn was a family favorite. Fanny's fondness for it is attested to by the beautiful harmonization that concludes her piano cycle *Das Jahr*, completed in 1841. All three chorales set by Fanny in this work ("Christ ist erstanden," "Vom Himmel hoch," and "Das alte Jahr") were set by Bach in the *Orgelbüchlein*.

Whatever the relationship between the *Orgelbüchlein* and Fanny's piano cycle, it cannot be coincidental that in December 1839, the same year in which Mendelssohn came into possession of Meissner's copy, Mendelssohn's close friend Robert Schumann published in his journal *Neue Zeitschrift für Musik* the same two *Orgelbüchlein* chorales admired by Mendelssohn: "Ich ruf zu dir" and "Das alte Jahr."[19] One can only conclude that Mendelssohn introduced Schumann to the *Orgelbüchlein* and recommended specific pieces for publication. (We know for a fact, of course, that Mendelssohn introduced Schumann to other Bach organ works, most notably the setting of "Schmücke dich, o liebe Seele" from the "Great Eighteen" Chorales.) The following June, Schumann published the *Orgelbüchlein* setting of "Durch Adams Fall," and there is evidence that this setting or at least this chorale was a favorite of Mendelssohn's, too: Charles Gounod reported that during a visit to Leipzig in 1842, Mendelssohn improvised for him at the Thomaskirche organ for two full hours on the chorale "Durch Adams Fall."[20] It is easy to believe that Mendelssohn got acquainted with the chorale tune through the *Orgelbüchlein* setting and that the setting—one of the richest in the collection—provided material for his improvisation. Only in the case of the last *Orgelbüchlein* chorale published by Schumann, "O Mensch, bewein dein Sünde gross," which appeared in the *Neue Zeitschrift* in December 1841, is there no evidence that the work was one of Mendelssohn's favorite *Orgelbüchlein* settings (but what organist does not count "O Mensch" a favorite work?).

Mendelssohn's edition of the *Orgelbüchlein* appeared first in London and then in Leipzig, two years before his death. One would like to state otherwise, but this landmark publication in the history of the *Orgelbüchlein*'s reception—the first complete edition of the collection—is of little scholarly or practical value. Although it follows the liturgical year, its ordering is far from authentic, and it contains a multitude of erroneous readings. No organist today would dare play from it.

By contrast, the Peters edition of the *Orgelbüchlein* by Conrad Friedrich Griepenkerl and Ferdinand Roitzsch that appeared in the following year is still in use. Its text is much more reliable than Mendelssohn's, primarily because it is based on the autograph. The Peters edition does not follow the order of the works in the autograph, however, since the editors were convinced that "Bach himself placed no importance on the order." They chose instead to order the works alphabetically and even to intersperse among the settings several short miscellaneous organ chorales. It was not until 1878, with the publication of the Bachgesellschaft edition, that an *Orgelbüchlein* edition appeared that was consistent with the text as well as the ordering of the autograph. This decade also witnessed the first comprehensive discussion of the *Orgelbüchlein* in print, in the first volume of Spitta's monumental biography *Johann Sebastian Bach*.

The most important *Orgelbüchlein* publications from the end of the nineteenth century are the piano transcriptions by Ferruccio Busoni and Max Reger, two of the most prolific Bach transcribers in music history (see Appendix 2, which lists all the published transcriptions of *Orgelbüchlein* chorales from the nineteenth and twentieth centuries).[21] Like the theorist A. B. Marx, who published transcriptions of *Orgelbüchlein* chorales about fifty years earlier, Busoni and Reger wished to introduce Bach's organ chorales to pianists and, ultimately, to the general public. In the prefaces to their transcriptions, both men professed their admiration for the music in unabashedly aesthetic terms. Busoni perceived a richness of "art, feeling, and fantasy," while Reger sensed in Bach's conception and interpretation of the chorale text a genius reminiscent of Richard Wagner, the composer against whom all others were measured at the time. For Reger, Bach's organ chorales were "symphonic poems in miniature" and nothing less than the "extract of Bach's art."

This is not the place for an analysis of Busoni's and Reger's methods of transcription. Suffice it to say that through various doublings and expressive devices, their *Orgelbüchlein* arrangements produce gorgeous piano sonorities in which the chorale tune stands out in the midst of a thick contrapuntal web. (This manner of playing is referred to by Busoni as "chamber style," in distinction to the more virtuosic "concert style" of his transcriptions of Bach's free instrumental works.) Of special interest, because of its relatively free elaboration of the model, is Busoni's transcription of "Ich ruf zu dir" (see Example 7–5), which has been recorded by both Dinu Lipatti and Vladimir Horowitz, among others.[22] Busoni extends the original version by four measures with a varied restatement of the last two chorale phrases, an addition that balances the restatement of the first two phrases on the repeat of the *Stollen*. In fact, this addition renders Busoni's phrase structure completely symmetrical (AB AB CDE FG FG), with a middle phrase (D) flanked on

Example 7–5. "Ich ruf zu dir, Herr Jesu Christ," BWV 639, as transcribed for piano by Ferruccio Busoni. ©1898, 1925 Breitkopf & Härtel, Wiesbaden— Leipzig. Used by permission.

either side by a single phrase (C and E) stated once and a pair of phrases (AB and FG) stated twice. Busoni varies the restatement of the last two phrases by transposing the chorale tune down an octave, thinning out the texture, and concluding with block chords. He also alters the final cadence of the initial statement of the last two phrases from F major to F minor and saves the Picardy third for the final cadence of the restatement—thus delaying the strongest sense of cadential repose until the very end of the transcription.

THE TWENTIETH CENTURY

Since 1900, we can observe a heightening of the trends that emerged in the nineteenth century. New editions have continued to appear, and transcriptions have become almost commonplace. As the field of musicology has grown, the scholarly literature on the *Orgelbüchlein* has swollen to unheard-of proportions. And as the *Orgelbüchlein* has become increasingly famous worldwide, it has piqued the interest of more performers and composers than ever before.

These trends converge in the person of Albert Schweitzer, doubtless the staunchest supporter of the *Orgelbüchlein* in the twentieth century. Schweitzer was already acquainted with the *Orgelbüchlein* by the time he arrived in Paris in 1893, at the age of eighteen, to study under Charles-Marie Widor. We know from Widor's preface to Schweitzer's book, *Jean-Sébastien Bach, le musicien-poète*, that Schweitzer immeasurably enhanced his new teacher's appreciation and understanding of Bach's organ chorales, especially with respect to text-music relationships. Surely this applies to the *Orgelbüchlein*. Indeed, it is tempting to believe that Schweitzer was largely responsible for the *Orgelbüchlein*'s popularity within Parisian organ circles at the turn of the century.

Perhaps Schweitzer was also responsible for Widor's particular attraction to the *Orgelbüchlein* setting of "O Mensch." Widor's fondness for this work was no secret among his students: allegedly it was Widor's favorite piece of music. Around 1894 he was presented with a photograph of four of his pupils gathered around the organ console at Saint Sulpice, with Louis Vierne playing "O Mensch" from the Peters edition.[23] Marcel Dupré played the work at Widor's funeral at the church in 1937.[24]

Schweitzer's championing of the *Orgelbüchlein* quickly spread beyond Paris. In his Bach monograph of 1905, published within six years' time in French, German, and English, Schweitzer proclaimed that the *Orgelbüchlein* was central to an understanding of Bach's music and one of the greatest of all musical works (see the quote in Chapter 3). The impact of this panegyric on the reception of the *Orgelbüchlein* cannot be overstated: Schweitzer's book is probably most responsible for the *Orgelbüchlein*'s worldwide popularity today. In addition, Schweitzer promoted the *Orgelbüchlein* throughout his life—and throughout the world—as a performer. He is credited with being the first organist to have audiences sing the chorale tunes of the organ chorales on his programs, always following the organ chorale.[25] These performances often included *Orgelbüchlein* settings. Thus one important aspect of Schweitzer's legacy as an advocate of the *Orgelbüchlein* is the modern tradition of playing the *Orgelbüchlein* chorales with a sung chorale melody or harmonization preceding or following the organ chorale.[26]

Very late in life, Schweitzer also edited the *Orgelbüchlein* for publication, as the penultimate volume of the so-called "Widor-Schweitzer" edition of Bach's organ music by G. Schirmer (New York). His *Orgelbüchlein* edition has not enjoyed a wide circulation in this country for the simple reason that by its publication date (1967), generations of American organists had grown accustomed to the edition by Albert Riemenschneider, published in 1933 by

Oliver Ditson (Philadelphia). Riemenschneider's edition of the *Orgelbüch-lein* is still the most widely used in America today.

Despite its maddening page turns, the Riemenschneider edition is both authoritative and practical. It closely follows the autograph, both in terms of text and order (indeed, the title of the edition is *The Liturgical Year*); chorale texts are given with translations; an alphabetical index is provided for ease of reference; and the edition is relatively inexpensive. Ironically, these are the very criteria for an edition of Bach's organ chorales laid down by Schweitzer in his monograph.[27] Riemenschneider adds a comprehensive preface; a list of all the chorale titles in the autograph, along with their liturgical associations; brief commentaries on the individual works; and harmonizations of all the chorale tunes. Add to these amenities the fact that the text is in English, and one can see how the edition meets virtually every need of the English-speaking player.[28]

A further edition of the *Orgelbüchlein* from the first half of this century is that of Marcel Dupré, published in 1940 by Bornemann (Paris) as volume 7 of Dupré's complete edition of Bach's organ compositions. By 1905, at the age of nineteen, Dupré had learned the whole collection, and it quickly became part of his regular concert repertory—always played, of course, from memory. Dupré may have been the first to perform the entire *Orgelbüchlein* in recital.[29] Like his teacher Widor, Dupré had a special attachment to "O Mensch." He was wont to play the work for his pupils as evidence that Bach could be expressive without a swell pedal.[30] And just as Dupré had played "O Mensch" at Widor's funeral at Saint Sulpice, Françoise Renet (Dupré's long-time assistant at the church) played the work, along with "Ich ruf zu dir," at Dupré's funeral there.

The *Orgelbüchlein* also circulated outside of organ circles in the early twentieth century—quite in contrast to today's musical scene, where organ music tends to be the exclusive property of organists. For the Second Viennese School of Arnold Schoenberg, Anton Webern, and Alban Berg, the *Orgelbüchlein* served as a compositional model, as evidenced by some newly discovered compositional exercises by Webern. One of Schoenberg's compositional assignments for Webern in 1906 was the harmonization of chorale tunes, to which Webern responded with chorale arrangements in block-chord as well as figured style.[31] One of the two harmonizations that has been published, a figured setting of "O Ewigkeit, du Donnerwort," is the very image of the *Orgelbüchlein*-type (see Example 7–6). The chorale tune is stated continuously and without embellishment in the soprano, while all three of the quasi-atonal accompanimental parts are derived from a single motive. The

Example 7–6. Anton Webern, "O Ewigkeit, du Donnerwort." ©1989. Reprinted with the permission of Cambridge University Press.

motive, furthermore, begins with a *suspirans* figure, and the constant statements of the motive result in continuous sixteenth-note motion.

Webern's arrangement, however, is an exceptional case. The greatest link between the *Orgelbüchlein* and nonorganists at this time was transcriptions. Let us mention only some of the most interesting and significant examples, in chronological order. The first, Max Reger's 1915 arrangement of "O Mensch" for string orchestra, spawned several other similar arrangements (see Appendix 2). For the sake of idiomatic string playing, Reger transposed the original down a half-step to D major. The chorale tune is assigned to the first violins and doubled at the lower octave by the first cellos, a scoring that, according to a contemporary review, "gives the already low-pitched melody even darker color, even more melancholy charm."[32] In keeping with the somber text, the arrangement has a hushed tone, despite building to *fortissimo* at the highest pitch of the ornamented chorale tune. Through extremely detailed dynamic markings, Reger achieves an infinitely wider range of expression than the original.

To cite other examples: in Alexander Kelberine's piano transcription of "Ich ruf zu dir" (1934), the chorale tune is generally transposed down an octave and played by the thumbs, while the original inner voice is transposed up an octave, played by the right hand. Mabel Wood-Hill's string transcriptions of "Puer natus in Bethlehem," "Christum wir sollen loben schon," and "Wir danken dir, Herr Jesu Christ" (1935) are noteworthy simply because they allow the chorale tune to sound without any interruptions. The four-hand piano arrangement of "Ach wie nichtig, ach wie flüchtig" by the opera impresario Boris Goldovsky (1940) is distinguished by an introductory chorale harmonization, played *pp*, and a work-long crescendo that culminates in massive chords, played *fff*. Anne Hull's four-hand rendering of "In dir ist Freude" (1950) contains as many fast octaves as a Liszt étude.

The most famous twentieth-century transcription of an *Orgelbüchlein* chorale, Leopold Stokowski's arrangement of "Ich ruf zu dir," remains unpublished. Fortunately, it is available in record form, on a "greatest hits" anthology of the Philadelphia Orchestra.[33] As is well known, Stokowski transcribed many of Bach's organ compositions—both free works and chorale settings—for the Philadelphia Orchestra during his tenure as conductor, and from 1916 to 1926 these arrangements were immensely popular fare on the orchestra's programs. Stokowski likened Bach's free organ works to "daring flights of imagination," while the organ chorales—and "Ich ruf zu dir" in particular—were equally dear to him for their "mystical beauty" and "concentrated essence of deep musical emotion."[34] Similar language had been used by Spitta and Schweitzer in describing the *Orgelbüchlein*.

Stokowski based his transcription of "Ich ruf zu dir" on Busoni's piano arrangement, for like Busoni, he restated the last two phrases and reserved the Picardy third for the end of the restatement. But Stokowski took even greater liberties. For one thing, he varied the instrumentation on the restatements of both the *Stollen* and the last two phrases by transferring the chorale tune from the violins to the woodwinds. Moreover, the arrangement contains material of Stokowski's own composition. For example, before Bach's first beat is heard, there is an introductory pedal point in the low strings, followed by two beats of sixteenth-note figuration derived from the inner voice of the original. On the initial statement of the last two phrases, a newly composed contrapuntal line (for oboe) emerges after the cadence of the penultimate phrase, only to dissipate by the final bar. And on the restatement of the last two phrases, Stokowski extends Bach's accompanimental figuration for the final cadence (whereas Busoni simplified the figuration to chordal texture) for one beat.

DEGREES OF POPULARITY

Our survey verifies that certain *Orgelbüchlein* chorales have been extraordinarily popular throughout the centuries. Four works stand out: "Ich ruf zu dir," "Das alte Jahr," "Durch Adams Fall," and "O Mensch."

Why these four pieces have attained such celebrity is one of the more interesting questions raised by the *Orgelbüchlein*, for in various respects the works are, ironically, among the least representative in the collection. It cannot be happenstance that two of them ("Das alte Jahr" and "O Mensch") are ornamental chorales, a very rare genre in the *Orgelbüchlein*, and that a third ("Ich ruf zu dir") contains more embellishment to the chorale tune than any other melody chorale in the collection. A lavishly decorated chorale tune simply appeals to players and listeners in ways that an unadorned melody cannot.[35] Furthermore, in these three works the chorale tune is played on a separate manual, an arrangement that highlights the chorale tune and creates a more variegated organ sonority as well. If forced to choose between this disposition and a one-manual scheme in which the chorale tune is played with the same registration as the accompanimental voices, most organists would select the former.

To be sure, these pieces also owe their popularity to harmonic style, since three of them are among the most chromatic and dissonant in the entire collection, inspired in each instance by a melancholy chorale text. "Das alte Jahr" and "O Mensch" display chromatic accompanimental figuration and chromatic coloring of the chorale tune, which depict, respectively, the passing of the old year and the agony of the Crucifixion. "Durch Adams Fall," with its unorthodox handling of chromaticism, is easily the most dissonant work in the *Orgelbüchlein*. The dissonance is clearly a metaphor for Original Sin. It is easy to see how the emotional intensity of these works attracted Schumann and Mendelssohn, especially considering their generation's obsession with sad subject matter. "Ich ruf zu dir" surely appealed to these artists for similar reasons, for the sense of longing expressed by its text was central to the movement of Romanticism.

Of the other *Orgelbüchlein* chorales, "In dir ist Freude" has been a particular favorite over the years. Its exuberant, virtuosic style has made it popular among organists and nonorganists alike (see the various transcriptions listed in Appendix 2). Organists often use it as a recital encore—something that cannot be said of any other *Orgelbüchlein* chorale. "In dir ist Freude" is also an anomaly within the *Orgelbüchlein*. Because of its extraordinarily free treatment of the chorale tune, it is the only piece in the collection that might be regarded as a chorale fantasy.

In considering additional settings that are especially popular today, one must take into account such external factors as liturgical usefulness, the familiarity of the chorale tune, and ease of performance. Generally speaking, the works most frequently played are those designated for a particular time in the church year (the *de tempore* chorales). Outside of Germany, precious few of the chorales set in the *Orgelbüchlein* have found their way into church hymnals. As a result, most of the settings cannot be used in conjunction with congregational singing. Still, it has become customary throughout North America and Europe to play the *de tempore* settings in church services (or on recitals) during the appropriate liturgical season.

Organists in the United States are also understandably attracted to those works with well known chorale tunes. The Easter setting "Christ lag in Todesbanden," for example, is played far more often than the Easter setting "Erstanden ist der heil'ge Christ." Most church organists here, though, do not play "In dulci jubilo," the setting whose chorale tune is undoubtedly the most famous in English-speaking lands. Although the melody is well known, as the popular Christmas carol "Good Christian Men, Rejoice," Bach's fiendishly difficult *Orgelbüchlein* setting is beyond the technique of many players. On the other hand, the setting of "Jesus Christus, unser Heiland" is based on a relatively obscure melody. But because it is one of the easiest settings from a technical standpoint, it is frequently performed.

Let us not, however, overlook the popularity of the collection as a whole. The *Orgelbüchlein* is the most frequently performed organ *collection* ever composed. It derives its huge success not from the popularity of a handful of pieces but from the accumulative appeal of forty-six masterworks.

Appendix 1

———————— ⚬ ————————

"Ich ruf zu dir, Herr Jesu Christ," BWV Anh. 73, attributed to C. P. E. Bach (arrangement of *Orgelbüchlein* chorale BWV 639).

Edited from: Staatsbibliothek zu Berlin—Preussischer Kulturbesitz, Musikabteilung, *Mus. ms. Bach P 1149*; and Musikbibliothek der Stadt Leipzig, *Ms. R 25*.

Title in *Ms. R 25: Vorspiel auf das / Lied / ich ruff zu dir Herr Jesu Christ / per il Organo auf 2. Manuale / und das Pedal. / dell Sig[nore] C. P. E. / Bach.*

Appendix 2

---✍---

Transcriptions of Orgelbüchlein *Chorales, in Chronological Order,*
According to Publication Date

TRANSCRIBER AND INSTRUMENTATION	BIBLIOGRAPHICAL CITATION	TITLE AND BWV NO. OF *ORGELBÜCHLEIN* CHORALE(S) TRANSCRIBED
Johann Nepomuk Schelble (d. 1837) (piano, four hands)	*Var. Choraele fürs P.f. zu 4 Haenden eingerichtet.* Vol. 1. Frankfurt/Main: Dunst, n.d.	"Christus, der uns selig macht," BWV 620a; Das alte Jahr vergangen ist, BWV 614; "O Mensch, bewein dein Sünde gross," BWV 622
Adolph Bernhard Marx (piano)	*Auswahl aus Sebastian Bach's Kompositionen, zur ersten Bekanntschaft mit dem Meister am Pianoforte, veranstaltet von Adolph Bernhard Marx.* Berlin: Challier, 1844.	"Das alte Jahr vergangen ist," BWV 614; "Christe, du Lamm Gottes," BWV 619
Ferruccio Busoni (piano)	*Orgelchoralvorspiele von Johann Sebastian Bach: Auf das Pianoforte im Kammerstyl übertragen von Ferruccio Benvenuto Busoni.* 2 vols. Leipzig: Breitkopf & Härtel, 1898.	"Ich ruf zu dir, Herr Jesu Christ," BWV 639; "Herr Gott, nun schleuss den Himmel auf," BWV 617; "Durch Adams Fall ist ganz verderbt," BWV 637; "In dir ist Freude," BWV 615

Max Reger (piano)	*Ausgewählte Choralvorspiele von Joh. Seb. Bach: Für Klavier zu 2 Händen übertragen von Max Reger.* Vienna: Universal Edition, 1900.	"O Mensch, bewein dein Sünde gross," BWV 622; "Durch Adams Fall ist ganz verderbt," BWV 637; "Ich ruf zu dir, Herr Jesu Christ," BWV 639; "Ach wie nichtig, ach wie flüchtig," BWV 644; "Das alte Jahr vergangen ist," BWV 614
Bernhard Friedrich Richter (piano, four hands)	*Joh. Seb. Bachs Werke. Nach der Ausgabe der Bachgesellschaft. Orgelbüchlein: 46 kürzere Choralbearbeitungen für Klavier zu vier Händen.* Leipzig: Breitkopf & Härtel, 1902.	complete collection
Max Reger (string orchestra)	*Johann Sebastian Bach: "O Mensch, bewein dein Sünde gross." Aria nach dem Choralvorspiel für Streichorchester bearbeitet.* Leipzig: Breitkopf & Härtel, 1915.	"O Mensch, bewein dein Sünde gross," BWV 622
Max Reger (violin and organ)	*Johann Sebastian Bach: "O Mensch, bewein dein Sünde gross." Air (Aria), nach dem Choralvorspiel bearbeitet für Violine mit Begleitung von Orgel (oder Harmonium oder Klavier).* In *Album für Violine mit Orgelbegleitung.* Leipzig: Edition Peters, 1915.	"O Mensch, bewein dein Sünde gross," BWV 622
Walter Rummel (piano)	*Adaptations.* Ser. 1 (*J. S. Bach*). London: J. & W. Chester, ca. 1922.	"Das alte Jahr vergangen ist," BWV 614
Vittorio Gui (orchestra)	*Due corali di J. S. Bach. Trascritti dall' organo per orchestra.* Vienna: Universal Edition, 1925.	"O Mensch, bewein dein Sünde gross," BWV 622; "In dir ist Freude," BWV 615

Harry Hodge (string orchestra)	*Johann Sebastian Bach: Organ Choral Preludes Arranged for Strings by Harry Hodge.* Glasgow: Paterson's Publications, ca. 1926.	"Ich ruf zu dir, Herr Jesu Christ," BWV 639; "Gott, durch deine Güte," BWV 600
William Murdoch (piano)	*J. S. Bach: Organ Choral Preludes Arranged for Pianoforte by William Murdoch.* 4 vols. London: Schott, 1928.	"O Mensch, bewein dein Sünde gross," BWV 622; "Ich ruf zu dir, Herr Jesu Christ," BWV 639
Marco Enrico Bossi (violin or viola and organ)	*Johann Sebastian Bach: "O Mensch, bewein' dein Sünde gross" (Choral).* Stuttgart: Edition Euterpe, 1929.	"O Mensch, bewein dein Sünde gross," BWV 622
Arthur Bliss, Herbert Howells, Constant Lambert (piano)	*A Bach Book for Harriet Cohen: Transcriptions for Pianoforte from the Works of J. S. Bach made by Granville Bantock, Arnold Bax, Lord Berners, Arthur Bliss, Frank Bridge, Eugene Goossens, Herbert Howells, John Ireland, Constant Lambert, R. Vaughan Williams, William Walton, and W. Gillies Whittaker.* London: Oxford University Press, 1932.	"Das alte Jahr vergangen ist," BWV 614 (Bliss); "O Mensch, bewein dein Sünde gross," BWV 622 (Howells); "Der Tag, der ist so freudenreich," BWV 605 (Lambert)
Harry S. Hirsch (oboe, clarinet, bassoon)	*Johann Sebastian Bach: I Call upon Thy Name O Jesus.* New York: Carl Fischer, 1934.	"Ich ruf zu dir, Herr Jesu Christ," BWV 639
Alexander Kelberine (piano)	*Joh. Seb. Bach: Organ Choral Prelude "Ich ruf' zu Dir, Herr."* Philadelphia: Elkan-Vogel, 1934.	"Ich ruf zu dir, Herr Jesu Christ," BWV 639
Mabel Wood-Hill (string quartet or string orchestra)	*J. S. Bach: Chorale Preludes.* Boston: R. D. Row, 1935.	"Christe, du Lamm Gottes," BWV 619; "Wir danken dir, Herr Jesu Christ," BWV 623; "In dir ist Freude," BWV 615

Eric DeLamarter (string orchestra)	*J. S. Bach: Chorale-Prelude Das alte Jahr vergangen ist.* New York: Ricordi, 1940.	"Das alte Jahr vergangen ist," BWV 614
Amedeo de Filippi (string orchestra or string quartet)	*Johann Sebastian Bach: Blessed Jesus, We Are Here (Chorale Prelude).* New York: Concord, 1940.	"Liebster Jesu, wir sind hier," BWV 633
Boris Goldovsky (two pianos)	*J. S. Bach: Oh, How Fleeting.* New York: J. Fischer & Bro., 1940.	"Ach wie nichtig, ach wie flüchtig," BWV 644
Felix Guenther (piano)	*Johann Sebastian Bach: Twenty-four Choral Preludes Compiled and Arranged for Piano Solo by Felix Guenther.* New York: Edward B. Marks, ca. 1942.	"Das alte Jahr vergangen ist," BWV 614; "Ich ruf zu dir, Herr Jesu Christ," BWV 639; "In dir ist Freude," BWV 615; "Wir danken dir, Herr Jesu Christ," BWV 623
Max Reger (piano)	*Johann Sebastian Bach: Drei Orgelchoralvorspiele, für Klavier bearbeitet.* Leipzig: Breitkopf & Härtel, 1943.	"Es ist das Heil uns kommen her," BWV 638; "Vom Himmel hoch, da komm ich her," BWV 606
Johanna and Roy Harris (piano)	*Bach Organ Preludes Transcribed for Piano by Johanna and Roy Harris.* New York: Mills Music, ca. 1946.	"Christ lag in Todesbanden," BWV 625; "Das alte Jahr vergangen ist," BWV 614; "Liebster Jesu, wir sind hier," BWV 633; "In dulci jubilo," BWV 608

C. H. Stuart Duncan (two pianos)	*Johann Sebastian Bach: Eleven Chorale Preludes from the Little Organ Book.* New York: G. Schirmer, 1949.	"Christ lag in Todesbanden," BWV 625; "Durch Adams Fall ist ganz verderbt," BWV 637; "Herr Christ, der ein'ge Gottessohn," BWV 601; "In dulci jubilo," BWV 608; "Liebster Jesu, wir sind hier," BWV 633; "Jesu, meine Freude," BWV 610; "Alle Menschen müssen sterben," BWV 643; "Christ ist erstanden," BWV 627; "Gott, durch deine Güte," BWV 600; "Lobt Gott, ihr Christen, allzugleich," BWV 609; "Vater unser im Himmelreich," BWV 636
Anne Hull (two pianos)	*Johann Sebastian Bach: Choral Prelude In dir ist Freude.* New York: Carl Fischer, 1950.	"In dir ist Freude," BWV 615
Wilhelm Kempff (piano)	*Johann Sebastian Bach: Ich ruf' zu dir, Herr Jesu Christ (Choralvorspiel).* Berlin: Bote & Bock, 1954.	"Ich ruf zu dir, Herr Jesu Christ," BWV 639

$\mathscr{N}otes$

CHAPTER 1

1. See Robin A. Leaver, "Bach and Hymnody: The Evidence of the *Orgelbüchlein*," *Early Music* 13 (1985): 227–36.

2. See Robert L. Marshall, *Luther, Bach, and the Early Reformation Chorale* (Kessler Reformation Lecture, Emory University, 1995), 1.

3. See Christoph Wolff, "Chronology and Style in the Early Works: A Background for the Orgel-Büchlein," in Wolff, *Bach: Essays on His Life and Music* (Cambridge, Mass., 1991), 297–305.

4. Bach's only extant setting of this chorale (BWV 725) spans 208 bars.

5. See *Johann Sebastian Bach's Werke*, 25/2, *Joh. Seb. Bach's Orgelwerke, zweiter Band*, ed. Wilhelm Rust (Leipzig, 1878), v.

6. Spitta, *Johann Sebastian Bach*, 3 vols., trans. Clara Bell and J. A. Fuller-Maitland (London, 1889; reprint, New York, 1951), 1:597–98, 647–56.

7. Dadelsen, *Beiträge zur Chronologie der Werke Johann Sebastian Bachs* (Trossingen, 1958), 80; and "Zur Entstehung des Bachschen Orgelbüchleins," in *Festschrift Friedrich Blume*, ed. Anna Amalie Abert and Wilhelm Pfannkuch (Kassel, 1963), 74–79.

8. Terry, "The 'Orgelbüchlein': Another Bach Problem," *The Musical Times* 58 (1917): 109.

9. See the preface to *Johann Sebastian Bach: Orgelbüchlein* (facsimile edition of the autograph), ed. Heinz-Harald Löhlein (Leipzig, 1981); and NBA IV/1, KB, 90–95.

10. Williams, *The Organ Music of J. S. Bach*, 3 vols. (Cambridge, 1980–84), 3:41–42.

11. Wolff, "Chronology and Style."

12. Marshall, *Luther, Bach, and the Early Reformation Chorale*, 1.

13. See Russell Stinson, "The Compositional History of Bach's *Orgelbüchlein* Reconsidered," *Bach Perspectives* 1 (1995): 43–78. To cite some findings of this study, until about 1714 Bach's tendency was: to cancel sharps with flats; to draw half notes that have been likened to the shape of a bird's head (downward stem) or ladle (upward stem); to use a symbol resembling the numeral "3" for soprano clefs;

to use a slanting symbol for the common-time signature; and to use small symbols in general. After 1714, he tended: to cancel sharps with naturals; to draw more conventional-looking half notes; to use a different, more ornate symbol for the soprano clef; to use an upright symbol for the common-time signature; and to write with larger symbols in general.

14. This threefold classification is derived from Robert L. Marshall, *The Compositional Process of J. S. Bach: A Study of the Autograph Scores of the Vocal Works*, 2 vols. (Princeton, 1972), 1:3–36.

15. The Neumeister version has thus far been published only in facsimile, in *The Neumeister Collection of Chorale Preludes from the Bach Circle*, ed. Christoph Wolff (New Haven, 1986); see also Russell Stinson, "Some Thoughts on Bach's Neumeister Chorales," *The Journal of Musicology* 11 (1993): 471–76. For editions of all other early versions of *Orgelbüchlein* chorales, see NBA IV/1.

16. So described by Peter Williams in his jacket notes to Peter Hurford's recording of the *Orgelbüchlein* (Decca - D228D 4, K228K: 1982).

17. See Stinson, "Some Thoughts on Bach's Neumeister Chorales," 471–72.

18. With respect to the canonic settings in the *Orgelbüchlein*, it bears pointing out that the contours of the chorale tunes set as canons at the fifth made a canon at the octave impossible. Thus, in addition to a penchant for more complex canonic writing, the chorale tunes themselves were a factor in Bach's move from canons at the octave to canons at the fifth.

19. Regarding ink types, it should be stated that only in the case of the Leipzig entries does this issue have any chronological bearing. Owing to certain restoration procedures, most pages of the autograph have a faded appearance, making it impossible to determine the ink's original color.

20. See Hans T. David and Arthur Mendel, eds., *The Bach Reader: A Life of Johann Sebastian Bach in Letters and Documents*, rev. ed. (New York, 1966), 218.

21. See Charles Sanford Terry, *Bach: A Biography*, rev. ed. (London, 1933), 85–86.

22. Figure 1–1 is based on Williams, *The Organ Music*, 3:124–25; and Winfried Schrammek, "Orgel, Positiv, Clavicymbel und Glocken der Schlosskirche zu Weimar 1658 bis 1774," in *Bericht über die Wissenschaftliche Konferenz zum V. Internationalen Bachfest der DDR in Verbindung mit dem 60. Bachfest der Neuen Bachgesellschaft*, ed. Winfried Hoffmann and Armin Schneiderheinze (Leipzig, 1988), 99–111. Schrammek's examination of Weimar court records shows that when the organ was rebuilt in 1707–8, it acquired the manual and pedal ranges given in Figure 1–1. These ranges remained unchanged until 1774, when the entire court chapel was destroyed by fire.

23. See Williams, *The Organ Music*, 3:118–19; and Lynn Edwards, "The Thuringian Organ 1702–1720: ' . . . ein wohlgerathenes gravitätisches Werk,'" *The Organ Yearbook* 22 (1991): 119–50.

24. See Williams, *The Organ Music*, 3:140–41.

25. See Schrammek, 99.

26. The other inscriptions on the title page stem from later owners of the autograph.

27. Translation adapted from Williams, *The Organ Music*, 2:3.

28. See NBA IV/1, KB, 106–7.

29. See David and Mendel, eds., *The Bach Reader*, 86.

30. The term "accompanimental" will be used throughout this book to designate any voice of a chorale setting other than that assigned the chorale tune.

31. See David and Mendel, eds., *The Bach Reader*, 75.

32. See NBA IV/1, KB, 107.

CHAPTER 2

1. Given the common assumption that most chorale melodies are in bar form, it is somewhat surprising that most of those set in the *Orgelbüchlein* are not.

2. As described by Giulio Cesare Monteverdi, the brother of Claudio Monteverdi, with reference to his brother's compositional style, in the preface to Claudio's *Scherzi musicali* (1607).

3. See Marshall, *The Compositional Process*.

4. Ibid., 1:69–89.

5. See David and Mendel, eds., *The Bach Reader*, 279.

6. Moreover, there survives in the manuscript SBB: *P 802* an organ chorale ("Jesu, der du meine Seele") notated in this manner and presumably composed by Krebs himself.

7. The inscription *Am Ende* at the left of the tablature is not autograph; it refers to a non-autograph transcription of the tablature passage, notated in score, found on the last page of the manuscript. It should also be pointed out that "Wir Christenleut" is characteristic of Bach's notational practice throughout the *Orgelbüchlein* autograph in a number of ways: the use of two instead of three staves, the notation of the upper staff in soprano rather than treble clef, the presence of a pedal cue (*p.* in m. 1) as opposed to a separate staff for the pedal part, and the use of "dorian" notation (the system in which minor flat keys are notated one flat short of modern practice).

8. Quote by the early Bach biographer Johann Nicolaus Forkel apropos Bach's tendency to revise his works. See David and Mendel, eds., *The Bach Reader*, 348.

9. There is plenty of evidence, though, judging from note size and note spacing, that Bach continued to embellish existing soprano passages on the first page in mm. 5 (beats 1–2 and 4), 7 (beat 2), 9 (beat 2), and 14 (beat 2).

10. Example 2–3 is based on Williams, *The Organ Music*, 2:60.

11. It is likewise by far the most common compositional revision in the early (ca. 1705) autograph of Bach's fragmentary organ chorale on "Wie schön leuchtet der Morgenstern," BWV 764. See Russell Stinson, "Bach's Earliest Autograph," *The*

Musical Quarterly 71 (1985): 235–63.

12. Wolff et al., *The New Grove Bach Family* (New York, 1983), 167.

13. In addition, Bach reportedly urged his pupils to compose "entirely from the mind." See David and Mendel, eds., *The Bach Reader*, 329.

CHAPTER 3

1. Spitta, 1:602.

2. Schweitzer, *J. S. Bach*, 2 vols., trans. Ernest Newman (orig. pub. as *Jean-Sébastien Bach, le musicien-poète*, New York, 1925; reprint, New York, 1966), 1:284; 2:54–55.

3. Marshall, "Chorale settings," in *The New Grove Dictionary of Music and Musicians* (London, 1980).

4. See Alexander Russell Brinkmann, "Johann Sebastian Bach's Orgelbüchlein: A Computer-Assisted Study of the Melodic Influence of the Cantus Firmus on the Contrapuntal Voices" (Ph.D. diss., Eastman School of Music, 1978).

5. *Johann Sebastian Bach: Orgelbüchlein*, ed. Robert Clark and John David Peterson (St. Louis, 1984), 10.

6. This term seems to have been coined by Willi Apel in the original *Harvard Dictionary of Music* (Cambridge, Mass., 1944).

7. See Elke Krüger, *Stilistische Untersuchungen zu ausgewählten frühen Klavierfugen Johann Sebastian Bachs* (Hamburg, 1970).

8. The use of a quarter rest here is also recommended in Marcel Dupré's "performing" edition of the *Orgelbüchlein*, hardly a surprise considering Dupré's general aversion to dissonance in Bach.

9. Williams, *The Organ Music*, 2:14.

10. Ibid., 2:254–55.

11. See Georg Philipp Telemann, *Zwölf leichte Choralvorspiele*, ed. Hermann Keller (Frankfurt, 1936).

CHAPTER 4

1. For complete translations of all the chorales set in the *Orgelbüchlein*, see Mark S. Bighley, *The Lutheran Chorales in the Organ Works of J. S. Bach* (St. Louis, 1986). Translations of first stanzas may be found in any English-language edition of the *Orgelbüchlein*, as well as in Hermann Keller, *The Organ Works of J. S. Bach: A Contribution to Their History, Form, Interpretation and Performance* (New York, 1967); and Williams, *The Organ Music*. In following the piece-by-piece commentaries in Chapters 4–6 of the present book, the reader will often find it helpful to refer to such translations.

2. Schweitzer, 2:63.

3. Bach, *Orgelbüchlein*, ed. Clark and Peterson, 40.

4. Spitta, 1:600.

5. Bach, *Orgelbüchlein*, ed. Clark and Peterson, 49.

6. Keller, *The Organ Works*, 205.

7. Williams, *The Organ Music*, 2:33.

8. See, for example, John O'Donnell, "*In dulci jubilo* from the *Orgel-Buechlein* Resolved!" *The Diapason* 67, no. 1 (December 1975): 4–6.

9. Although a literal translation of the opening line of the chorale would be "As Jesus *stood at* the cross," the biblical context is definitely that of Jesus *hanging on* the cross.

10. See Albert Riemenschneider, ed., *The Liturgical Year (Orgelbüchlein) by Johann Sebastian Bach* (Bryn Mawr, 1933), 73.

11. Max Reger called attention to this lyricism by designating his string transcriptions of "O Mensch" as "arias"; see Appendix 2.

12. Stauffer, "Boyvin, Grigny, D'Anglebert, and Bach's Assimilation of French Classical Organ Music," *Early Music* 21 (1993): 83–96.

13. Still, the manuscript copy by Bach's pupil Meissner (private possession) contains the unqualified heading *Canon*. See NBA IV/1, KB, 50–51.

14. Budday, "Musikalische Figuren als satztechnische Freiheiten in Bachs Orgelchoral 'Durch Adams Fall ist ganz verderbt,'" *Bach-Jahrbuch* 63 (1977): 139–59.

15. Snyder, *Dieterich Buxtehude: Organist in Lübeck* (New York, 1987), 269.

CHAPTER 5

1. Bach, *Orgelbüchlein*, ed. Clark and Peterson, 29.

2. Bach, *The Liturgical Year*, ed. Riemenschneider, 4; Schweitzer, 2:65.

3. Keller, *The Organ Works*, 202.

4. Spitta, 1:602.

5. See Michael Murray, *Marcel Dupré: The Work of a Master Organist* (Boston, 1985), 120.

6. Bach, *The Liturgical Year*, ed. Riemenschneider, 84.

7. Michael Murray's 1992 recording, *Bach at St. Bavo's* (Telarc CD-80286), contains renditions of "Christ lag" in both the "French" manner (duration of 2:04) and in the exuberant style favored today (duration of 1:30). It bears pointing out that Murray was one of Dupré's pupils.

8. Williams, *The Organ Music*, 2:68.

9. For a version of the work with written-out ornamentation throughout, see Gerhard Krapf, *Bach: Improvised Ornamentation and Keyboard Cadenzas* (Dayton, 1983), 62–64.

10. Richter, *Orgelchoral und Ensemblesatz bei J. S. Bach* (Tutzing, 1982), 181–200.

11. The unsimplified version of the motive, though, appears several times in the pedal solo of Bach's Toccata, Adagio, and Fugue in C Major, BWV 564.

12. The harmonic as well as motivic writing brings to mind a passage (m. 24) at the end of Bach's setting of "Von Gott will ich nicht lassen" from the "Great Eighteen" Chorales.

13. See Stinson, "Some Thoughts on Bach's Neumeister Chorales," 464–67.

CHAPTER 6

1. Bach, *Orgelbüchlein*, ed. Clark and Peterson, 57.

2. Keller, *The Organ Works*, 206.

3. Schweitzer, 2:67.

4. Bach, *The Liturgical Year*, ed. Riemenschneider, 47.

5. Williams, *The Organ Music*, 2:56.

6. See Keller, *The Organ Works*, 215.

7. Spitta, 1:601.

8. Evidently, BWV 633 is the first of the two versions listed in the BWV because it represents the final, "definitive" version. The BWV considers BWV 634 a "variant."

CHAPTER 7

1. Table 7–1 is based on NBA IV/1, KB, 108–11.

2. See George B. Stauffer, "J. S. Bach as Organ Pedagogue," in *The Organist as Scholar: Essays in Memory of Russell Saunders*, ed. Kerala J. Snyder (Stuyvesant, N.Y., 1994), 25–44.

3. Published in Gotthold Frotscher, ed., *Orgelchoräle um Joh. Seb. Bach* (Frankfurt, 1937).

4. Published in Hermann Keller, ed., *Achtzig Choralvorspiele deutscher Meister des 17. und 18. Jahrhunderts* (Frankfurt, 1937); and Carl F. Pfatteicher and Archibald T. Davison, eds., *The Church Organist's Golden Treasury*, 3 vols. (Bryn Mawr, 1949–51), 3:6.

5. Published in *Johann Caspar Vogler: Chorale Preludes*, ed. Ewald Kooiman (Hilversum, 1988); and Karl Straube, ed., *Choralvorspiele alter Meister* (Leipzig, 1907). The work is listed in the BWV as BWV Anh. 57.

6. According to *Bach-Dokumente 2: Fremdschriftliche und gedruckte Dokumente zur Lebensgeschichte Johann Sebastian Bachs 1685–1750*, ed. Werner Neumann and Hans-Joachim Schulze (Leipzig, 1969), no. 324.

7. See David and Mendel, eds., *The Bach Reader*, 237.

8. See *Bach-Dokumente 3: Dokumente zum Nachwirken Johann Sebastian Bachs*, ed. Hans-Joachim Schulze (Leipzig, 1972), no. 725.

9. On the publication history of the *Orgelbüchlein*, see NBA IV/1, KB, 108–11; and BWV, pp. 563–64.

10. See NBA IV/1, KB, 122–24; and Peter Janson, "The Eighteenth-Century Chorale Prelude with Solo Wind Instrument," *The Diapason* 79, no. 10 (October

1988): 10–13. Janson's argument that the arrangement is for organ and solo instrument, with the chorale tune played by the latter, is simply unfounded. There is no evidence that the instrumentation is anything other than that prescribed by both sources: organ, with two manuals and pedals.

11.   See BWV 683a, based on the small setting of "Vater unser im Himmelreich" from *Clavierübung* III; and BWV 691a, based on the miscellaneous setting of "Wer nur den lieben Gott lässt walten," BWV 691.

12.   See Williams, *The Organ Music*, 2:10–11.

13.   See E. Eugene Helm, *Thematic Catalogue of the Works of Carl Philipp Emanuel Bach* (New Haven, 1989).

14.   Johann-Sebastian-Bach-Institut, Göttingen: no shelf number. See NBA IV/1, KB, 60.

15.   See Kirsten Beisswenger, "An Early Version of the First Movement of the *Italian Concerto* BWV 971 from the Scholz Collection?" in *Bach Studies 2*, ed. Daniel R. Melamed (Cambridge, 1995), 5–13.

16.   "Das Ganze drückt lebhafte kräftig-sichere Bewegung aus: Ober- und Unterstimme erzählen die freudige Begebenheit der Auferstehung des Herrn. Daher auch alle Stimmen der verschiedenen Claviere in Thätigkeit gesetz worden." Ritter singles out the soprano and bass, obviously because they state the chorale tune and thus imply the chorale text.

17.   For the original German, see NBA IV/1, KB, 65.

18.   For the original German, see NBA IV/1, KB, 67.

19.   In October 1839, Schumann's editorial colleague Oswald Lorenz published in the *Neue Zeitschrift* a review of the anthology *Orgel-Archiv* (see Table 7–1), in which Lorenz praised the two *Orgelbüchlein* chorales contained in the publication as "extremely valuable" ("höchst kostbare").

20.   See Rollin Smith, "Charles Gounod and the Organ," *The American Organist* 27, no. 10 (October 1993): 54–57.

21.   Appendix 2 does not list what is in effect a further *Orgelbüchlein* piano transcription by Busoni, the two-fold arrangement of "Lob sei dem allmächtigen Gott" in his *Fantasia nach Johann Sebastian Bach*.

22.   See, respectively, Columbia Masterworks ML 4633 and Sony Classical SK 53466 ADD.

23.   The photograph is published in John R. Near, "Charles-Marie Widor: The Organ Works and Saint-Sulpice," *The American Organist* 27, no. 2 (February 1993): 53.

24.   See Murray, *Marcel Dupré*, 160–61. Unless otherwise noted, all further references to Dupré are based on Murray's book.

25.   See Keller, *The Organ Works*, 174.

26.   As Helmuth Rilling's recording of the *Orgelbüchlein* on the Nonesuch label demonstrates, either of these practices is valid. This recording shows as well that many of the *Orgelbüchlein* chorales are adaptable to a wide variety of registrations—

some of them are just as effective played full organ as with softer registrations—a testament to the music's transcendence over performing medium.

27.   The first edition of the *Orgelbüchlein* to include chorale texts (and chorale harmonizations), that of Hermann Keller (1928), is expressly based on Schweitzer's criteria.

28.   An even more authoritative and practical edition of this type is that published by Concordia (1984), edited by Robert Clark and John David Peterson.

29.   The first person to accomplish this feat in America was Lynnwood Farnam, in 1928, followed by E. Power Biggs in the late 1930s. See Barbara Owen, *E. Power Biggs: Concert Organist* (Bloomington, 1987), 41–43.

30.   See Bach, *The Liturgical Year*, ed. Riemenschneider, ix.

31.   See Martin Zenck, "Tradition as Authority and Provocation: Anton Webern's Confrontation with J. S. Bach," in *Bach Studies*, ed. Don O. Franklin (Cambridge, 1989), 301–8.

32.   See Johannes Lorenzen, *Max Reger als Bearbeiter Bachs* (Wiesbaden, 1982), 212.

33.   *Landmarks and Legends of Those Fabulous Philadelphians: Celebrated Performances by the Philadelphia Orchestra* (Columbia Masterworks MGP 17).

34.   Stokowski, *Music for All of Us* (New York, 1943), 145–47.

35.   Thus the only other ornamental setting in the *Orgelbüchlein*, "Wenn wir in höchsten Nöten sein," is likewise especially popular.

Bibliography

MUSICAL EDITIONS AND FACSIMILES

Bach, Johann Michael. *Sämtliche Orgelchoräle / The Complete Organ Chorales.* Edited by Christoph Wolff. (Stuttgarter Bach-Ausgaben.) Neuhausen-Stuttgart: Hänssler, 1988.

Bach, Johann Sebastian. *44 kleine Choralvorspiele für die Orgel.* Edited by Felix Mendelssohn Bartholdy. Leipzig: Breitkopf & Härtel, 1845.

———. *The Liturgical Year (Orgelbüchlein).* Edited by Albert Riemenschneider. Bryn Mawr: Oliver Ditson, 1933.

———. *I. Orgelbüchlein, II. Sechs Choräle, III. Achtzehn Choräle.* Edited by Wilhelm Rust. (*Joh. Seb. Bach's Orgelwerke*, 2 = Vol. 25/2 of *Johann Sebastian Bach's Werke* [Bachgesellschaft edition].) Leipzig: Breitkopf & Härtel, 1878.

———. *Orgelbüchlein.* Edited by Ivor Atkins, with an introduction by Ernest Newman. Revised by Walter Emery. (*The Organ Works of J. S. Bach*, 15.) Borough Green: Novello, 1957.

———. *Orgelbüchlein: BWV 599–644.* Edited by Heinz Lohmann. Wiesbaden: Breitkopf & Härtel, 1983.

———. *Orgelbüchlein.* Edited by Robert Clark and John David Peterson. St. Louis: Concordia, 1984.

———. *Orgelbüchlein.* Facsimile edition of the autograph, edited and with an introduction by Heinz-Harald Löhlein. (*Faksimile-Reihe Bachscher Werke und Schriftstücke*, 17.) Leipzig: VEB Deutscher Verlag für Musik, 1981.

———. *Orgel-Büchlein - Choralvariationen.* Edited by Friedrich Conrad Griepenkerl. (*Johann Sebastian Bach's Kompositionen für die Orgel*, 5.) Leipzig: C. F. Peters, 1846.

———. *Orgelbüchlein - 18 grosse Choralbearbeitungen, Anhang: Varianten.* Edited by Heinz Lohmann. (*Sämtliche Orgelwerke*, 7.) Wiesbaden: Breitkopf & Härtel, 1968.

———. *Orgelbüchlein, Sechs Choräle von verschiedener Art (Schübler Choräle), Choralpartiten.* Edited by Heinz-Harald Löhlein. (*Neue Bach-Ausgabe*, Serie IV, Band 1.) Kassel: Bärenreiter; Leipzig: VEB Deutscher Verlag für Musik, 1983. *Kritischer Bericht*, 1987.

————. *Orgelbüchlein und andere kleine Choralvorspiele*. Edited by Hermann Keller. Kassel: Bärenreiter, 1928.

————. *Orgelchoräle der Neumeister Sammlung / Organ Chorales from the Neumeister Collection*. Edited by Christoph Wolff. New Haven: Yale University Press; Kassel: Bärenreiter, 1985.

————. *Quarante cinq chorals du petit Livre d'Orgue*. Edited by Marcel Dupré. (*Oeuvres complète pour orgue*, 7.) Paris: Bornemann, 1940.

Busoni, Ferruccio. *Fantasia nach Johann Sebastian Bach*. Leipzig: Breitkopf & Härtel, 1909.

Emery, Walter, ed. *A Vocal Companion to Bach's Orgelbüchlein*. 3 volumes. Borough Green: Novello, 1969–75.

Frotscher, Gotthold, ed. *Orgelchoräle um Joh. Seb. Bach*. Frankfurt: C. F. Peters, 1937.

Keller, Hermann, ed. *Achtzig Choralvorspiele deutscher Meister des 17. und 18. Jahrhunderts*. Frankfurt: C. F. Peters, 1937.

Pachelbel, Johann. *Ausgewählte Orgelwerke*. Edited by Karl Matthaei. 4 volumes. Kassel: Bärenreiter, 1936.

Pfatteicher, Carl F. and Davison, Archibald T., eds. *The Church Organist's Golden Treasury*. 3 volumes. Bryn Mawr: Oliver Ditson, 1949–51.

Telemann, Georg Philipp. *Zwölf leichte Choralvorspiele*. Edited by Hermann Keller. Frankfurt: C. F. Peters, 1936.

Straube, Karl, ed. *Choralvorspiele alter Meister*. Leipzig: C. F. Peters, 1907.

Vogler, Johann Caspar. *Chorale Preludes*. (*Incognita Organo*, 36.) Edited by Ewald Kooiman. Hilversum: Harmonia, 1988.

Walther, Johann Gottfried. *Ausgewählte Orgelwerke*. Edited by Heinz Lohmann. 3 volumes. Wiesbaden: Breitkopf & Härtel, 1966.

Wolff, Christoph, ed. *The Neumeister Collection of Chorale Preludes from the Bach Circle*. Facsimile edition, with an introduction by Christoph Wolff. New Haven: Yale University Press, 1986.

LITERATURE

Apel, Willi. *The History of Keyboard Music to 1700*. Translated and revised by Hans Tischler. Bloomington: Indiana University Press, 1972. (Originally published as *Geschichte der Orgel- und Klaviermusik bis 1700*. Kassel: Bärenreiter, 1967.)

Apel, Willi, ed. *Harvard Dictionary of Music*. Cambridge, Mass.: Harvard University Press, 1944.

Arfken, Ernst. "Zur Entstehungsgeschichte des Orgelbüchleins." *Bach-Jahrbuch* 52 (1966): 41–58.

Bach-Dokumente 1: Schriftstücke von der Hand Johann Sebastian Bachs. Edited by Werner Neumann and Hans-Joachim Schulze. Kassel: Bärenreiter; Leipzig: VEB Deutscher Verlag für Musik, 1963.

Bach-Dokumente 2: Fremdschriftliche und gedruckte Dokumente zur Lebens-geschichte Johann Sebastian Bachs 1685–1750. Edited by Werner Neumann and Hans-Joachim Schulze. Kassel: Bärenreiter; Leipzig: VEB Deutscher Verlag für Musik, 1969.

Bach-Dokumente 3: Dokumente zum Nachwirken Johann Sebastian Bachs. Edited by Hans-Joachim Schulze. Kassel: Bärenreiter; Leipzig: VEB Deutscher Verlag für Musik, 1972.

Beisswenger, Kirsten. "An Early Version of the First Movement of the *Italian Concerto* BWV 971 from the Scholz Collection?" In *Bach Studies 2*, edited by Daniel R. Melamed, 1–19. Cambridge: Cambridge University Press, 1995.

Benitez, Vincent. "Musical-Rhetorical Figures in the *Orgelbüchlein* of J. S. Bach." *Bach (The Journal of the Riemenschneider Bach Institute)* 18, no. 1 (January 1987): 3–21.

Bighley, Mark S. *The Lutheran Chorales in the Organ Works of J. S. Bach*. St. Louis: Concordia, 1986.

Breig, Werner. "Bachs Orgelchoral und die italienische Instrumentalmusik." In *Bach und die italienische Musik*, edited by Wolfgang Osthoff and Reinhard Wiesend, 91–109. (*Centro Tedesco di Studi Veneziani Quaderni*, 36.) Venice: Centro Tedesco di Studi Veneziani, 1987.

———. "Die geschichtliche Stellung von Buxtehudes monodischem Orgelchoral." In *Dietrich Buxtehude und die europäische Musik seiner Zeit*, edited by Arnfried Elder and Friedhelm Krummacher, 260–74. (*Kieler Schriften zur Musikwissenschaft*, 35.) Kassel: Bärenreiter, 1990.

———. "Textbezug und Werkidee in Johann Sebastian Bachs frühen Orgelchorälen." In *Musikkulturgeschichte: Festschrift für Constantin Floros zum 60. Geburtstag*, edited by Peter Petersen, 167–82. Wiesbaden: Breit-kopf & Härtel, 1990.

———. "Zum geschichtlichen Hintergrund und zur Kompositionsgeschichte von Bachs 'Orgel-Büchlein.'" In *Bachs 'Orgel-Büchlein' in nieuw perspectief*, edited by Paul Peeters, 7–20. (*Kerkmuziek & Liturgie*.) Utrecht: Hogeschool Voor Die Kunsten, 1988.

Brinkmann, Alexander Russell. "Johann Sebastian Bach's Orgelbüchlein: A Computer-Assisted Study of the Melodic Influence of the Cantus Firmus on the Contrapuntal Voices." Ph.D. dissertation, Eastman School of Music, 1978.

Budday, Wolfgang. "Musikalische Figuren als satztechnische Freiheiten in Bachs Orgelchoral 'Durch Adams Fall ist ganz verderbt.'" *Bach-Jahrbuch* 63 (1977): 139–59.

Buelow, George J. "Rhetoric and music." In *The New Grove Dictionary of Music and Musicians*, edited by Stanley Sadie. Vol. 15: 793–803. London: Macmillan, 1980.

Bukofzer, Manfred F. *Music in the Baroque Era: From Monteverdi to Bach.* New York: Norton, 1947.

Butt, John. *Bach Interpretation: Articulation Marks in Primary Sources of J. S. Bach.* (*Cambridge Musical Texts and Monographs.*) Cambridge: Cambridge University Press, 1990.

Clement, Albert. "'Alsdann ich gantz freudig sterbe . . . ' Zu J. S. Bachs Deutung des 24/16 Taktes." *Musik und Kirche* 61 (1991): 303–11.

Dadelsen, Georg von. *Beiträge zur Chronologie der Werke Johann Sebastian Bachs.* (*Tübinger Bach-Studien,* 4/5.) Trossingen: Hohner, 1958.

———. "Die 'Fassung letzter Hand' in der Musik." *Acta Musicologica* 33 (1961): 1–14.

———. "Zur Entstehung des Bachschen Orgelbüchleins." In *Festschrift Friedrich Blume zum 70. Geburtstag,* edited by Anna Amalie Abert and Wilhelm Pfannkuch, 74–79. Kassel: Bärenreiter, 1963.

Dähnert, Ulrich. "Organs Played and Tested by J. S. Bach." In *J. S. Bach as Organist: His Instruments, Music, and Performance Practices,* edited by George Stauffer and Ernest May, 3–24. Bloomington: Indiana University Press, 1986.

David, Hans T. and Arthur Mendel. *The Bach Reader: A Life of Johann Sebastian Bach in Letters and Documents.* Revised edition. New York: Norton, 1966.

Daw, Stephen. "Copies of J. S. Bach by Walther and Krebs: A Study of the Manuscripts P 801, P 802, and P 803." *The Organ Yearbook* 7 (1976): 31–58.

Dietrich, Fritz. "J. S. Bachs Orgelchoral und seine geschichtlichen Wurzeln." *Bach-Jahrbuch* 26 (1929): 1–89.

Dirst, Matthew. "Tradition, Authenticity, and a Bach Chorale Prelude." *The American Organist* 25, no. 3 (March 1991): 59–61.

Disselhorst, Delbert. "The *Orgelbüchlein:* Bach's Organ Method." In *Bach-Stunden: Festschrift für Helmut Walcha zum 70. Geburtstag überreicht von seinen Schülern,* edited by Walther Dehnhard and Gottlob Ritter, 36–42. Frankfurt/Main: Evangelischer Presseverband in Hessen und Nassau, 1978.

Dürr, Alfred. *Johann Sebastian Bach: Seine Handschrift—Abbild seines Schaffens.* Wiesbaden: Breitkopf & Härtel, 1984.

Edwards, Lynn. "The Thuringian Organ 1702–1720: ' . . . ein wohlgerathenes gravitätisches Werk.'" *The Organ Yearbook* 22 (1991): 119–50.

Eller, Rudolf. "Thoughts on Bach's Leipzig Creative Years." Translated and annotated by Stephen A. Crist. *Bach (The Journal of the Riemenschneider Bach Institute)* 21, no. 2 (Summer 1990): 31–54. (Originally published as "Gedanken über Bachs Leipziger Schaffensjahre." In *Bach-Studien* 5, edited by Rudolf Eller and Hans-Joachim Schulze, 7–27. Leipzig: VEB Breitkopf & Härtel, 1975.)

Emery, Walter. "A Note on Bach's Use of Triplets." In *Bach-Studien* 5, edited by Rudolf Eller and Hans-Joachim Schulze, 109–11. Leipzig: VEB Breitkopf & Härtel, 1975.

Faulkner, Quentin. "Information on Organ Registration from a Student of J. S. Bach." *The American Organist* 27, no. 6 (June 1993): 58–63. (Originally published in *Early Keyboard Studies Newsletter* 7, no. 1 [January 1993]: 1–10.)

———. *J. S. Bach's Keyboard Technique: A Historical Introduction.* St. Louis: Concordia, 1984.

Franklin, Don O. "Bach's Keyboard Music in the 1730s and 1740s: Organs and Harpsichords, Hildebrandt and Neidhardt." *Early Keyboard Studies Newsletter* 6, no. 1 (October 1991): 1–14.

Geiringer, Karl. *Johann Sebastian Bach: The Culmination of an Era.* New York: Oxford University Press, 1966.

Godman, Stanley. "Bach's Copies of Ammerbach's 'Orgel oder Instrument Tabulatur' (1571)." *Music and Letters* 38 (1957): 21–27.

Grossmann-Vendrey, Susanna. *Felix Mendelssohn Bartholdy und die Musik der Vergangenheit.* (*Studien zur Musikgeschichte des 19. Jahrhunderts,* 17.) Regensburg: Gustav Bosse Verlag, 1969.

Harriss, Ernest C. *Johann Mattheson's Der vollkommene Capellmeister: A Revised Translation with Critical Commentary.* (*Studies in Musicology,* 21.) Ann Arbor: UMI Research Press, 1981.

Helm, E. Eugene. *Thematic Catalogue of the Works of Carl Philipp Emanuel Bach.* New Haven: Yale University Press, 1989.

Hiller, Ferdinand. *Mendelssohn: Letters and Recollections.* Translated by M. E. von Glehn. With an introduction by Joel Sachs. New York: Vienna House, 1972.

Horn, Victoria. "French Influence in Bach's Organ Works." In *J. S. Bach as Organist: His Instruments, Music, and Performance Practices,* edited by George Stauffer and Ernest May, 256–73. Bloomington: Indiana University Press, 1986.

Hunt, J. Eric. *A Companion to Bach's "Orgelbüchlein."* London: J. Compton Organ Co., 1949.

Janson, Peter. "The Eighteenth-Century Chorale Prelude with Solo Wind Instrument." *The Diapason* 79, no. 10 (October 1988): 10–13.

Jauernig, Reinhold. "Johann Sebastian Bach in Weimar: Neue Forschungsergebnisse aus Weimarer Quellen." In *Johann Sebastian Bach in Thüringen: Festgabe zum Gedenkjahr 1950,* edited by Heinrich Besseler and Günther Kraft, 49–105. Weimar: Thüringer Volksverlag, 1950.

Joelson-Strohbach, Harry. "Nachricht von verschiedenen verloren geglaubten Handschriften mit barocker Tastenmusik." *Archiv für Musikwissenschaft* 44 (1987): 91–140.

Jung, Hans Rudolf. *Johann Sebastian Bach in Weimar 1708 bis 1717*. (*Tradition und Gegenwart: Weimarer Schriften*, 16.) Weimar: Rat der Stadt Weimar, 1985.

Karstadt, Georg. *Thematisch-systematisches Verzeichnis der musikalischen Werke von Dietrich Buxtehude (Buxtehude-Werke-Verzeichnis)*. Wiesbaden: Breitkopf & Härtel, 1974.

Kast, Paul. *Die Bach-Handschriften der Berliner Staatsbibliothek*. (*Tübinger Bach-Studien*, 2/3.) Trossingen: Hohner, 1958.

Keller, Hermann. *The Organ Works of Bach: A Contribution to Their History, Form, Interpretation and Performance*. Translated by Helen Hewitt. New York: C. F. Peters, 1967. (Originally published as *Die Orgelwerke Bachs: Ein Beitrag zu ihrer Geschichte, Form, Deutung und Wiedergabe*. Leipzig: Edition Peters, 1948.)

Kobayashi, Yoshitake. *Die Notenschrift Johann Sebastian Bachs: Dokumentation ihrer Entwicklung*. (*Neue Bach-Ausgabe*, Serie IX, Band 2.) Kassel: Bärenreiter; Leipzig: VEB Deutscher Verlag für Musik, 1989.

————. "Diplomatische Überlegungen zur Chronologie der Weimarer Vokalwerke." Unpublished paper delivered at the Bach-Kolloquium Rostock 1990.

Krapf, Gerhard. *Bach: Improvised Ornamentation and Keyboard Cadenzas—An Approach to Creative Performance*. Dayton: The Sacred Music Press, 1983.

Krüger, Elke. *Stilistische Untersuchungen zu ausgewählten frühen Klavierfugen Johann Sebastian Bachs*. Hamburg: Karl Dieter Wagner, 1970.

Kupferberg, Herbert. *Those Fabulous Philadelphians: The Life and Times of a Great Orchestra*. New York: Charles Scribner's Sons, 1969.

Leaver, Robin A. "Bach and Hymnody: The Evidence of the *Orgelbüchlein*." *Early Music* 13 (1985): 227–36.

Leisinger, Ulrich and Peter Wollny. " 'Altes Zeug von mir': Carl Philipp Emanuel Bachs kompositorisches Schaffen vor 1740." *Bach-Jahrbuch* 79 (1993): 127–204.

Lorenzen, Johannes. *Max Reger als Bearbeiter Bachs*. (*Schriftenreihe des Max-Reger-Instituts Bonn-Bad Godesberg*, 2.) Wiesbaden: Breitkopf & Härtel, 1982.

Marshall, Robert L. "Bach the Progressive: Observations on His Later Works." *The Musical Quarterly* 62 (1976): 313–57. (Reprinted, with a postscript, in Marshall, *The Music of Johann Sebastian Bach: The Sources, the Style, the Significance*. New York: Schirmer Books, 1989.)

————. "Chorale settings." In *The New Grove Dictionary of Music and Musicians*, edited by Stanley Sadie. Vol. 4: 323–38. London: Macmillan, 1980.

————. *The Compositional Process of J. S. Bach*. 2 volumes. Princeton: Princeton University Press, 1972.

————. *Luther, Bach, and the Early Reformation Chorale*. Kessler Reformation Lecture, Emory University, 1995.

————. "Tempo and Dynamics: The Original Terminology." In Marshall, *The Music of Johann Sebastian Bach: The Sources, the Style, the Significance*. New

York: Schirmer Books, 1989. (Originally published as "Tempo and Dynamic Indications in the Bach Sources: A Review of the Terminology." In *Bach, Handel, Scarlatti: Tercentenary Essays*, edited by Peter Williams, 259–75. Cambridge: Cambridge University Press, 1985.)

Mattheson, Johann. *Der vollkommene Capellmeister*. Hamburg: Christian Herold, 1739. Reprint, Kassel: Bärenreiter, 1954.

May, Ernest. "Breitkopf's Role in the Transmission of J. S. Bach's Organ Chorales." Ph.D. dissertation, Princeton University, 1974.

———. "Eine neue Quelle für J. S. Bachs einzeln überlieferte Orgelchoräle." *Bach-Jahrbuch* 60 (1974): 98–103.

———. "J. G. Walther and the Lost Weimar Autographs of Bach's Organ Works." In *Studies in Renaissance and Baroque Music in Honor of Arthur Mendel*, edited by Robert L. Marshall, 264–82. Hackensack, N.J.: Joseph Boonin; Kassel: Bärenreiter, 1974.

———. "The Types, Uses, and Historical Position of Bach's Organ Chorales." In *J. S. Bach as Organist: His Instruments, Music, and Performance Practices*, edited by George Stauffer and Ernest May, 81–101. Bloomington: Indiana University Press, 1986.

Murray, Michael. *Marcel Dupré: The Work of a Master Organist*. Boston: Northeastern University Press, 1985.

Near, John R. "Charles-Marie Widor: The Organ Works and Saint-Sulpice." *The American Organist* 27, no. 2 (February 1993): 46–59.

Neumann, Frederick. *Ornamentation in Baroque and Post-Baroque Music: With Special Emphasis on J. S. Bach*. Princeton: Princeton University Press, 1978.

Niedt, Friederich Erhardt. *The Musical Guide: Parts 1 (1700/10), 2 (1721), and 3 (1717)*. Translated by Pamela L. Poulin and Irmgard C. Taylor. (*Early Music Series*, 8.) Oxford: Oxford University Press, 1989.

O'Donnell, John. "*In dulci jubilo* from the *Orgel-Buechlein* Resolved!" *The Diapason* 67, no. 1 (December 1975): 4–6.

Owen, Barbara. *E. Power Biggs: Concert Organist*. Bloomington: Indiana University Press, 1987.

Petzsch, Christoph. "Ein unbekannter Brief von Carl Philipp Emanuel Bach an Ch. G. von Murr in Nürnberg." *Archiv für Musikwissenschaft* 22 (1965): 208–13.

Plantinga, Leon. *Schumann as Critic*. (*Yale Studies in the History of Music*, 4.) New Haven: Yale University Press, 1967. Reprint, New York: Da Capo Press, 1976.

Randel, Don Michael, ed. *The New Harvard Dictionary of Music*. Cambridge, Mass.: Harvard University Press, 1986.

Richter, Klaus Peter. *Orgelchoral und Ensemblesatz bei J. S. Bach*. (*Münchner Veröffentlichungen zur Musikgeschichte*, 37.) Tutzing: Hans Schneider, 1982.

Ritchie, George and George Stauffer. *Organ Technique: Modern and Early.* Englewood Cliffs: Prentice-Hall, 1992.

Ritter, August Gottfried. *Kunst des Orgelspiels.* Erfurt, 1844.

Sachs, Klaus-Jurgen. "Die 'Anleitung . . . , auff allerhand Arth einen Choral durchzuführen,' als Paradigma der Lehre und der Satzkunst Johann Sebastian Bachs." *Archiv für Musikwissenschaft* 37 (1980): 135–54.

Schmieder, Wolfgang. *Thematisch-systematisches Verzeichnis der musikalischen Werke Johann Sebastian Bachs (Bach-Werke-Verzeichnis).* Revised edition. Wiesbaden: Breitkopf & Härtel, 1990.

Schrammek, Winfried. "Orgel, Positiv, Clavicymbel und Glocken der Schlosskirche zu Weimar 1658 bis 1774." In *Bericht über die Wissenschaftliche Konferenz zum V. Internationalen Bachfest der DDR in Verbindung mit dem 60. Bachfest der Neuen Bachgesellschaft,* edited by Winfried Hoffmann and Armin Schneiderheinze, 99–111. Leipzig: VEB Deutscher Verlag für Musik, 1988.

Schulenberg, David. *The Keyboard Music of J. S. Bach.* New York: Schirmer Books, 1992.

Schulze, Hans-Joachim. "Johann Sebastian Bach und Christian Gottlob Meissner." *Bach-Jahrbuch* 54 (1968): 80–88.

———. *Studien zur Bach-Überlieferung im 18. Jahrhundert. (Musikwissenschaftliche Studienbibliothek Peters.)* Leipzig: Edition Peters, 1984.

Schweitzer, Albert. *J. S. Bach.* Translated by Ernest Newman. 2 volumes. New York: Macmillan, 1925. Reprint, New York: Dover, 1966. (Originally published as *Jean-Sébastian Bach, le musicien-poète.* Leipzig: Breitkopf & Härtel, 1905.)

Seebass, Tilman. *Musikhandschriften in Basel.* Basel: Basler Berichthaus, 1975.

Sitsky, Larry. *Busoni and the Piano: The Works, the Writings, and the Recordings. (Contributions to the Study of Music and Dance,* 7.) New York: Greenwood Press, 1986.

Snyder, Kerala J. *Dieterich Buxtehude: Organist in Lübeck.* New York: Schirmer Books, 1987.

Smith, Rollin. "Charles Gounod and the Organ." *The American Organist* 27, no. 10 (October 1993): 54–57.

Spitta, Philipp. *Johann Sebastian Bach: His Work and Influence on the Music of Germany, 1685–1750.* Translated by Clara Bell and J. A. Fuller-Maitland. 3 volumes. London: Novello, 1889. Reprint, New York: Dover, 1952. (Originally published as *Johann Sebastian Bach.* 2 volumes. Leipzig: Breitkopf & Härtel, 1873–80.)

Stauffer, George B. "Bach as Reviser of His Own Keyboard Works." *Early Music* 13 (1985): 185–98.

———. "Boyvin, Grigny, D'Anglebert, and Bach's Assimilation of French Classical Organ Music." *Early Music* 21 (1993): 83–96.

———. "J. S. Bach as Organ Pedagogue." In *The Organist as Scholar: Essays in Memory of Russell Saunders,* edited by Kerala J. Snyder, 25–44. Stuyvesant, N.Y.: Pendragon Press, 1994.

————. *The Organ Preludes of Johann Sebastian Bach.* (*Studies in Musicology,* 27.) Ann Arbor: UMI Research Press, 1980.

Stiller, Günther. *Johann Sebastian Bach and Liturgical Life in Leipzig.* Translated by Herbert J. A. Bouman, Daniel F. Poellot, and Hilton C. Oswald. Edited by Robin A. Leaver. St. Louis: Concordia, 1984. (Originally published as *Johann Sebastian Bach und das Leipziger gottesdienstliche Leben seiner Zeit.* Berlin: Evangelische Verlagsanstalt, 1970.)

Stinson, Russell. *The Bach Manuscripts of Johann Peter Kellner and His Circle: A Case Study in Reception History.* (*Sources of Music and Their Interpretation: Duke Studies in Music.*) Durham, N. C.: Duke University Press, 1990.

————. "Bach's Earliest Autograph." *The Musical Quarterly* 71 (1985): 235–63.

————. "The Compositional History of Bach's *Orgelbüchlein* Reconsidered." *Bach Perspectives* 1 (1995): 43–78.

————. "Some Thoughts on Bach's Neumeister Chorales." *The Journal of Musicology* 11 (1993): 455–77.

Stokowski, Leopold. *Music for All of Us.* New York: Simon and Schuster, 1943.

Strauss, Joseph N. *Remaking the Past: Musical Modernism and the Influence of the Tonal Tradition.* Cambridge, Mass.: Harvard University Press, 1990.

Talevich, Susan. "Form and Structure in the Chorale Preludes of the Orgelbuechlein of J. S. Bach." M. A. thesis, California State University, 1975.

Terry, Charles Sanford. *Bach: A Biography.* Revised edition. London: Oxford University Press, 1933.

————. "The 'Orgelbüchlein': Another Bach Problem." *The Musical Times* 58 (1917): 109.

Thistlewaite, Nicholas. *The Making of the Victorian Organ.* (*Cambridge Musical Texts and Monographs.*) Cambridge: Cambridge University Press, 1990.

Tusler, Robert L. *The Style of J. S. Bach's Chorale Preludes.* (*University of California Publications in Music,* 1.) Berkeley and Los Angeles: University of California Press, 1956.

Walther, Johann Gottfried. *Musikalisches Lexikon.* Leipzig: Wolffgang Deer, 1732. Reprint, Kassel: Bärenreiter, 1953.

————. *Praecepta der Musicalischen Compositionen.* Edited by Peter Benary. (*Jenaer Beiträge zur Musikforschung,* 2.) Leipzig: VEB Breitkopf & Härtel, 1955.

Weiss, Wisso and Yoshitake Kobayashi. *Katalog der Wasserzeichen in Bachs Originalhandschriften.* (*Neue Bach-Ausgabe,* Serie IX, Band 1.) 2 volumes. Kassel: Bärenreiter; Leipzig, Deutscher Verlag für Musik, 1985.

Williams, Peter. *The Organ Music of J. S. Bach.* (*Cambridge Studies in Music.*) 3 volumes. Cambridge: Cambridge University Press, 1980–84.

————. *Playing the Organ Works of Bach: Some Case Studies.* New York: American Guild of Organists, 1987.

————. Program notes to recording of the *Orgelbüchlein* by Peter Hurford. Decca - D228D 4, K228K: 1982.

Wolff, Christoph. "Bach's Organ Music: Studies and Discoveries." *The Musical Times* 126 (1985): 149–52.

———. "Chronology and Style in the Early Works: A Background for the Orgel-Büchlein." In Wolff, *Bach: Essays on His Life and Music*, 297–305. Cambridge, Mass.: Harvard University Press, 1991. (Originally published as "Zur Problematik der Chronologie und Stilentwicklung des Bachschen Frühwerkes, inbesondere zur musikalischen Vorgeschichte des Orgelbüchleins." In *Bericht über die Wissenschaftliche Konferenz zum V. Internationalen Bachfest der DDR in Verbindung mit dem 60. Bachfest der Neuen Bachgesellschaft*, edited by Winfried Hoffmann and Armin Schneiderheinze, 449–55. Leipzig: VEB Deutscher Verlag für Musik, 1988.)

———. "The Deathbed Chorale: Exposing a Myth." In Wolff, *Bach: Essays on His Life and Music*, 282–94. Cambridge, Mass.: Harvard University Press, 1991. (Originally published as "Johann Sebastian Bachs 'Sterbechoral': Kritische Fragen zu einem Mythos." In *Studies in Renaissance and Baroque Music in Honor of Arthur Mendel*, edited by Robert L. Marshall, 283–97. Hackensack, N.J.: Joseph Boonin; Kassel: Bärenreiter, 1974.)

———. "Die Rastrierungen in den Originalhandschriften Joh. Seb. Bachs und ihre Bedeutung für die diplomatische Quellenkritik." In *Festschrift für Friedrich Smend*, 80–92. Berlin: Merseburger, 1963.

Wolff, Christoph, et al. *The New Grove Bach Family*. New York: Norton, 1983.

Zehnder, Jean-Claude. "Giuseppe Torelli und Johann Sebastian Bach: Zu Bachs Weimarer Konzertform." *Bach-Jahrbuch* 77 (1991): 33–95.

Zenck, Martin. "Tradition as Authority and Provocation: Anton Webern's Confrontation with Johann Sebastian Bach." In *Bach Studies*, edited by Don O. Franklin, 297–322. Cambridge: Cambridge University Press, 1989.

Zietz, Hermann. *Quellenkritische Untersuchungen an den Bach-Handschriften P 801, P 802 und P 803 aus dem "Krebs'schen Nachlass" unter besonderer Berücksichtigung der Choralbearbeitungen des jungen J. S. Bach.* (*Hamburger Beiträge zur Musikwissenschaft*, 1.) Hamburg: Karl Dieter Wagner, 1969.

General Index

Index to Cited Works of Bach